Making Sense of the Sacred

Making Sense of the Sacred

The Meaning of World Religions

James L. Rowell

FORTRESS PRESS
MINNEAPOLIS

MAKING SENSE OF THE SACRED
The Meaning of World Religions

Cover design: Brice Hemmer

Print ISBN: 978-1-5064-6808-2
eBook ISBN: 978-1-5064-6809-9

Contents

Introduction

Life is like a jigsaw puzzle. Not all of the pieces are easy to find, nor do they always seem to fit together. For a long time, we may be searching for a piece and cannot find it. We despair, we think it is lost, until finally, after a long search, we find it and put it in place. And then we go on our merry way, looking for the next piece of the puzzle. We are looking for certain pieces of the puzzle of our lives, and they do not come together at predictable times and places. We are looking for the right job, one that will make us happy and successful. And so we obsess about school, experience, and money. We may be looking for a spouse or a romantic partner and have had relationships that ended badly in the past. But we keep looking, and the missing pieces keep multiplying—where should we live, how should we pass our spare time, and what should we believe? *What should we believe*? Indeed, what?

Religion, too, is like a puzzle, or it seems so to me. In the modern world, we are aware that there are a lot of different religions out there, and when we study them, they do not seem to add up to one cohesive picture. What is the meaning of life, of the puzzle of life, when Christians, Muslims, Jews, Hindus, Buddhists, Taoists, Confucians, and Jains all see the religious life quite differently? How are we to make sense of the big picture when the pieces do not seem to add up to one?

I have always been a "big picture" type of person. I am a teacher, an academic, and have studied world religions for many years. Trying to make sense of the big picture of life and the world has been my job, and I have tried to leave nothing out. This has led me to look beyond the confines of the Christian religion with which I was raised to study other religions and philosophies. What I discovered was a very difficult puzzle involving history, philosophy, and religion. It is a very hard picture to assemble, just as the smaller puzzle of our own lives can be. This book is intended to help you make sense of the puzzle of world religions. Like you, I am searching for meaning, for a sense of the bigger picture to finally come into resolution. And while I have learned much in my search, there are many parts of the religion puzzle left to work out. So let us begin.

When assembling a puzzle, we look for familiar shapes. We grab certain pieces, they almost fit, but then we put them back as we see the shape and the colors do not match. The search goes on until we find the right piece. One thing that is a constant aid in assembling the puzzle is the image on the box. You use it as a reliable map to construct the puzzle before you. But what is the common image that allows *all persons of all religions* to put together the viewpoint of this world's life? Arguably, this image is quite faint, or absent altogether, for the average human being. A person might come to know well their own religion, but is there really anything like a common image that binds *all of them* together? After all, they are all different in many ways.

Let's give a few examples of the dissenting images. Christians follow Jesus and think of him as the Messiah, while Muslims may see Christ as a prophet but not as divine; Muslims follow Muhammad and the Qur'an instead. Jews will not commonly recognize Jesus or Muhammad in their traditions, and many are still awaiting a messiah. These three religions are traditions called "Abrahamic faiths" because they descend from the patriarch Abraham and believe in a single God. Yet Hinduism has a vast variety of gods and goddesses, something Islam strictly frowns upon, and while Hinduism seems polytheistic, some Hindus see these deities as faces or manifestations of one God. They may consider themselves to be monotheists. Buddhists will not commonly recognize the idea of God, the immortal soul, or the permanent self, which is something that Jews, Christians, Muslims, and Hindus all believe. What I have just described to you does not seem like any coherent image at all; in fact, it seems so different, it is impossible to imagine how they fit together. They may be puzzles that add up separately, but they do not seem to add up together.

And yet they are all products of one earth, whose histories are relevant but not well connected in our minds. They are all part of our world's civilizations, and these religions have encountered one another, sometimes learned from one another, and at other times fought one another, or among themselves. Too often we might think that each religion is focused only upon *its own history*, *its own perspective*, and not on any common perspective or history that unites them to the soil of this earth. For an alien visitor from space, this might be one of the first questions asked—How do all these religions fit together? In what way do they add up to make life meaningful here on earth? This is an important question to ask to make sense of the puzzle, and while the alien visitor would ask it early on, it seems a question we rarely ask ourselves. We are too busy with our few parts of the puzzle—with Christianity, Judaism, Islam, Hinduism, Buddhism, or another religion. We want to know what life on earth means through the lens of any *one* of those religions but not whether they add up to anything coherent. When we do this, we fail to ask what we have in common as a people of one shared world.

There is something that religions can agree upon, there are some common themes and beliefs that run through them, and there are also striking contrasts and differences. So the grand picture of the puzzle of this world's religions is not fully envisioned, not fully understood, and that makes the task of making a meaningful whole of all of them quite difficult. And yet in the modern world, I would argue it is absolutely imperative because the days of our isolation are long over; young people today grow up knowing and encountering a pluralistic world, a world of many puzzling beliefs and believers. Young people—and old, for that matter—want some help and aid in resolving a very simple question: *Does it all really make sense?* Or is it just the chaotic jabber of conflicting civilizations and their religions unable to resolve their differences?

Religions can agree upon *general moral precepts*. These are moral guidelines that can give one a strong moral bearing and focus on what is right, what is wrong, and what is essential. The moral precepts that religions of our world seem to share are as follows:

1. Follow the Golden Rule—do unto others as you would have them do unto you, or love your neighbor as yourselves.
2. Accept God or a Sacred Purpose in your life.
3. Do not lie.
4. Do not kill, or more specifically, murder.
5. Do not commit adultery or "unchaste acts."
6. Do not steal.

These are some of the basics, and scholars such as Hans Küng, Eric Erickson, Huston Smith, and others have also supported some idea of shared norms.[1] I would add a few others, however, that can be found in some form in the world's religions:

1. I first encountered the idea that all religions advocate the norms "do not lie, kill, steal, or commit adultery" in Hans Küng, *A Global Ethic: The Declaration of the Parliament of World Religions* (New York: Continuum, 1995), 55.

7. Do not be possessive of or greedy about material things.
8. Respect one's elders, or authorities.

The last one reflects the Ten Commandments' law of "honoring your mother and father" but also the Confucian ethic of respect and deference to elders. More generally, it is reflected in the first law, the Golden Rule of respect for other human life. The seventh, too, is universal. Religions constantly tell us that material possessiveness is not a good thing, that it is altogether shallow and insignificant when compared with a spiritual life. One can dispute that, and indeed, the world today is filled with an abundance of images celebrating materialism, ownership of countless mindless things and commodities. We are repudiating ancient norms. There is an abundance of greed in our world, and if we are honest, we may confess to greed in ourselves. Greed, inner desire, is highly contagious and resistant to its cure.

The second law, to "accept God or a Sacred Purpose in your life," must be explained. Not all religions believe in a God, and some have many gods or goddesses. For religions like Buddhism that do not formally have a God, there is still a "Sacred Purpose" of escaping reincarnation and attaining nirvana. So this law must be carefully worded and understood. I also accept that atheists, seeing neither God nor nirvana, may believe that living a good life while our feet are on this earth is an essential thing, a secular form of a sacred end. Conceptions differ, but I think a common *moral and humane* purpose must unite us in terms of this second law.

Laws three through eight are really logical and rational reflections of the first law, which demands a level of good reciprocal treatment. We do not want to be lied to, murdered, cheated, or stolen from, so we should not do those things to others. It deprives them of the peace, honor, and tranquility of living. Bad behaviors erode the basis of civilization that requires decency to stave off chaos and war. One does not even have to accept that these laws have a godly or sacred source, but if examined rationally, they pass the test as well. Immanuel Kant suggested that one must "always act in such a way that the maxim of one's actions should become universal law."[2] I like to rephrase it: "Do the right thing that would be the right thing for any other person to do." It is a very sensible and important test. All ethics have to be reasonable and have some common basis by which they can be

2. Immanuel Kant, *Grounding for the Metaphysics of Morals*, trans. James W. Harrington, 3rd ed. (Cambridge, MA: Hackett, 1993), v.

shared with others. It is totally unsurprising that what religions agree upon can be defended by reason. Because of this, atheists may argue religion is unnecessary.

The good news is that there is a common vision, but it is not quite as simple as that. What have been described are *general moral precepts*, or ideas about right and wrong that are formulated on a very basic level. The exact wording about these moral ideas is not identical in every religious text, nor are they always observed in the same way. For example, regarding the idea of spurning possessions, a certain sect of the Jain religion in India, called the Digambaras, believes that attachment to material possessions is so bad, so ensnaring of the soul's path to liberation, that only sheer and complete nudity will set them free. Nakedness is mandatory for male Jain monks, and it is believed that only males can attain this end. Not all Digambara Jains are monks, and another sect called the Svetambara Jains neither requires complete nudity nor thinks that only men can attain this. In short, their *specific ethical interpretation* is different. They understand and apply the norm differently.[3] We may agree materialism is bad but disagree about how far we should go to avoid it.

The same applies to many other religions that warn against materialism. Not being covetous, not having too much, and living a comparatively modest life are standards accepted by many world religions. Indeed, the *lay* Jains (those who are not monks) also share a lot of this view. Ethical interpretations, meaning individual understanding of moral norms, are quite varied, so the appearance of the general agreement on morality either seems to be less real or (others might argue) has essentially disappeared. I do not think it has disappeared entirely, but more on that soon.

Differences in ethical interpretation and application of this general moral consensus can be illustrated with every one of the shared norms described above. The injunction of "do not kill" appears in every major religious tradition, but it is not observed with the same intensity or in exactly the same manner. For example, is abortion a form of murder? Should capital punishment be allowed? Can war be justified? We all agree that *killing* is morally bad and should be avoided but disagree (ethically) in terms of specific applications of or exemptions from that rule.

3. For a general overview of Jainism, see Jeffrey Long, *Jainism: An Introduction* (New York: I. B. Tauris, 2009).

The Jain religion that was just mentioned is also very strict about ahimsa, or "nonviolence." This nonviolence is so strict for the Jains that even killing a bug should be avoided if unnecessary, and Jains will generally be vegetarians so as not to do violence to life. Now Mahatma Gandhi also stressed the idea of ahimsa, but he derived its values from the Hindu Bhagavad Gita, though he was also partly influenced by Jains. And while Gandhi also abstained from eating meat, he did not have the exact same ideas about nonviolence as the Jains did. In one case, for example, Gandhi allowed for the killing of poisonous snakes that were a threat to members of his ashram, or "living community," when he was in Africa. It was a practical matter he thought could not be avoided.[4]

There are many other disagreements about nonviolence and abstention from killing in Christianity, Judaism, and Islam. The people of these religions are not vegetarian, though Jews and Muslims generally refrain from eating pork, while Christians do not. Muslims can, however, kill the cow and eat beef, but the cow is a sacred animal for Hindus. During Gandhi's independence movement, the killing of cows at one point was a major moral and spiritual issue. It is very difficult when one culture sees an animal as sacred and another kills it for food, but this is written not to pass judgment on either Hindus or Muslims, only to illumine the real difference. Christians and Muslims have gone to war for religious reasons much more frequently than the traditions of Buddhism and Jainism. Not only has there emerged in Islam and Christianity a dialogue about what constitutes justified warfare, but there has also been perversion and abuse of this principle; the worst violence in the Christian Crusades and the 9/11 attacks might be taken as examples. Buddhists, however, do not have such a developed tradition about war in this regard, and Jains in particular have strenuously rejected violence. Yet some Jain monks have engaged in the practice of *sallekhana*, or a spiritual fasting unto death.[5] This is an idea or tradition that Jews, Christians, and Muslims, as well as many others, emphatically reject and a violence to the self that they would condemn as unnecessary.

Therefore, to claim there is general moral consensus among the world's religions without also admitting unique interpretations and dissent is to offer a too-rosy and

4. M. K. Gandhi, *Satyagraha in South Africa*, trans. Valji Govindji Desai from Gujarati, 6th ed. (Ahmedabad, India: Navajivan, 2001), 229–31.
5. Long, *Jainism*, 110–11.

misleading picture. There *can be* agreement among the various world religions, but that agreement and understanding need to be consciously worked at; they do not automatically preexist. Consensus or agreement among the various religions cannot be assumed; it requires work and ongoing dialogue. Yet the general moral overlap and agreement are significant.

If we do not lie, do not steal, do not kill or cheat, and generally respect and treat our neighbor as we might also wish to be treated (these are all good rational ethics), then we should expect a state of relative peace and harmony for all individuals regardless of their background. Political, social, and economic factors are always concerns, of course, and can make a good ideal possibly much worse. Strictly speaking about the general moral norms of religion, however, they can allow for harmony and peace if properly observed and practiced. Within that sphere of peace, all sorts of great things are possible. Religions can give us a way to respect and live with our neighbors.

Religions do not exist independently of human beings, however, and human beings are always flawed and imperfect. This seems to be something of a ninth truth that religions agree upon, that we are not perfect. We need constant reminders of the moral norms that we should observe, because we have been diagnosed as sinful (Christianity), rebellious toward God (Jews and Muslims), ignorant of God's wisdom (Hinduism), or otherwise attached and desirous of transitory worldly things (Buddhism and Jainism). The root cause of our problem is stated differently in different world religions, but there seems to be a problem, a constant misalignment between the moral norms we set for ourselves and the paths we actually follow.

I would add another moral diagnosis to this list. We are both social and *self-full* at once, each a competing aspect of our minds. The social aspect of human nature recognizes necessary moral norms and understands we are part of a larger human race and dependent upon other humans for happiness and survival. *Survival* is a key word here. For as products of evolution, we have competitive, survival instincts, things not inherently *selfish* but that invite that possibility. Instead, I call them *self-full* because while we may have our neighbors and the rest of humanity in mind, our attention is constantly pulled toward our own self-interest and welfare. Being preoccupied with oneself, being self-full, can lead to selfishness, but it does not always do so. Sometimes being self-full can mean just being productive, writing a book or building a set of wooden cabinets. It can, of course, lead in other moments to a negative selfishness, where our minds and hearts are numbed to the needs of others. Selfishness can cause us to break away and forget our common links with other human beings. We can champion ourselves or our kind, resulting in racism, sexism, discrimination, and every other form of belief that touts the self-identity at the expense of others. We can also be altruistic. Human beings are a mixed bag of selfless and selfish motivations, each constantly competing for our attention.

That is why we need to remember the possible harmony and unity present among the world's religions—so that our self-fullness does not turn into nasty selfishness. We are not biological robots. If we were and our morality could be programmed for us to follow, then human conflict would have ended centuries ago. That human conflict did not end centuries ago is indicative of our freedom and capacity to choose either good or evil. We are creatures of fleeting existence, pursuing and tempted by good and evil, selflessness and selfishness, and the only way out of that predicament would seem to be an unpalatable one: to be deprived of our freedom and given a perfect mental programming that we followed slavishly. That kind of automatous behavior repulses us deep in our nature, and this is also perhaps an argument that God gave us free will knowing it would make a better, more interesting world.

Religions therefore are like our spiritual workshops; we need to enter into them for routine spiritual maintenance. Although we may not be like cars, or automatons following mechanically some slavish code set in our minds, we need spiritual maintenance and tuning. Everything in nature is at risk of falling into a state of disrepair if it is not maintained and properly cared for. Like weeds growing through cracks in the pavement, moral doubts and problems can easily take root in the crevices of our minds if we do not uproot and eradicate them. This is the constant battle between our social and selfish selves.

The choice we have to make, however, is not just between the social and selfish side of ourselves. It is a choice about making sense of life itself. Whether we are brought up in a religious tradition or not, we are exposed to other religions and perspectives that may fill us with doubt or cause us to rethink some of our basic ideas about the world. It is hoped that this book might help with that.

Hans Küng once observed that there would be "no peace among the nations without peace among religions. No peace among the religions without dialogue between the religions. No dialogue between the religions without investigation of the foundations of the religions."[6] Küng was correct that religious understanding, a common vision or set of values, is imperative as we move into the future. Reinhold Niebuhr observed in relation to our social and sinful, or selfish, selves, "Man's capacity for justice makes democracy possible, but man's inclination to injustice makes democracy necessary."[7] In a multicultural world, we need a view of the common values that hold the individual pieces of our puzzles of life together. We have three choices: theism, that the religious puzzle pieces make some sense; atheism, that they really do not; or agnosticism, in which case we are not sure.

This book has been written not to champion any particular religion, nor to exalt theists, agnostics, or atheists. Rather, it was written so that you might treat all of them more seriously. Let me explain. First, atheists try to describe the world as they see it. We know we die, and we aren't too certain if there is anything beyond that. In terms of what the senses immediately perceive, atheism may be compelling. Agnosticism, however, refuses to decide upon the religious question. Given that there is much we don't know about the universe and much not understood about religion, agnosticism is a rational choice too. Then there is theism. Believers feel a moral compulsion and a spiritual guidance, which their religions provide. Believers do not have absolute proof of their views, but that is not needed. As long as their religion provides a healthy measure of guidance and hope for a world too often embroiled in war or chaos, that is enough. Logically, all three points of view can be defended.

My own point of view is that of a "Christian Universalist." I believe foremost in the Christian religion, but I do not see it as an exclusive truth that renders all others worthless. If there is a sacred heart in the cosmos, or a God who is compassionate and just, I hope persons from all faiths and perspectives all over the world are loved and preserved. It isn't my business to set up a litmus test of salvation but rather my hope that our common humanity shares a benevolent and higher aim. I see my Christianity as part of a larger whole and hopefully have made connections of my own beliefs to those of others. While I hope to promote my viewpoint, I also want to illuminate the wisdom in others.

6. Hans Küng, *Islam: Past, Present and Future*, trans. John Bowden (Oxford: Oneworld, 2007), xiii.
7. Reinhold Niebuhr, *The Children of Light and Darkness* (New York: Charles Scribner's Sons, 1944), xiii.

I wanted to write a book about religion that was short and sensible. This is it. I begin (chapters 1 and 2) with the important question of "trilemma," the choice of the three perspectives: atheism, agnosticism, and theism. These first two chapters will discuss the philosophical problems of *making sense of the sacred* and finding *the meaning of world religions*, while subsequent chapters examine the sense of the sacred in specific religious traditions.

Within each chapter you will find an introduction to the religion, as well as very succinct parts about "What Fits" and "What Doesn't Fit" with other religions. These are my suggestions about making sense of the puzzle. I have kept these sections short. The intent is to begin the conversation rather than to exhaust it. An exhaustive study of religion would tire the reader and miss my aim of brevity. Therefore, let this be my contribution to an already vast ocean of words on the subject. It will drift in time, in place, and to persons and things I cannot anticipate.

1 Religious Trilemma: The Puzzling Choice

When making a puzzle with family or friends, finding the right piece is a joy, not a nasty competition. Among friends, we don't swat another's hand away from a puzzle piece; we delight that they have found it. Finding and putting together the puzzle pieces of life as a civilization is a different thing. Competing, we often claim that only our views and pieces matter in assembling the puzzle. Putting a piece in a puzzle among friends is fun, but putting the pieces together as a civilization can be a fight. Has anyone, however, *fully seen* the picture on the "box of life," from which all our puzzle pieces of this world came? No one *for certain* has seen this picture and knows how to assemble the pieces of life, save perhaps God. Religions and people compete because they have different views and claims of the big picture: the picture on the puzzle box of the world itself. Where did it come from? How was it all put together?

This puzzle is before us, and we have three ways of looking at it: (1) the pieces of the puzzle make sense *religiously* and can fit together, (2) the pieces of the puzzle do not add up to any true *religious* picture, (3) we are unsure either way. In the first case, if we claim that the pieces of the puzzle add up *religiously*, then we are theists, or believers. If, in the second case, they do not add up or are not meaningful, we reject them as atheists. If, in the third case, we are unsure, we are agnostics. There is a "trilemma" before us about whether there is a greater picture of life to resolve into sharper clarity. We need to have that hunch, that picture, to continue our puzzle making.

To elucidate the trilemma simply, let me put forward the following. To claim theism is, on the one hand, a good thing because this view asserts meaning, purpose, and hope for our lives. On the other, to support theism also begs the question, Which religion do you believe? Some religions have one God, some have many, and some do not have any gods, and this plunges us into a confusing world: Which religion is true? One religion? Two or three? Many of the world's religions or none? How can we "verify" which religions are good or true? Largely, I suspect, it will be in terms of their plausibility as well as the moral good and hope they offer. Also, to a large extent, it will be based on whether we were brought up in that tradition. Being born into a religious tradition, you inherit the puzzle image of your parents or culture and begin to assemble. Perhaps also you acquire a nuanced view of it or reject that view.

One can oppositely conclude that because religions disagree about God, the soul, and the afterlife, this proves that they are human made, stemming from our imagination. Religions emerge from our creative minds and have evolved much as language and culture did. They are shaped by a regional view of spiritual truth, not truth once and for all. Karl Marx (1818–83) and Sigmund Freud (1856–1939) argued that religion was an invention—and one that we are better off without. By taking this choice, however, a scary void seems to open in the human heart. What is our purpose? What has become of our lost loved ones? Is the final end to our lives simply grim death and decay? The choice to espouse atheism is by no means easy or comfortable.

Finally, the choice to remain unconvinced leads to agnosticism. Here, Thomas Huxley (1825–95) offers some compelling points. It can be argued that there is no flaming "signature of god" on any one religion, no final way to credit or discredit them, and a hint of uncertain humility about truth is invaluable. Remember, however, religion involves also a strong emotional pull; it is not pure rational calculus. The philosopher William James (1842–1910) suggested the choice to believe must be *living*, *forced*, and *momentous*, meaning that it was alive and rooted deeply in one's mind.[1] I would add that this choice might be like an emotional gravity not easily resisted or ignored. To remain wholly rationalistic about religion, to remain uncommitted, isn't easy. Simply put, humans may have an innate want and need to believe *something*. Putting off the choice or refraining from it is possible but could be difficult.

Nine Perspectives on Religion

This chapter will clarify a few puzzlers' *perspectives* on how we assemble the picture of life. If there is a greater truth, the vision of the picture puzzle will lead

1. William James, *The Will to Believe and Human Morality* (New York: Dover, 1956), 3.

one to theism. If there is not, one's vision of the truth of life will lead them to atheism. Both paths are different ways of working out the picture puzzle of life, of assembling meaning in different manners. There is a great freedom and blessing in this possibility: that we can agree to disagree. There is, however, also a danger in becoming alienated from those around us when vastly contrasting images of life imply equally deep gulfs in values and commitments. Again, puzzle making among family and friends is fun, but puzzle making between civilizations and religions has often been a fight. We'd like to avoid that in the future. That is why common understanding is so essential.

Here I will discuss at least nine different views of the puzzle of life. They are the following:

Theism

1. Militant theism: the angry puzzle maker
2. Traditional exclusivism: the conservative puzzle maker
3. Inclusivism: the moderate puzzle maker
4. Universalism: the progressive puzzle maker
5. Deism: the spirited and rational puzzle maker

Agnosticism

6. Agnosticism: the cautious puzzle maker

Atheism

7. Soft atheism or humanism: the tolerant puzzle maker
8. Hard atheism: the critical puzzle maker
9. Militant atheism: oppressor of the religious puzzle maker

This list is not intended to be definitive or final but captures at least some of the great complexity of views on this matter. Each will now in turn be further explained.

In terms of theism, the *militant theist* is the angry puzzle maker. They are so convinced of the absolute truth found in their religious view that they are willing to use violent force or coercion to promote it. Militant theists are often aggressive toward anyone not representing their own views, including possibly someone of the same religion. Christians have fought Christians, Muslims have fought Muslims,

Muslims and Christians have battled each other, and sometimes Jews have also been fighting or suffering in between. In India at partition in 1947, Hindus and Muslims fought one another due to deep fear and mutual mistrust. Gandhi was repulsed, but against his will, religious identity during that time was turned into a tool of violence.[2] In many traditions, the militant theist is one possessed by blind zeal: terrorism, crusades, intolerance, and violence always accompany the militant theist. Militants have lost all sight that anyone else might have a meaningful part or puzzle piece of life. The first lesson of religion should be to never yield to this deplorable militancy.

A vast gulf separates militancy from the *traditional* or *exclusive theist*. These are the conservative puzzle makers, who think that their religious view is right and preferred to all others but will never use force to promote it. The traditional theist may use argument, preaching, sermons, or other nonviolent means to convince others of their truth but will refrain from coercion. They really see truth as contained in one and only one tradition. The puzzle of life for them is only resolved by one religion. For the exclusive theist, their religion tells them all they need to know, and they are satisfied with it as a guide and spiritual compass. Nothing else can substitute. The traditional view might seem arrogant to others, but this is not necessarily true. The danger of too prideful an exclusive belief is that it disdains others who do not accept it. Many traditionalists simply coexist and agree to disagree.

The *inclusive theist* may have a slightly broader view. Instead of one tradition having *all* the pieces, there are a few religions that have the best perspective. These puzzle makers are moderates. For them, perhaps a few religions have it right, such as those that believe in the one God of Abraham (Judaism, Christianity, and Islam) or alternately those that affirm reincarnation (such as Hinduism, Jainism, or Buddhism). In any case, the inclusive theist takes a broader view than just one religion and thinks two or a few religious perspectives are best but that certainly all are not equal. The inclusive thinker will think that some religions have a better grasp of the puzzle of life than others; this seems to be natural to many of us. Seeing wisdom in a few religious perspectives, this moderate thinker will just not be persuaded that there is truth in many religions.

2. An excellent source on this conflict is Yasmin Khan, *The Great Partition: The Making of India and Pakistan* (New Haven, CT: Yale University Press, 2007).

The *Universalist* or *progressive theist* will think this, however. The Universalist is very well exemplified by Mohandas Gandhi (better known as Mahatma Gandhi). Gandhi believed that all religions were pathways up the same mountain, that it did not matter so much whether we were Buddhist, Hindu, Christian, Muslim, or Jew, but that the purpose of each religion propelled us to a sacred truth and better morality. Gandhi believed "all the principal religions are equal in the sense that they are true. They are supplying a felt want in the spiritual progress of humanity."[3] Gandhi thought that religions pursue a higher truth. He said, "To me God is Truth, and Love, God is ethics and morality, God is fearlessness. . . . He is all things to all men. . . . He is ever forgiving for He always gives us the chance to repent. He is the greatest democrat the world knows for He leaves us 'unfettered' to make our own choice between evil and good."[4]

This is a wonderful and warming view. It suggests we are all wanted, loved, or saved in the end. All puzzle makers have an equal and good role in assembling a meaningful picture of life. Perhaps our moral commitment and our integrity are most divine. Gandhi seemed to think so. There are of course difficulties with the Universalist view. It tends to sweep under the carpet, or at least set aside as unresolved, some very real differences: Was Christ divine or not? Was Muhammad a prophet? Is there a God? Is there a soul and final afterlife, as Muslims and Christians assert, or is there no God and no permanent soul, as Buddhists believe? World religions state very different things about the final nature of truth and sometimes also about morality. The universal perspective is warm and welcoming but leaves many things unresolved. Universalism succeeds at finding moral common grounds but struggles to reconcile real differences in professed faith.

Deism has much in common with the Universalists. Deists are trying to make the images and pieces of religion fit and accord with rationalism and science. For Deists, the spirit of religion must not contradict the dictates of science and reason. Deism does not look to any tradition for an infallible truth but may see the works of God, sometimes called "Providence" by Deists, as clearly evident in the natural world. Thomas Paine, while scathing and critical of established religious traditions,

3. Mohandas Gandhi, *The Selected Works of Mahatma Gandhi*, ed. Shriman Narayan (Ahmedabad, India: Navajivan, 1968), 6:266.
4. Louis Fischer, ed., *The Essential Gandhi: An Anthology of His Life, Works, and Ideas* (New York: Vintage Books, 1983), 228–29.

admitted that the grandeur of creation testified to divine Providence. Critical of any notion of revelation being found in a particular text, Paine wrote, "The word of God is the Creation we behold; and it is in this word, which no human invention can counterfeit or alter, that God speaks universally to man."[5] Deists have not wanted to sacrifice the warm hope of religion to the sometimes cold calculus of science and reason. Deists may still see God as evidenced by nature.

Not all Deists were equally critical of conventional religion. Many of the American Founding Fathers were Deists. Thomas Jefferson believed Christianity had been corrupted and misinterpreted but that it contained an important truth. He wrote, "To the corruptions of Christianity I am, indeed, opposed, but not to the genuine precepts of Jesus himself. I am a Christian in the only sense in which I believe Jesus wished any one to be; sincerely attached to his doctrines, in preference to all others; ascribing to himself every human excellence, and believing he never claimed any other."[6] Deists believe that there is something divine, that it may not be fully understood in any particular tradition, and that the pursuits of science and reason may help clarify our image of the world. Trying to bring religion in harmony with reason, Deists de-emphasize miracles. For them, miracles violate natural law and are therefore not compatible with a scientific worldview. In Deism, God is often conceived as a watchmaker who created the world but does not intervene in it.

Among religious believers, a split exists between liberals and fundamentalists. A religious *liberal* takes their religion seriously but more symbolically and less literally than a fundamentalist. The religious liberal takes seriously secular or scientific views but still adheres to religion as a moral and spiritual guide, insisting that religion is good but not infallible. In this respect, religious liberals may be "neo-Deists," who seek to make religion breathe with the modern spirit of the times rather than a wooden adherence to tradition.

On the other side of the split is the *fundamentalist*, who considers religious liberalism to be a watered-down version of religion. The fundamentalist insists upon the literal, authentic, and authoritative understanding of text and tradition. Without true belief, faith is dissolute, flabby, and weak. Caving in to the temptations

5. Thomas Paine, *The Age of Reason* (Sioux Falls, SD: NuVision, 2007), 47: "speaks" as modern English here is a substitute for "speaketh."
6. David L. Holmes, *The Faiths of the Founding Fathers* (New York: Oxford University Press, 2006), 83.

of the modern world would lead to abandoning the true faith. The fundamentalist belongs to the exclusivist school of religious thinking described above.

Agnosticism literally means "without knowledge" of the divine or sacred. Thomas Huxley has been credited with coining the term, as it expressed his belief that neither the theists nor the atheists had a definitive argument to settle the matter. As Huxley wrote, "Why trouble ourselves about matters of which, however important they may be, we do not know and can know nothing? We live in a world which is full of misery and ignorance, and the plain duty of each and all of us is to try to make the little corner he can influence somewhat less miserable and somewhat less ignorant than it was before he entered it."[7] In his view, agnosticism was the most rational position to take regarding the sacred. Agnosticism, he argued, "appears to me to be the only position for people who object to say that they know what they are quite aware they do not know."[8] This really explains why I have called them the "cautious" puzzle maker, for they refuse to affirm what they believe the mind cannot know.

There are shades or dispositions of agnosticism, but I have not chosen to classify them further. Agnosticism contains an essential element of rational humility, but remaining out of the fray and not taking sides in this tremendously emotional debate is difficult. Huxley himself might be criticized for not being as neutral or impartial as he imagined.

People who are basically *secular* and have no firm attachment to religion may feel close to agnosticism. Secular people are nonreligious, are comfortable in worldly experience, and may have had little exposure to religion when they were growing up. Others simply drifted away from their religious heritage as they aged. Secular mass media culture often avoids religion for fear of stirring up certain passions or disagreements.

The next puzzle-making perspective is atheism. Atheists are interested in religion, at least so they can better understand and refute it. In the *hard atheist* perspective, the picture puzzle of religion never added up to any vision of the world that was good, true, or meaningful. The hard atheist has given up on the religious view and is building another puzzle altogether based on things that are thought

7. Thomas Henry Huxley, *Agnosticism and Christianity—and Other Essays* (New York: Prometheus Books, 1992), 90.
8. Huxley, 118.

to be more reasonable. Hard atheists try to be persuasive in attacking religion and its influence on society. They perceive that religious visions are false, that the best puzzle made is the one made by us, according to a reasoned view.

One example of hard atheism is the philosopher Bertrand Russell (1872–1970). He argued that religion brought out the bad aspects of human nature and that a better future was one where people were less religious. For the hard atheist, no measure of physical force needs to be applied in this endeavor, simply the force of solid argument. For example, the idea that a benevolent God could have created such an evil world is a proposition Russell found to be absurd. In a particularly powerful and concise argument, he wrote, "Do you think that, if you were granted omnipotence and omniscience and millions of years in which to perfect your world, you could produce nothing better than the Ku Klux Klan or the Fascists?"[9] This pithy question captures the problem of evil effectively: Why would a good and all-powerful Creator fashion a world that allowed for the stupidity, savagery, and inhumanity of the Nazis? Theists might respond that this is a part of free will and that Russell's observation also omits the many good aspects of God's creation. No argument, however—theistic or atheistic—really has the final word. A cautious measure of doubt is ever the wise companion of a genuinely held and rationally evaluated conviction.

Psychology has taken differing views regarding the sacred. Sigmund Freud thought that religion was largely wish fulfillment based on a deep psychological need for security and patriarchy. He believed religion was essentially an illusion that we can and should dispense with. Like Russell, Freud embraced a hard-atheistic point of view. Carl Jung (1875–1961), however, took a more positive approach toward the psychology of religious belief. He argued that religion tapped into certain archetypes of human psychology, which are basic units of meaning and value to the species. Psychologists have at times been appreciative of or hostile to religion.

Karl Marx believed that religion was a false distraction from the real economic oppression that overwhelmed us. He famously said that religion was the "opium" of the people:

9. Bertrand Russell, *Why I Am Not a Christian: And Other Essays on Religion and Related Subjects*, comp. Paul Edwards (New York: Simon & Schuster, 1957), 10.

> Religious distress is at the same time the expression of real distress and the protest against real distress. Religion is the sigh of the oppressed culture, the heart of a heartless world, just as it is the spirit of a spiritless situation. It is the opium of the people.
>
> The abolition of religion as the illusory happiness of the people is required for their real happiness. The demand to give up the illusions about its condition is the demand to give up a condition which needs illusions. The criticism of religion is therefore in embryo the criticism of the vale of woe, the halo of which is religion.[10]

Marx thought that once economic relations were changed, the need to believe in religion would be gone. Religion itself was both a distraction from and an apology for the savage inequalities of capitalism. He was a hard-nosed atheist, but whether Marxism itself is *militantly atheist* (convinced of atheism and willing to use force to promote it) is debatable. His ire was directed at the state and economic relations. Religion would wither and die once the state and economy had changed. Marx himself was never in any position of power to do this and died long before Communism emerged in Russia or China. Unquestionably, however, some of his ideological heirs, like Joseph Stalin and Mao Zedong, used the political powers of the state coercively and violently against religion. That Marxism invites the militant atheism of the latter Stalin or Zedong is a defensible proposition.

The atheistic perspective can take a different tone: *soft atheism* or *tolerant humanism*. Like other atheists, the tolerant or soft atheist does not personally believe in religion but is not persuaded that it is essentially harmful either. They are tolerant puzzle makers, willing to build a rationalist view alongside but separate from a religious one. The *soft atheist* coexists with and may be positive about some religious views but is simply doubtful of their truth. The humanistic perspective may go even further and affirm that religious values and thinking, while not completely true, are beneficial or useful. The sociologist Emile Durkheim (1858–1917), for example, studied tribal religions, and though he did not believe them to be true, he observed that their values were customary totems that regulated and ordered the behavior of society in beneficial ways. Even if its central claims about "God" or

10. Karl Marx and Friedrich Engels, *On Religion* (New York: Dover, 2008), 42.

absolute truth are wrong, religion may be useful in terms of its values and social functions. One can be critical of religion's claim to speak to the capital T Truth but also think it offers something valuable in terms of capital M Moral importance. Indeed, whether the final impact and importance of religion lie in its moral importance or its metaphysical claims is a topic of debate. Einstein, Isaac Asimov, and others have been critical of the literal truth of religion while appreciating much of its moral and cultural heritage.

The list of different ways of thinking about religion presented in this chapter does not pretend to be exhaustive. *Existentialists*, for example, would argue that it is essentially up to us to provide the vision of life and puzzle through its meaning. There have been, however, religious as well as atheistic existentialists. My nine types introduce a framework for how we assemble answers to the big question: the picture on the puzzle box of life. In *Making Sense of the Sacred*, we must all at some point consent to disagree, but we should have a better framework of common understanding. All of our answers will seem partial, but collectively appraised, our wisdom may at least point the compass needle in some direction. It tilts the seesaw of belief one way or the other. That process itself will probably not cease. It is the work of a lifetime.

Seven Reasons Why Religion Matters

Why does religion matter? Protestant theologian Reinhold Niebuhr long ago wrote *Does Civilization Need Religion?* There he argued that religion demonstrates its value to society when it responds to modern questions and moral problems. I agree that religion is needed in our world; I also agree with Gandhi that God's love of people and divine wisdom extends to all families of the world's religions.

Let us outline, then, why religion matters. Whether you happen to be an atheist, theist, or agnostic, religion matters for (at least!) seven major reasons. These reasons are (1) hopeful, (2) moral, (3) political, (4) human, (5) cosmic, (6) comic, and (7) imaginative. Let us look briefly at each.

The hopeful reason: Death is a grim truth all of us face, and religion offers a hopeful answer that death might not be the end. When facing death, everyone wonders if there is an afterlife or something beyond. Is death the end or just a new beginning? Is there heaven, hell, judgment, or a new cycle of life? Religion's hope reaches the very depth of human experience. It touches our shared fear of death and offers us a positive and consoling response. Because we all face the certainty of death, we all have to consider religion at some point in our lives as we figure out its meaning. I've often thought, *If all religions were false, I would wish for some form of them to be true.* Hope springs eternal from religion. This light of hope is never a bad thing, but it should not be a blinding thing either.

The moral and political reasons for religion's value are deeply related. Religion should be a spiritual guide and moral compass, giving us instructions to behave humanely. This, sadly, is not always the case. Often, darkly motivated religion exalts immoral and murderous behavior. Whether we behave humanely has a real political impact. A society full of moral persons is going to have different political results than one full of immoral persons. We must ask, How *should* we behave? Is religion giving us the best answers? Religion matters because it can transform people and their behavior and firm up the very bones of political society. Bad or darkly motivated religion might also erode those bones. In short, religion is not just about the next world; it is about what we should do in this one. In that respect, it is a source of hope and peace but also real conflict. Even when we fail its better standards, religion is a wellspring of both morality and politics.

The "human" reason for inquiring into religion is more psychological and sociological. Why do we believe these things? What does it say about our human nature? The study of religion is a way to learn more about human beings. Myths are tales of human origins, of the cosmos, that often try to explain and give meaning to the world we live in. Understanding religion and its myths is like trying to grasp the basic compass of human existence. When we read these stories, we may decipher a moral and symbolic meaning that provides us with a compass and map for where we are going. The human reason to study religion is to better understand ourselves.

The "cosmic" reason for religious value looks at the stories of creation and of God. Such stories are responses to questions like "How did we get here?" and "What is the meaning of our existence?" Religions invariably speak of the cosmos and how or why it came about. These stories needn't be perfect, nor even scientifically exact, if their simple intent is to situate us in the world and explain something about why it is here. Even a religion with no creation story has something to say about human life and the human world. But religious creation stories have sometimes courted ridicule. Comedians and humorists have drawn attention to possible absurdities of religious belief. A laugh, a good satire, can also evoke rich meaning, for what is absurd or funny tells us also something about our human values. Humor rebukes our stupidity while also consoling us about our capacity to make mistakes. The comic reason for religious value helps us laugh at ourselves and forget our woes. If we all retained at least some measure of humor and an ability to laugh at ourselves and even our beliefs, the world would be a less hostile place.

Finally, we come to the imaginative value of religion. Modern science has explained much of our world and our existence. Yet even modern science has explanatory limits. If we remain the fallible, mortal creatures I am familiar with, science will never be able to explain everything. There will be a part of the cosmos left unexplained, unfathomable, and mysterious. Imagination and religion forever abide in this realm, in the part of life we do not understand. Imagination and hope then take us to religion, to our vision of the world as we wish it to be.

Does religion matter? It certainly seems to! Personally, spiritually, socially, culturally, morally, politically, rationally, imaginatively, and scientifically religion touches upon all dimensions of our lives, and we are engaged with the questions of why we believe, how we believe, and what kind of evidence or arguments we use to support those beliefs. Religion matters. It matters everywhere, and all we have to do is open our eyes and minds to see why. Religion provides us a view to puzzle together and make sense of the sacred, giving us vision and courage to challenge the injustices of our society when they fail to meet up to our highest ideals. To creatively reparaphrase Gandhi's autobiography, religion matters and is of great consequence in our lives, and if all the words I have expended in the effort to make that clear have not been convincing, I shall deem those words to have been in vain.

2 Religious Trilemma: Making the Right Choice

Where do we find the right puzzle pieces to make sense of life? Do they fall out of the sky, like snowflakes? Like falling snowflakes, I suspect we might have to hustle in order to catch all of them. Or they might just unexpectedly fall into our hands at an unforeseen time and place. Sometimes the pieces of meaning come from a sacred scripture, a wise parent or teacher, a friend, or maybe an unforgettable experience. We can learn from books, people, and just living life. Religious traditions are in part all three of these. Once we have found enough pieces, there is the tough job of assembling them: a "trilemma" of theism, atheism, and agnosticism. This chapter explores that choice further. I'll try to make a tough choice easier. My choice may not be the same as yours, but even if it is not, we can at least muster enough common understanding to reconcile our differences. That theme runs to the very core of this book.

Let's begin with the miracle of now, this moment. Sometimes it seems as if science and computer technology have been Formula One race cars and religion has been a farmer's cart with a donkey in the modern world. Transformations in society have come so fast that they make a simpler world seem irrelevant or antiquated. Yet while we are quick to adapt transformations, we are also easily numbed to some of the classical values of religion. Religion *isn't* a slow, obsolete donkey, but it has much to adapt to in the modern world.

Science has indeed transformed the globe with new technologies. Two hundred years ago, the Industrial Revolution introduced mass production and overabundance. Seventy-five years ago, the atomic age began. Sixty years ago, we entered the space age. Not long after, we had personal computers and satellite-directed phones, navigation all across the globe, and genetically modified foods on the grocery shelves. In pharmacies and convenience stores everywhere, you can get your favorite candy bar or beer, and a product available in Iowa is also found in Boston, Moscow, or Paris. It is an age of scientific and industrial wonders, the miracle of this moment now.

But will the methods of science, critical thinking, and reason displace religion in the modern world? Science and reason are increasingly a common language based on demonstrable facts, theories, and empirical data. They have united scientists and men and women of reason across the globe regardless of nationality. Will this new common understanding wring the last drops of religious passion from the fabric of our civilization? Will the language of science and reason simply shatter old national, cultural, and religious boundaries? Science and modernity might appear as rivals to religion, but it may not be that simple. Religion and science may not be in mutual opposition to one another.

Martin Luther King Jr. once commented that religion and science are not in fact rivals: "There may be a conflict between soft-minded religionists and tough-minded scientists, but not between science and religion. Their respective worlds are different and their methods dissimilar. Science investigates; religion interprets. Science gives man knowledge which is power; religion gives man wisdom which is control. Science deals mainly with facts; religion deals mainly with values. The two are not rivals. They are complementary. Science keeps religion from sinking into the valley of crippling irrationalism and paralyzing obscurantism. Religion prevents science from falling into the marsh of obsolete materialism and moral nihilism."[1]

King's words pack in a lot of meaning, but the most significant point is that religion and science are complementary forms of knowledge, not rivals. Einstein famously observed that "science without religion is lame, and religion without science is blind."[2] Religion and science might therefore be viewed as interdependent.

Reexamining all perspectives on truth, one is left with several different ways of trying to make meaning of life. There is more than one picture of the world and its history to use to guide the assembling of the various pieces of the puzzle of life. Which will be the most compelling *worldview*, the Weltanschauung, as it has been called? A worldview that sets our feet on the ground in history, orients us, and gives us a map of where we have been and a compass direction for where we are going is needed. It will transform the baffling puzzles of life into a meaningful whole with which we can move forward toward a more peaceable and stable

1. Martin Luther King Jr., A *Testament of Hope: The Essential Writings and Speeches of Martin Luther King, Jr.*, ed. James M. Washington (New York: HarperCollins, 1986), 483.
2. Max Jammer, *Einstein and Religion: Physics and Theology* (Princeton, NJ: Princeton University Press, 1999), 11.

world future. Not everyone needs to have the same worldview; progress can be made without that absolute unity. But when worldviews collide badly, however, the results can be disastrous.

The globe we live on today is full of promises and wonder. We have technologies and wealth undreamed of in our past, but inequality and oppression still lead to turmoil and revolt. Dictators, tyrants, lying and manipulative rulers come and go. Our world of promise is also a world filled with peril. That is why attempting a common understanding is so essential. Religion is one of the primary ways of establishing that understanding and therefore must be part of the dialogue. It cannot be left out in an arbitrary preference to science or rational philosophy. Neither can religion set aside science and reason if it is to be fully engaging and compelling.

When I was a young man, there were 4.5 billion persons on this earth. Today, there are over 7.7 billion people. Many of them are poor and illiterate, without much opportunity to further themselves or escape the whims and dictates of their country or leader. I would be wealthy by their standards, having a home and a computer and a car and so much at my disposal, but by the standards of my own country, I am just middle class, and my means are virtually indistinguishable from any on my block or millions of other people. With so many disparate social and political contexts, one might despair of having any meaningful conversation about common values or ethics, let alone some kind of worldview with which we can all engage.

Despair is never a promising answer. In failing to explain our world, its religions and philosophies, we simply shrug and dismiss the task as impossible or futile, leaving it for future generations to tackle. Yet to do so would be irresponsible. So much would not have been invented or accomplished if we gave in to such temptations. Therefore, let us set despair aside and set into ink some meaningful *worldviews*. Building on what I've written, let's focus on a few perspectives.

Before we go any further, I want to formalize my definition of religion. Religion is, simply put, "belief in God(s), Goddess(es), or the sacred." Some religions have a God or various gods or goddesses. Others do not have a personal deity but assert that there is something sacred about human life or its ends. A fuller definition would be this: "Belief in a deity, deities, or the sacred, which provides a spiritual and moral compass." Religion is more than belief; it also gives us a direction and bearing for living.

In exploring the different choices of the religious *trilemma*, I will begin with a backward approach by investigating each proposition as if it were true and then considering its likelihood based on the evidence and implications. In terms of making sense of the sacred, or God, one can give an answer in at least four ways:

1. Atheism: God or the sacred is not true; we just make truth for ourselves.
2. Exclusivism: God or the sacred is represented best by only one tradition.
3. Inclusivism: God or the sacred is represented by a few but not all traditions.
4. Universalism/pluralism: Sacred truth or God is found in a great many religious traditions.

Atheism is the belief that God does not exist, and so the truth is not reflected in any of the world's religious traditions. Religions are either false and harmful (as the hard atheist claims) or reflections of human values that are useful for living (as the soft atheist claims). For the hard atheist, religions speak of things false in themselves: wish fulfillments as Freud spoke of them, opiates as Marx made them out to be, or delusions as Richard Dawkins has argued. Moreover, in the hard atheist view, the morality advocated by religion is imperfect, harmful, or even false. Reason should be the basis for morality because it alone is the firm ground on which we can plant our feet and understand the world. All else is a commitment to superstition or nonsense.

Humanists take a different stand. There may be no God or sacred, but religious traditions have captured meaning anyway. Religion has a social function and serves good ends. It can speak to some of the key values humans cherish, and so the soft atheist or humanist is not against all things that come from a religious tradition, only against the deeper affirmation that religious final truth (metaphysical) claims are real.

Humanists also point toward a less religious world. For while religions contain good values, once people deny that they are rooted in a final truth, they uproot those values from the emotional soil that gives them life. Religions are organically rooted in heart and mind, but if either heart or mind is consumed with doubt, religions are likely to wither. To say that religions uphold good values without also acknowledging that they have final truth in their end claims (such as the afterlife or belief in God, for example) is to pull them from the soil of our self that gives them life.

Atheism is possibly true, but no one has proven that it is true or offered a definitive argument that it is not. We must be prepared to live with a level of uncertainty. No single person possesses all the facts or a perfect theory about how to arrange them. The scope of our mind's horizons is simply too narrow to honestly affirm an idea with fixed and invariable certainty. A new development, a theory, an unforeseen shift in the sands beneath us could wash away all that we are sure about. Awareness of our limited perception should humble our views. Atheism might not be true. Its key problem is that it robs humans of a powerful motivational force without the absolute certainty that such force is false. There is still hope, I think, that there is a divine truth to this world. Of this, I cannot be sure, but it has led my mind (however narrow or broad you may think it to be) to pursue horizons and pictures different from that of atheism.

The second possibility is exclusivism: God or the sacred is best represented by just one religion. The rest of them may have captured something important but are in some way false or misleading. Religious truth is zero-sum. If the Buddhists are correct, then the Muslims are not. If the Christians are correct, then the Jews are not. The same goes for the exclusive claims of the Jains of India, the Hindus, the Zoroastrians, or the Mormons. One faith is true religion, and the rest are imposters. But with so many possible choices, which religion is true? If we are raised in a particular religion and adopt the habits of our culture and our parents, it is difficult to change our minds. How are we to know if we have been born into the religion that is true? Can we abandon the comfortable ways in which we are raised for some other tradition or idea that is wholly foreign to us? And why would God or the sacred allow some to be born to truth and others not? If one was not *born* into the religious tradition that is "true," why should one be judged by this? Why would God see fit to endow all wisdom to one place and not to another? It seems cruel that God would give one tribe of earth a monopoly on truth and leave the rest of us in the dark.

Such a God is possible, of course, even if that possibility is unpalatable. Moreover, the assumption that "God or the sacred" should act like we would is just that, an assumption. It is an anthropomorphism that compels God to act in ways we can conventionally understand. But God or the sacred is under no such limitation.

Buddhism does not have a personal God, nor does Jainism, and it is possible that the analogy made to God or the sacred as a loving parent or wise governor is a false one, even if we want it to be true. Much of the traditional religious world has tended toward exclusivism. The exclusive, traditional view embraces one religion out of a deep commitment that its teachings and rituals are indispensable.

Why would many people be predisposed to an exclusive view? Because human nature understands what is most familiar and close, what is sensible to us. There isn't often much time and leisure to *puzzle* and contemplate unfamiliar ideas. Work compels us to put in long hours to earn a living for home and family. When work is done, basic jobs around our house need doing, we need to rest and to relax, and there really isn't a lot of time to study one religion, let alone the whole family of world religions and philosophies.

Most people have proclivities, interests, and personal biases. We are not infinitely malleable and open-minded toward all things. We all tend to like some things more than others, however arbitrary or unfair that may seem. Personal biases are inherent in human nature, and thus they are both to be expected and completely understandable. It is common to find people attached to one tradition while also being unfamiliar or unacquainted with a variety of others. Human nature is inclined to assemble and make sense of the pieces of the puzzle of life that are most immediate and familiar to us. Those are the pieces inherited by one's family and nation of birth.

I am not compelled to follow this traditional or exclusive view. I have moved in a quite opposite direction. Why should any single tradition claim *all* the meaningful puzzle pieces, especially when some are quite well matched by other traditions? Perhaps a basic moral decency can be found in almost every tradition. I think this is possible. The traditional thinker may strongly disagree here. The traditional or exclusive thinker does not *necessarily* think less of others outside of their tradition. They simply follow their religion without thinking badly of others in any conscious way. That is so, unless they have been consumed by too much arrogant pride.

The real danger comes from the angry militants. They are ready to sweep aside others with contempt and inhuman violence. They claim their puzzle pieces are correct and absolute, sweeping all other pieces off the table as irrelevant. They've forgotten that the pieces are not mere pieces, however. They are human beings.

There is a third possibility. God or the sacred exists and is reflected in more than one but not all religious traditions. There are some religions that are "right" and on the "right track," and there are other religions that are wrong. This might seem a difficult view to sustain, but with further description, it may come more clearly into focus.

Religions of the world come in certain families or types. There are those religions that believe in one God, such as the "Abrahamic faiths" of Judaism, Christianity, and Islam. All three have scriptural and traditional connections to Abraham, who was called out of Ur of the Chaldees to journey to the promised land of Israel. Another family of religions is those of India, which believe in reincarnation: Hinduism, Jainism, Sikhism, and Buddhism. In the religions of East Asia, such as Daoism and Shinto, there is a pantheistic conception of the divine inherent in nature, in trees, rocks, water, and so forth. A sacred energy is believed to permeate based on the Dao in China, and in Shinto, the spiritual energy, or ki, is important. Some religions have common truths, and it is therefore possible to accept a few religions as being "closer to a divine truth" than others.

For example, in Islam, the Qur'an speaks about "People of the Book," or Jews and Christians and Sabeans, teaching that they will be saved on the day of judgment. The Qur'an 2:62 reads, "Believers, Jews, Christians, and Sabeans—whoever believes in God and the Last Day and does what is right—shall be rewarded by their Lord; they have nothing to fear or to regret."[3] The Qur'an also suggests, however, that a person who chooses a religion other than Islam will have regrets.[4] It is thus possible (but not automatic) for Muslims to view other monotheists as close to their own religion.

But if one sincerely believes in reincarnation, as the religions of India do, how can one seriously embrace the idea of a final judgment, as the Abrahamic faiths proclaim? I have also encountered Christians who have great respect for other monotheistic faiths but who think that the East Asian religions are nonsense. Mohandas Gandhi would have been repelled by these notions. He thought all religions were coequal, speaking of the same God. Gandhi's tolerance and pluralism have not always been favored, nor have they always prevailed. Gandhi cannot be

3. N. J. Dawood, trans., *The Koran* (New York: Penguin, 2003), v. 2:62, or p. 15.
4. Dawood, v. 3:83, or p. 44.

held up as a final arbiter of truth, and it is possible that some religions are more on track than others. It is possible to see a few religions as close to your own, which are more familiar, nearer to the sacred camp, pursuing a viable spiritual goal. An inclusivist thinker is not so adamant that one religion only is true but insists that some religious ideas and conceptions are better than others. For the inclusivist, some of the world's religions are really just barking up the wrong tree. This is wonderful news for those belonging to those sacred camps but not so good if you are on the outside.

What seems most difficult about either the inclusive or the exclusive viewpoint is this: How can a variety of religions speak to good and essential ethics and still be false? Is it the ultimate truth claims of a religion that matter or the good life they help us follow? If we observed the basic norms—the Golden Rule, don't lie, don't kill, don't commit adultery, don't steal—it would be hard to condemn a person for believing in other religious particulars that can be neither proved nor disproved.

In ways distinct from either the exclusivist or the inclusivist viewpoint, the Universalist or pluralist view of religion has this going for it: people everywhere are bonded together by a shared sense of good moral purpose. What the Universalist or pluralist model has going against it is a clear picture of what is true or sacred. Is there one God? Is there reincarnation? A Universalist does not proclaim to know and can only say that religious ideas are useful or good, even if they are not all absolutely true. Some religions observe one God, and others do not. Some religions affirm an eternal soul, which may reincarnate or strive for the afterlife. Others do not.

The fact that there is some moral agreement, however small it might be, is some consolation. Humans are beings that love life and want to live, to nurture families and thrive. If we can set aside the contrasting pictures we have of God or the sacred, which can be quite profound, it is possible to live together in peace. Gandhi, a great champion of the idea that religions are compatible, strove for this common understanding, and at the end of his life, he was distressed about the violence between Hindus and Muslims. He fasted, putting his life on the line to stop it, and ironically, he was assassinated by a Hindu who thought he was too biased toward Muslims.

A Universalist sees that there are many good and moral puzzle pieces scattered throughout the religious traditions of the world. The sacred message or truth is more broadly dispersed; no religion or culture has a monopoly on it. Since all traditions have good meaning, all can earnestly make good efforts in making sense of the sacred. We needn't argue that all religions are absolutely equivalent, just that no one is left in the dark. There is an additional proposition that the Universalist covertly accepts: the ultimate truth is beyond all partial grasp.

There will always be critics. Religions do not see eye to eye. Some seek salvation, and others escape from reincarnation; some have many deities, and others have one God; some believe in a soul, while others do not. The atheist might argue that religions evolved in separate and distinct ways, similar to the way languages have developed. Different human contexts match the unique spiritual climate. This is all religions are, speculations based on ignorance or an incomplete understanding of the cosmos. Science will wash those differences away.

That view has traction, but one need not embrace it. There have been attempts to explain and reconcile the differences between the various world religions. In Buddhism, from the Pali Canon, the Buddha warned against the absolute and certain claims made by various persons about religion. He told a parable of an elephant entering a village and a variety of blind men grabbing the elephant and coming to differing conclusions about it. One man got a hold of the trunk of the elephant and thought it was like a thick snake; another grabbed a tusk of the elephant and thought he held a spear. Still, a third blind man grabbed an ear of the elephant and thought he had a fan. A blind man who wrapped his arms around a leg of the elephant thought he had a tree trunk, and the man who grabbed the tail of the elephant believed he held a rope. Each man had a partial tactile sensation of what the elephant felt like, and according to what their hands grappled and felt, this was interpreted to be true. So too our minds only grapple with part of the truth we have seen.[5]

It is a classic parable, and its wisdom still extends to us today from across many centuries. Each of us can become too strident and sure of our beliefs, and we mistake the strength of our intellect with the certainty that is timeless and perfect. Buddhism is not the only religion from India to warn about this tendency. Jainism speaks of *anekantavada* as a doctrine of multiple viewpoints, which must be kept in mind. Too often we forget we are just one grain of sand on an endless beach,

5. Pali Canon excerpt from Bhikku Bodhi, ed., *In the Buddha's Words: An Anthology of the Pali Canon* (Boston: Wisdom, 2005), 214–15.

and we think that we know it all, when in fact we do not. Pride leads us to assume we are correct, when humility should call on us to admit we may not be.

Can the parable also reconcile the differences in the various world religions? When Christians experience the divine, it feels like the suffering Messiah Jesus, who died for the forgiveness of our sins. Jews do not perceive Jesus in the same way. Muslims accept Jesus as a prophet but not as divine. For them, Muhammad experienced a revelation that made important corrections to both of these religions. Buddhists might argue all three religions are mistaken and that there is no God, permanent self, or soul. Is it possible that these and other religions are partially true and partially mistaken, like the blind men have a partial religious understanding of the elephant (of truth)? All are grabbing just an edge or a corner of a sacred tapestry and cannot perceive the whole thing.

In the past, I thought that this parable was effective for explaining religious differences. But while it has some promises, it also some limitations. As a warning against personal absolutism and certainty, it does a good job. A level of humility or uncertainty, borrowed from the agnostic, is a good vaccination against excessive pride and certainty. The parable has some limitations, however. Can the divine or sacred really feel both like God (for Abrahamic religions) and also like no God (for Buddhism and Jainism)? Can we be certain we have a soul, while other religions deny the soul's existence? Are we really going to an afterlife and a *final* judgment after we die, or is death just a step in the journey to the next reincarnation? What kind of morality and what kind of faith profession are necessary to push us to the highest summit, to reconcile us with God, or to redeem us from the spiritual shackles of our world? These are very different ideas, and the fact remains that even with the Buddhist parable in mind, some religions may be wrong about some things, while others may be right. Either there is a God or there is no God, and either there is reincarnation or there is final judgment; one cannot have it both ways. Universalism can affirm we are all morally good but not offer a fully coherent picture of the puzzle of life. There is always a gap in the puzzle that is not understood.

Moreover, the parable asserts that religions are partially blinded, but this is not what religions have claimed to be. Religions purport to be keys to an everlasting bliss or eternally deep understanding. They have strong truth claims that they are extremely reticent to give up. No one likes being told that they are blind to the full truth, that they have only a partial answer. The parable of the blind men will continue to remind us of the limitations of our minds, but it may not suffice to surmount the entrenched spiritual differences of religion. So we must do more searching.

It has also been said that the religions are pathways up the same mountain. All religions, in spite of their differences, offer us spiritual and moral elevation toward a sacred goal—we are trying to raise ourselves to a spiritual summit and become better people. There is some merit to this metaphor because of the common general morality religions share: don't lie, don't kill, don't steal, and so forth. There are at least some aims that we do appear to have in common in basic standards of behavior.

Instead of climbing the *same* mountain, however, it seems more accurate to describe religions as climbing a common *mountain range*, or perhaps mountain ranges not so far removed from one another. Having studied many religions, the spiritual journeys of Christians, Jews, Hindus, Muslims, and Buddhists are not identical and do not seem to be going up an identical path or even the same mountain peak. Some seek an end to the cycles of reincarnation, while others are concerned with a final judgment. They do share the striving to become better, more moral, and elevated in terms of the standards of their religion. I think those standards of self-improvement can translate to moral progress on the whole in a wide variety of the world's faiths. Shared moral progress, however, does not imply a shared place of consensus. Finding *that* summit requires more work. A Hindu who follows his religion well and elevates his soul may see on a nearby summit a Christian who has done the same for her religion or a Jew who has done well in his. In some cases, based on the paths chosen by these spiritual hikers, the summits may be near one another. We may be surprised by how much we do have in common and how often we encounter each other on the way up. Because pathways up the same mountain may look very different at the base, we may be surprised who we meet at the top.

There is one concrete thing that the analogy tells us: religions set a moral goal or standard that is better than the one we currently have and help us work toward achieving it. This is what moral mountain climbing is all about. The mountain-climbing analogy may leave a level of complexity out. The critic charges that because religions are so specific in their rites, rituals, and beliefs, it is only when we *descend* from the heights of our religions and into a more generally shared space of the valleys that we find the common values. We must move away from specific ethical interpretations to get to the general moral precepts, such as the prohibitions against lying, killing, stealing, and adultery. It is only when we strip away the complexity of religions that we find the common traits among them. But, as previously said, simplifying and stripping our cultural heritage and religion away from us often uproot it from the soil that sustains belief.

The puzzle-making analogy is the one I am fond of because it implies a difficulty in trying to put things together and that it is a *really hard* puzzle that no one has been able to fully complete. No one has really agreed about the picture itself. We are all left with some personal bafflement in explaining the larger picture because there are some with beliefs that don't seem to fit into a common view of the picture puzzle as we imagine it. In public discourse we can be polite and civil, but in private we wonder, *How can this person believe in that*? There are a few of the puzzle pieces and values that fit together and are held in common, but there are quite a few others that don't fit. The common picture, the big idea of what unites all religions *outside* of their own perspectives, is going to remain elusive.

Nonetheless, the idea that all religious traditions have some redeeming moral vision or wisdom that can be used to enlighten others is the reason I have chosen the last option: Universalism. God or the sacred has given wisdom to a wide variety of religious and philosophical traditions so that we may learn from each other. We may not figure it all out, and we will be mystified and perplexed by much, but there is equal importance to exercising and improving our minds as there is to improving and elevating our moral selves. That some part of the world's traditions is "left out," excluded, without hope, is a rationally and morally unappealing idea to me.

This is why I think the puzzle-making analogy is the most honest and compelling metaphor for navigating the religious trilemma, however we choose to answer it. It tells us that progress in mutual understanding can and has been made but that the whole picture still eludes us. Belief systems are not just ways of making sense of meaning and moral progress; they are very real and entrenched parts of our social and political landscapes. With nearly eight billion people in the world, a wide disparity in the allocation of resources, and increasing demand, our planet is a place of both great promise and peril. Among those nearly eight billion people, there are myriad points of fragility where serious fractures can take place and violent conflicts erupt. Disagreement in worldviews can compound our differences and exacerbate our problems. While religion has not been the only cause of conflict in the past, religious disagreement remains real and dangerous. Making sense of our lives together is so important because collectively, so much is at stake.

We can look to a person outside our tradition, try to take them *seriously*, and learn from them at the risk of rethinking and reevaluating some of our own views and perspectives. We can look to the values of another religion or perspective and take them *casually* and not be so compelled to reflect on our own values, but we will not learn much either. If we look to the other and treat them *dismissively*, we risk reducing or belittling their humanity, which can lead to oppression and violence. Pressures in our society and politics can influence us to look at other peoples and cultures with varying levels of depth, and none of us exists outside of these pressures.

In navigating the religious trilemma, we will be left with pieces of the puzzle and gaps in the image that are not fully explained. But we should be patient and good-willed. We should try to go on puzzle making as best we can. The project is not in service of some grand picture that exists only in our minds. The project involves the very integrity and stability of earth's civilization, which can be either brought together in greater harmony or fractured along one of eight billion points of vulnerability. It is hoped that the religions of the world have something important to teach and to learn from each other. Take your own perspective seriously, but if you also reflect seriously on the perspective of another, you will learn twice as much.

3 Judaism

Summary of Judaism

Is Judaism the one true religion? Does it have all the puzzle pieces needed for human existence? Some Jews think so, particularly the Orthodox. Of course, Christians, Muslims, Sikhs, and many others make competing claims. Reform Jews who may be open to these other religions still insist that Judaism deeply inspires. Its message can improve justice and happiness for the whole world. Whether Judaism is the one true religion or not cannot be settled here, but it is likely that Jews are right that it has much to offer to the world.

The Hebrew Bible opens with the following words, "In the beginning when God created the heavens and the earth, the earth was a formless void and darkness covered the face of the deep, while a wind from God swept over the face of the waters. Then God said, 'Let there be light'; and there was light. And God saw that the light was good; and God separated the light from the darkness. God called the light Day, and the darkness he called Night. And there was evening and there was morning, the first day" (Gen 1:1–5). On subsequent days, God created the waters and the sky and caused dry land to appear. He created plants and animals that brought forth all sorts of living creatures. He created "cattle and wild animals of every kind," and "then God said, 'Let us make humankind in our image, according to our likeness; and let them have dominion over the fish of the sea, and over the birds of the air, and over the cattle, and over all the wild animals of the earth" (Gen 1:26). God told them to "be fruitful and multiply" (Gen 1:28). God did all of this in six days, and on the seventh day, he rested and blessed that day as hallowed.

God created the garden of Eden and told the first humans, Adam and Eve, not to eat from the tree of knowledge of good and evil and that if they did, they would surely die. The serpent persuaded them to eat from the tree of knowledge, and they became aware of their nakedness and their shame. When God confronted Adam, he said it was Eve who had given him the fruit of the tree of knowledge; she said she had been tricked by the serpent. So God punished the serpent by making him crawl on his belly, punished Eve with great pains in childbirth, and cursed Adam so that his toil would be hard and that only by the sweat on his face he would eat. And God banished them forever from Eden.[1]

This is one of the most famous stories in history and one of the most ancient accounts of human origins. But while traditional Jews and Christians feel a strong attachment to it, the story itself is out of sync with the findings of modern evolutionary biology. That we *evolved* and have a special relationship with other animals in a vast tree of life is the great insight of the nineteenth-century English biologist Charles Darwin. Bishop Samuel Wilberforce condemned Darwin's theory outright as incompatible with the Christian religion. During the famous 1925 *Scopes Monkey Trial*, the populist politician and prosecutor William Jennings Bryan said, "If evolution wins, Christianity goes—not suddenly, of course, but gradually, for the two cannot stand together."[2] What is a threat to Christianity could equally be a threat to Judaism. If we are not created by God, then the integrity of the Bible seems reduced or deflated.

Among both Jews and Christians, there are two major poles of religious interpretation regarding the passage. The literal view rejects evolution outright and asserts that the world is between six and ten thousand years old. This directly contradicts modern science, which tells us that the human species is at least a hundred thousand years old, our *Homo habilis* and *Homo erectus* ancestors are over one million years old, and the earth itself has been forming since at least 4.5 billion years ago.[3] According to modern science, the story of our world is much different from the one told in the Hebrew scriptures. Fossil remains, skeletal remains, radiocarbon and other forms of dating, and the study of the stars in the skies all seem to confirm that the world is much more ancient than the literal interpretation allows.

The more liberal religious believers, however, do not read the Genesis story literally but see it as inspired. Inspired stories need not be word-for-word true in every detail, and parts may be interpreted mythically or metaphorically. Myths evoke symbols or ideas but don't need to be literally true to be meaningful. Inspired, liberal readings of the Genesis story as an ancient myth tell us that God created humanity and that we rebelled against God. The struggles we have faced since the

1. Gen 2:15–3:20.
2. Clyde Wilcox and Carin Robinson, *Onward Christian Soldiers: The Religious Right in American Politics* (Boulder, CO: Westview, 2011), 29.
3. Richard Leakey, *The Origin of Humankind* (New York: Basic Books, 1994), preface and chaps. 1–3.

exile from Eden—our perils, labors, and hardships—go back to being in some state of rebellion and exile. But the liberal reading of the Genesis story as *myth* also has difficulties. A Reform Jew or a liberal Christian may be able to call parts of the Bible *myths*, to be read metaphorically for their moral or spiritual meaning, but what then becomes of the integrity of the Bible? What parts of the Bible must be read as *myth*, and what parts are concrete historical narrative? What is word-for-word truth and actually happened, and what parts are symbolic? The Bible, which has been a document of great authority and inspiration for centuries, suddenly becomes marshy. The Bible is not the only religious scripture facing this problem of interpretation. Many other religious scriptures can be added as well. No exact reading, no precise interpretive method, can fully answer these questions. Religion and science may be more compatible than they sometimes seem. But the peace and reconciliation between science and religion are neither easy nor permanent.

Like many ancient religions, the Hebrew Bible contains both a creation narrative and a flood narrative, in which much of what was initially created is destroyed. The story of Noah is arguably the best known of these ancient flood narratives. But like the story of creation, the modern liberal believer treats the flood account as myth and not literal history. The flood story begins with God's grim recognition that "the wickedness of humankind was great in the earth, and that every inclination of the thoughts of their hearts was only evil continually" (Gen 6:5). According to the narrative, "the Lord was sorry that he had made humankind on the earth, and it grieved him to his heart. So the Lord said, 'I will blot out from the earth the human beings I have created—people together with animals and creeping things and birds of the air, for I am sorry that I have made them.' But Noah found favor in the sight of the Lord" (Gen 6:6–8).

God instructed Noah to build an ark and fill it with pairs of the earth's animals, saving a remnant of what was good in creation. For forty days, torrential rains covered the earth. Noah and the inhabitants of his ark survived, and God's covenant was reestablished through him. But why this grisly, wet apocalypse? Why would a good and omniscient God regret his own creation so much that there was a need to blot out humanity? To the fundamentalist Christian or Orthodox Jew, these events happened. In the most liberal, mythic interpretation, if they did not literally happen, they tell us of the human capacity for rebelliousness and sin and God's redemptive action.

It is a tale both troubling and hopeful. It suggests an inconceivable error of a Creator but balances this with a statement of hope and promise at the end. Yet the flood story also resonates with a theme explored throughout the Hebrew Bible: an eternal, tested covenant or promise between God and humankind. That covenant takes this formula: God extends a promise and human beings fail to live up to it. There is a consequent punishment, but the covenant continues with another generation or a prophetic leader. God never closes the door on humankind, even in the flood story. God always finds some who have been worthy of the promise.

What is clear in the Hebrew Bible is that God chooses the Jews for a special purpose. They are to embrace his covenant and follow his commands. Abram and Sarai, the ancestral parents of the Jewish faith, are summoned to the promised land that will be known as Israel. God gives them both new names: Abram is renamed Abraham and Sarai is renamed Sarah. Abraham fathers a son, Ishmael, through his wife's handmaid, Hagar. It is from Ishmael that Muslims trace their lineage, which is why Islam connects with Judaism as an Abrahamic faith. Abraham eventually has a son named Isaac through Sarah. God tests Abraham's faith, telling him to sacrifice his son Isaac as an offering to the Lord. Abraham begins to do so, but at the last moment, God stays Abraham's hand, telling him that he has passed the test of his faith.

Why would God do this? Why would God promise Abraham many descendants and then ask him to kill the child of that promise? Atheists and critics cite this text as evidence for their view that religion is immoral. There are no easy rebuttals, but skeptics are not the only ones who wrestle with the morality of this story. Theologians and believers have tried to make sense of it for thousands of years. It remains that God does not, in fact, make Abraham commit the repugnant deed. God also tells Abraham that although he and his descendants will be greatly blessed by God's covenant (Gen 12:1–3), they will also face trials and tribulations (Gen 15:13–14). But because God is faithful to the covenant, he will never abandon them.

The covenant between God and the Jewish people is a major theme of the Bible, and it is well reflected in the Shema, or the "Hear Prayer" of Judaism:

> Hear O Israel: The Lord is our God and the Lord Alone. You shall love the Lord your God with all your heart, and with all your soul, and with all your might. Keep these words that I am commanding you today in your heart.

> Recite them to your children and talk about them when you are at home and when you are away, when you lie down and when you rise. Bind them as a sign on your hand, fix them as emblems on your forehead and write them on the doorposts of your house and on your gates.[4]

These are the words Moses offers to the newly freed Hebrews after he received God's law on Mount Sinai. They are reflected in the Jewish tradition of the black prayer box worn during prayers, known as tefillin. They are also inside the mezuzah, or prayer box at the threshold of Jewish homes.

According to Genesis, Isaac himself had two sons: Jacob and Esau. Jacob fathered many sons who were to become the patriarchs of the twelve tribes of Israel. Of these sons, Joseph had his father's favor. The jealousy of Joseph's brother turns to treachery, and they throw him into a pit, sell him into slavery, and tell their father that Joseph had been killed. In slavery in Egypt, Joseph experiences further travail but also triumph. Through his capacity for interpreting dreams, Joseph is brought to the attention of Pharaoh, who was disturbed by a dream he'd had about seven fat cows and seven skinny ones emerging from the river Nile. Joseph interprets Pharaoh's dream and explains that there will be seven years of plentiful crops in Egypt followed by seven years of famine in the land. Pharaoh is so impressed with Joseph that he frees him from captivity and makes him his adviser. Joseph helps Pharaoh prepare Egypt for the impending famine.

While Joseph is busy in Egypt, his brothers back in Israel are not prepared for the famine and are forced to come to buy provisions in Egypt. They encounter Joseph but do not recognize him at first. Putting them to a test, Joseph finally reveals who he is. After a long and bittersweet reconciliation with his brothers, he forgives them.

The book of Exodus opens by telling the reader that shortly later in Egyptian history, a pharaoh came to power who did not remember Joseph's good deeds. The Hebrew descendants of Joseph and his brothers are enslaved. Instead of a great promised land and freedom, the Jews become oppressed in bondage. In this context, the Hebrew Bible tells us of the next inheritor of the covenantal promise: Moses.

To keep control over the growing slave population, Pharaoh had ordered that the male firstborn of Jewish households be put to death. But Moses had been put into

4. Wayne A. Meeks, ed., *The HarperCollins Study Bible* (New York: HarperCollins, 1993), Deut 6:4–9.

a reed basket in the river Nile, was discovered by Pharaoh's daughter, and was raised as an Egyptian in Pharaoh's house. It is a famous tale, but there is actually a Mesopotamian one much like it in which Sargon the First was put into the river Euphrates and later became a great ruler over Akkadia.[5] In Moses's story he grows up within the court of Pharaoh, then becomes angry with an Egyptian taskmaster for beating a Hebrew slave. He strikes and kills the guard and is then forced to flee into Midian, where he meets a man named Jethro and marries his daughter Zipporah.

Moses's tale has captivated our attention for centuries. Famous actors such as Charlton Heston, Ben Kingsley, and Christian Bale have portrayed him in movies. Whether one believes in the tale or not, it is a deeply memorable one filled with twists, turns, villains, and danger. Pharaoh is the primary villain. God calls out to Moses from a burning bush and instructs him to return to Egypt to confront Pharaoh and to set his people free. It is an overwhelming task.

When Moses confronts Pharaoh, he does not want to let the Jews go, and there is a contest of power between Moses and Pharaoh's court magicians. Moses wins this battle, but not until ten devastating plagues have been unleashed upon the Egyptians: the river turns to blood; there is a plague of frogs, gnats, and lice; there are swarms of flies and animals; and there is pestilence over livestock. There are also boils, hail, and locusts sent upon Egypt. Curiously, the text also says that God "hardened Pharaoh's heart," as if he wanted the Egyptians' suffering to continue. But after the angel of death causes the death of all the firstborn (the Jews are able to escape this fate by marking the threshold of their doors with the blood of a lamb), Pharaoh agrees to let the Hebrews go free. The Jewish holiday Passover commemorates this time when God set his people free from Egypt.

But curiously, God again "hardened the heart of Pharaoh" (Exod 14:8) against his own decision to release the Jews. This was the decision God apparently wanted him to make. So why change Pharaoh's mind? The Bible tells us that it was done to show God's power and demonstrate clear signs of God's supremacy. But did this have to be done? Can God make us move about like marionettes on a string? Reading the exodus narrative literally raises important and difficult philosophical questions about free will and Providence.

5. Robert Chadwick, *First Civilizations: Ancient Mesopotamia and Ancient Egypt* (Oakville, CT: Equinox, 2005), 52.

The Bible is full of both amazing and disturbing images: tales of miracles but also of massacres. We cannot easily today imagine worshipping a God who finds the aroma of sacrificial animals "pleasing." It seems our conception of God has changed and with it our understanding of the Bible's narratives.

One of the most famous images in the Bible is Moses's parting of the Red Sea, allowing the Jews to escape. The pursuing Egyptians are then consumed by collapsing waters that drown Pharaoh's army. It is a miraculous story. Did it really happen? Are there nonmiraculous ways of explaining it? Some have claimed, for example, that the Red Sea was the marshy sea of *reeds* (rather than the actual Red Sea), which the Hebrews could cross but in which Pharaoh's heavy army got bogged down. Accepting miracles that one has not witnessed and that defy human experience requires some faith and imagination. Does this require too much? Should the Bible be taken literally here? Perhaps the primary moral and theological lesson is instead this: God's guiding hand is essential to setting his people free. In reading any story, we interpret it, edit it in our minds, and either cast it into the rubbish heap of dim memories or make it our own. We appropriate reported facts, values, and ideas to ourselves and discard what we cannot process or accept. No two people read any text the same way.

What is very central to the Jewish story of the exodus is the reception of the law on Sinai. Moses ascends the fiery mountain for forty days and nights, but below, the Hebrews begin to despair in his absence. They ask Aaron to make a golden calf to worship instead, and when Moses comes back down from the mountain, divine wrath and bloody reckoning follow. Many of the faithless are killed for having so quickly strayed from God's path and promise. How can faith be so weak? How can God be so vengeful? Why did any of this need to happen? Questions like these are hard to answer. In the Bible, clearly faith is sternly required and a hard test to pass.

The covenant between God and his people does not end there, however. It never does. For while God can be wrathful and vengeful, as depicted in the Jewish Bible at least, he also reconciles and forgives. Indeed, the covenant is even renewed and intensified with the granting of the law to Moses, the most famous being the Ten Commandments, relayed here in abbreviated form:

1. I am the Lord your God; you shall have no other gods.
2. You shall not make for yourself an idol or graven image.

3. You shall not take the Lord's name in vain.
4. Remember the Sabbath, to keep it holy.
5. Honor your father and your mother.
6. You shall not commit murder.
7. You shall not commit adultery.
8. You shall not steal.
9. You shall not lie or bear false witness.
10. You shall not covet your neighbor's wife or possessions.[6]

As we've seen in earlier chapters, commandments five through ten resonate strongly with other religious traditions. The moral law of the Jews is universal, reflected across the world. Commandment five, to honor one's father and mother, is reflected, for example, in Confucian practices of reverence for one's ancestors. Many cultures do the same. Not *all* that is in the Ten Commandments is universally reflected, however. The ideas of keeping a Sabbath, of worshipping one high Creator God, and of not making any idols are not so widely reflected in other religions. There are areas of agreement and disagreement between Judaism and other traditions. Puzzling through this, I wonder if there is room for growth: by considering seriously our differences, we learn deeply from neighbors unlike us. The picture of life deepens.

The Ten Commandments are a precious gem of moral wisdom. If they were followed more regularly and routinely, then the world might be a better place. Their human, moral parts (laws six through ten) can be defended on the basis of reason. Like many other gems, however, closer study reveals a flaw, or at least something that deeply *troubles* human reason. The *full text* of the second commandment is rarely printed, and many have never read it in its entirety. It reads as follows: "You shall not make for yourself an idol, whether in the form of anything that is in heaven above, or that is on the earth beneath, or that is in the water under the earth. You shall not bow down to them or worship them; for I the Lord your God am a jealous God, punishing children for the iniquity of parents, to the third and the fourth generation of those who reject me, but showing steadfast love to the thousandth generation of those who love me and keep my commandments."[7] The supreme irony of course is that this is the very commandment that was violated even when

6. Exod 20:1–17.
7. Exod 20:4–7.

the faithless Hebrews at the foot of Sinai asked Aaron to make the golden calf. But questions remain: Why is God *jealous*? Should we ascribe that petty human trait to a divine and omnipotent being? What kind of sadistic God would punish four generations of innocent descendants who had no part in their ancestors' decisions? By reasonable standards, this God seems unjust and unfair. What can explain it?

Some have tried to explain away the punishments for violating the second commandment as a "divine bluff" meant to warn and keep people on track but never actually to be put into practice. But in the context of Judaism at the time, it might also be explained as a move to purify the emerging faith from rival or competing gods, such as Baal or El. Hence it reflects the theological interests of that time. One can try to explain it, one can outright reject it, but at minimum one has to think about it. Do religious scriptures really have to be *perfect*, or just meaningful? Personally, I can't say that I've ever read a *perfect* text, but I have read many meaningful ones. Trying to defend a text or tradition as *perfect* and *absolute*, for me, has been a much higher and harder bar to achieve than defending it as good or meaningful.

I often think of critically reading the scriptures of our past as looking into a fiery bed of hot coals and embers mixed with dying ash. Some of the things you encounter will still shine brightly and inspire centuries after they were written because they touch upon things that are essentially human. Other things may seem like lifeless ash, part of a time or culture that is no longer alive. We no longer keep slaves and avoid brutal punishments. These things clearly are ashes to us. Other parts of our past come to us like hot coals that still enlighten us or shine like diamonds. For now, let us return to the story.

After years of leading the Hebrews through the wilderness, Moses is able to see the promised land at a distance but dies before he can enter it. When his people enter, though, several major religious holidays are born: Shavuot, an annual celebration of the giving of the law on Sinai; Sukkot, or the Day of Tabernacles, remembers the temporary living arrangements endured during the journey to the promised land; and of course Pesach, or Passover, recalls the escape from Egypt.

When the Hebrews come back to the promised land, they soon demand a government to administrate the affairs of the state. After the period of the judges, God gives the Israelites a king. King Saul is the first king to rule over all the tribes. King David succeeds Saul. And Solomon succeeds King David. Saul leads the Israelites as they fight and reconquer the land that had been occupied in their absence. He embarks on a hasty military campaign without God's prophetic guidance and loses God's favor. He plays out a cat-and-mouse chase with his ultimate successor and God's new anointed one, David. David has the opportunity to kill Saul at one point but doesn't. He is one of the most famous and memorable kings of the Jews.

It is David who slays Goliath, the mighty and towering Philistine. Goliath had been the strongest warrior among the Philistines, yet with a sling and a stone, David lays him low. David receives great blessing from God, but David is flawed. When he is king, David sees Bathsheba bathing from afar, is filled with lust and desire, and commits adultery with her. To cover up his crime, he tries to get her husband Uriah to sleep with her to conceal the paternity of the child illicitly conceived. But Uriah is too steadfast a soldier and declines, so David sends him to the front lines of the fight, and he is killed. God then sends Nathan to remind David of his crime, and he is punished with the death of his firstborn child. Again, one must ask, Why is it the innocent child who has to die here for the crimes of the parents? Not all that is written in the Bible agrees with modern senses of morality. In any case, David is crestfallen. He repents, and God forgives him. Despite his moral failings, he helped redeem the promised land for the Jews and is widely esteemed for many of his other just actions.

God grants to David's son and successor, Solomon, a wise and discerning mind along with great prosperity. Solomon has the honor of building the first great temple for the Jews in the promised land. This point in Jewish religious and political history is a golden age. Things are back where they belong. The Israelites have a good king ruling over them, and by biblical accounts, they are prosperous. And yet within a few generations, the kingdom is conquered by Assyrians, then the Babylonians, and the people are swept away into exile. But why? Weren't they God's chosen people?

The Jewish view has been that while they have always been God's chosen people, they have at times neglected to fulfill the central tenet of loving God: the basic commandment of the Shema prayer. Solomon, despite all his great wisdom, is an all-too-human character and, like the rest of us, makes mistakes. Solomon's mistake is not his polygamy (the Hebrew Bible says that he had some seven hundred wives and three hundred concubines); rather, he sinned in allowing the worship of other gods and goddesses to creep into his household and into the nation. His many foreign wives brought their deities with them to Israel, and that, from a Jewish perspective, is the biggest problem. One must serve God and no other.

Therefore, the kingdom was swept away. After Solomon's death, the nation of Israel divided into two kingdoms, with ten tribes of Israel in the north under King Jeroboam and two tribes in the south under King Rehoboam. First, the northern kingdom was conquered by Assyrians in 722 BCE, and its ten tribes were taken captive. Then, in 586 BCE, the Babylonians conquered the kingdom of Judah in the south. This began the Babylonian captivity, a second exile for the Jews, and a partial explanation for their Diaspora, a term that refers to the Jewish spread outside from the promised land. In exile, Jews encountered other religions, including Zoroastrianism, a similar but distinct monotheist faith. Eventually, the Persian king Cyrus allowed many Jews to return to Judea, and they built a second temple. With the construction of the Second Temple, the Jews were back in the promised land once again.

Alexander the Great soon conquered the known world, and the Jews came under Greek rule. A revolt by the Maccabees, celebrated each year during the Chanukah festival, provided a period of brief autonomy before the Roman general Pompey began a new occupation in 63 BCE. A final attempt at revolt from Rome in the year 66 CE failed, and in the year 70 CE, the Second Temple was destroyed. The Wailing Wall in modern Jerusalem is the ruins of the Second Temple. It is a place sacred to Jews. It allows them to commemorate their past, both their tragedies and their triumphs.

Through the centuries, the Jews have been trying to hold on to their religious traditions and beliefs in spite of incredibly hard circumstances. What are the core values that they pass on to us? The Ten Commandments are indeed a precious contribution to human civilization. Much but not all of their morality is seen in other religions. Jews try always to remember God and his covenant by keeping his laws. But what is the essence of the law? A parable about Rabbi Hillel instructs us.

According to the story, a man comes one day to the elders of the Sanhedrin, the Jewish high court of the first century. The man mockingly asks the rabbis to summarize the heart of the Torah while standing on one foot. Rabbi Shammai dismisses the man and sends him away, but Rabbi Hillel says that he is up to the challenge and delivers a beautiful response: "What is hateful to you, do not do to others. The rest is commentary, go and learn it." The man is impressed and is converted on the spot.[8] Hillel's commentary invokes what is sometimes called the "silver rule."

As a student of world religions, it is fascinating to me how widely spread the rule is. Confucius, a Chinese philosopher whom Shammai did not know, had a similar rule that stands at the heart of Confucianism. Confucius called it *shu*, or "Do not impose on others what you do not want yourself."[9] It is an inversion of the Golden Rule, which enjoins us to do unto others as you would have them do unto you, and it is a reasonable and defensible commandment. A vast number of world religions contain some expression of it. That a common vision of the moral life can emerge from among the various religions of the world is a hopeful prospect.

Tragically, the Jews have had to endure the horrible burdens of anti-Semitism. They have been pulled from their promised land and have lived scattered in Diaspora across Asia, Europe, the United States, and elsewhere. The anti-Semitic climate became so intense that figures like Theodor Herzl and his successor Chaim Weizmann decided it was necessary to find a homeland for the Jews. In the nineteenth and twentieth centuries, the Zionist project to establish a homeland for the Jews took off with great energy, and through many labors and the leadership of figures like David Ben-Gurion, a new state was founded in Palestine. Amid conflict, Israel was reborn in 1948. Of course, the Palestinians have objected that they were unjustly displaced from their land, and Arabs have argued that the injustice done to Jews elsewhere, infamously by the Nazis during the Holocaust, does not justify the injustice done to the Muslim Palestinians who had been living there for centuries. It has become a difficult and intractable conflict, and there are just arguments that can be made for both sides.

It is remarkable, even amazing, that a group of people so small in number has had such a disproportionately huge impact upon the world. There are not many Jews, nor a huge number of practitioners of Judaism, but the daughter religions of Christianity and Islam descend from the tradition of Abraham, and without that connection, there are vast historical gaps in Christianity and Islam. The promise made to Abraham by God that his descendants would be innumerable has come true. The direct descendants of the Jews *and* the indirect descendants of

8. Stephen Wylen, *Settings of Silver: An Introduction to Judaism* (New York: Paulist, 2000), 201–2.
9. Roger T. Ames and Henry Rosemont, trans., *The Analects of Confucius—a Philosophical Translation* (New York: Ballantine Books, 1999), 189.

Christianity and Islam add to over 3.6 billion people. The impact of the Jews and their Abrahamic faith has been felt on almost half of the peoples of earth. In addition, the capacity for Jewish people to hold on to their heritage, to preserve their culture and tradition, in spite of the great difficulties imposed on them is nothing short of remarkable. Whether or not the Jews are indeed God's "chosen" people, it is evident that their great strength and perseverance have kept their tradition alive. Of course, Judaism and its beliefs are not for everyone. There are secular and atheistic Jews, as there are skeptics in all cultures and traditions. Even in this brief review of the religion, we've seen a number of beliefs and values shared with other religions and a number of things that do not fit.

What Fits?

What pieces of the puzzle of Judaism fit with other religions and our ideas about the kind of world we want to live in? The Ten Commandments and the silver rule (and its Golden counterpart) would top the list. Even a compact version of the Decalogue—"don't lie, don't kill, don't commit adultery, don't steal"—represents values cherished across the world. Humanity's well-documented history of lies, murder, pain, betrayal, and theft is clear evidence that we are not always up to following this ethic. Our human nature is indeed split, part selfish, part social, but always in need of a moral alignment to keep our minds and hearts straight. Morally speaking, Judaism has a lot to offer.

The timeless narrative of how God created the world and gave us a central place in it strikes an important heart chord. Deep down, perhaps in an archetypical fashion, we connect with the idea that we are here for a reason. We want to believe, even if we have doubts, that our lives are meaningful, are purposeful, and have clear directions. This is a view of the world that Christians, Muslims, and Zoroastrians could get behind, and many Hindus and other religious people could share in it as well, though their narratives about creation are not identical. There is some vital shared meaning in the idea that we are here because a loving God wanted it that way.

But this idea, this timeless narrative, has to reckon with the modern world. Imagine that you are a peasant in the fourteenth century, maybe partly literate if you are lucky, having no idea about Galileo or Darwin. All you really immediately know is that the Bible told you why you are here and how to behave. In such a world, the narratives from the Hebrew Bible were not challenged. But that peasant from the fourteenth century is no more. Today, we have modern evolutionary biology and astronomy. Our cell phones can put them at our fingertips in seconds. Presently, we struggle to put the pieces of meaning together, and there are a lot of pieces! The moral law and its sacred meaning are only two of the things that could fit this puzzle. There are many more. If the narrative of creation is not taken literally, it can still be taken symbolically or metaphorically. It can tell us about ourselves, our rebellious and often sinful ways, but also of the hope that we can overcome them. This is the story of Judaism, a promise made by God, human failure to live up to it, and the times of great triumph and awful tragedy that follow. In many ways it is still simply the story of ourselves as we stumble and climb to higher peaks.

What Doesn't Fit?

Judaism's narrative is not one that gels immediately with everyone. Its metaphysics doesn't fit well with Buddhism, which disavows the idea of a creator God. Jewish rules against making idols or graven images are not a Hindu concern. Hindus make countless images of God, but they are just symbols, and Hindus do not fret over them. God transcends the idols of Hinduism, and Hindus understand this. Muslims are much closer to Jews than Hindus in this respect. They emphasize God's transcendence and prohibit any kind of depiction of God. Critics from scientists like Richard Dawkins or psychoanalysts in the spirit of Sigmund Freud have argued that the religious creator idea is a false one that we should discard. For those like Freud or Dawkins, empirical reality is all there is. As a result, they build the puzzle of life in a much different way than many theists. Science is now an equal contestant with religion in the arena of life that tries to establish its meaning.

Additionally, some parts of the Jewish Bible do not fit with modern ethical understandings. For example, directly after the Ten Commandments, the book of Exodus enumerates rules for keeping, selling, and managing slaves. Now why would a sacred text bother to spell out rules for keeping slaves if slavery is inherently immoral? Slavery may have been accepted at the time of Moses, but

God is timeless and would know what is right and what is wrong for that time or any other. The Bible was used to justify slavery in the United States. Slave owners said it was a good Christian thing to do. Abolitionists have also used the Bible to condemn slavery, arguing that it does not live up to the norms of human justice, to the Golden Rule (or silver if you prefer). Slavery fails Kant's categorical imperative, as well as the test of justice and good ethics in many other philosophies. The fact remains that slavery exists in the Bible. How one addresses that fact is determined by how one interprets the text. And there are multiple interpretive traditions.

Different schools of interpretation exist in every religion I have ever studied. They exist in Judaism too. For the Orthodox Jew, the Bible is to be taken seriously such that all the rituals and laws that were incumbent upon Jews thousands of years ago should be a duty for Jews today. Yet even the Orthodox Jew today does not imagine keeping a slave. The Orthodox Jew does, however, hope to keep the integrity and spirit of the tradition alive to the highest possible degree. The Reform Jew sees things differently. The Reform school of Judaism believes that it is the moral spirit and heritage of the Torah that is essential but that parts of it may have applied with more force in ancient times. Adaptation and reinterpretation are required in accord with Reform Judaism's acceptance of an evolutionary point of view. Reform Jews therefore try to live according to the spirit of the religion but not so much the direct letter. In between these two schools, Conservative Judaism offers a third interpretation. Taking the Bible seriously but not so intensely at certain parts as the Orthodox Jew, the Conservative Jew still tries to maintain the tradition. The Conservative observes the kosher dietary restrictions and many of the rules of the Orthodox Jew. They may see the Orthodox as too rigorous in parts and the Reform as too liberal.

All of us are in the same boat here, making some negotiations and compromises in interpreting our religions and different philosophical or scientific perspectives. We are oftentimes forced to confront things that do not fit well together, puzzle pieces that do not make sense or do not belong, and sometimes we put them together in ways that do not quite fit until we find the right piece later. We are doing this all the time in life, trying to figure out the picture around our personal life and the bigger life surrounding that. Unlike the peasant or the priest of many centuries ago, we have a larger, more bewildering intellectual universe to assemble. The physical challenges of survival may be easier now than they were then, but the mental ones are immensely more challenging.

Puzzler's Conclusion

For my part, I cannot accept a literal reading of the Bible. I affirm that evolution happened and that parts of the Bible are not direct factual reports. But as ancient myths, many still have a great core of meaning. An inspired, more liberal reading of Judaism allows me to preserve much of its moral meaning while rejecting ideas that seem contrary to good moral conscience or scientific reasoning. One might therefore affirm evolution, but that God may have had a hand in beginning or perhaps even guiding it. Further, one can affirm moral norms and values that have a classic antiquity while avoiding others that seem obsolete. A treasure of moral wisdom emerges from Judaism, but moral tragedies, which belong to the heritage of past cultures, should have no place in modern life. I cannot accept that an omnipotent God would fashion the institution of slavery and make recommendations for its continued management. Slavery and discrimination represent a failure of human culture, not divine wisdom. I read the Bible as a part of the tapestry of world history and find in it divine sparks, notions of what God must be like, but the whole picture continues to be elusive. We are still assembling it.

To be fair to the opposing view, an Orthodox Jew or more literalist Christian would reject these ideas, seeing them as a danger that waters down the authority of ancient texts and risks perverting them. Traditional cultures and ideas must be preserved, it might be argued, to keep people from going astray and manufacturing their own false gods, just as Aaron was persuaded to do in the biblical account. This, however, is an idea that the liberal or inspired view might also share: that if we don't take good norms and values seriously, we are in danger of creating false ones; norms that ask too little of us or cause us to follow wrong ends.

To conclude, I think the challenge to prove *any* religion is absolute and perfect is a high bar to meet. Even if one were able to prove such a religion perfect and true, it would trouble me what that might imply for the rest of us. For me, the lower bar of seeing a religion as potentially good and meaningful is more plausible and more compatible with other religious or philosophical views. Despite tragedy and persecution, Jews have kept alive their culture and traditions, both of which have made an impact on world history. Disagreement about *any* religious idea must not automatically be interpreted as an insult or injury. If our skin becomes too thin, then we have no way of reconciling and negotiating with our neighbors. If one sees flaws in the interpretation of another view or vision, one must also contritely admit flaws in one's own.

4 Christianity

Summary of Christianity

Jesus is perhaps the most famous person in world history. He can also be controversial. Worldwide, two billion Christians revere him as the Messiah. Among 1.6 billion Muslims, his message (albeit not the final one) is also affirmed as prophetic. Jews do not recognize Jesus as a messiah, though many appreciate his words and ministry. Hindus and Buddhists have sometimes admired Christ, while others have gone their own way. But what did Jesus say that mattered?

Jesus emphasized the imperative to love and forgive: "You have heard that it was said, 'You shall love your neighbor and hate your enemy.' But I say to you, Love your enemies and pray for those who persecute you, so that you may be children of your Father in heaven; for he makes his sun rise on the evil and on the good, and sends rain on the righteous and on the unrighteous. For if you love those who love you, what reward do you have? Do not even the tax collectors do the same? . . . Be perfect, therefore, as your heavenly Father is perfect" (Matt 5:43–48). The famous Beatitudes add, "Blessed are the merciful, for they will receive mercy. Blessed are the pure in heart, for they will see God. Blessed are the peacemakers, for they will be called children of God" (Matt 5:7–9). Instead of seeking vengeance or harboring anger, Jesus taught a message of forgiveness: "You have heard that it was said, 'An eye for an eye and a tooth for a tooth.' But I say to you, Do not resist an evildoer. But if anyone strikes you on the right cheek, turn the other also; and if anyone wants to sue you and take your coat, give your cloak as well; and if anyone forces you to go one mile, go also the second mile" (Matt 5:38–41).

There is a forgiving and merciful tone to Christ's words but also a hard edge. Jesus commands forgiveness: "Do not judge, so that you may not be judged. For with the judgment you make you will be judged, and the measure you give will be the measure you get" (Matt 7:1–2). But Jesus also warned that some things may not be forgiven: "Whoever is not with me is against me, and whoever does not gather with me scatters. Therefore I tell you, people will be forgiven for every sin and blasphemy, but blasphemy against the Spirit will not be forgiven" (Matt 12:30–31). This verse is troubling, for it suggests that there are ideas our minds might harbor that could set us outside of these great promises. Furthermore, there is an exclusive tone in Christian Scripture: "For God so loved the world that he gave his only Son, so that everyone who believes in him may not perish but may have eternal life" (John 3:16).

Right here we have challenging ideas to think about. Does this litmus test for salvation mean that only Christian believers can be saved? What if we have doubts about Jesus's identity? What becomes of Jews, Muslims, Buddhists, and Hindus? Many Christians would answer that to be saved, one must accept Jesus and his teachings in full measure. Other Christians are Universalists. They ask a compelling question: How can God be omnipotent and good and yet leave some people out of salvation? Would an all-powerful, benign parent do that? The Christian author Rob Bell once asked, "Will all people be saved, or will God not get what God wants? Does this magnificent, mighty, marvelous God *fail* in the end?"[1] In Bell's book *Love Wins*, he argued that Christian love can overcome all barriers in the end. Eric Stetson also embraces a more Universalist Christianity, stating, "God's love is infinite and can overcome all obstacles. The cross of Christ is God's way of proving the unfathomable depth and invincible power of His love for us—for *all* of us—so that we can know for sure that God's love can never fail."[2] Christians remain split on this matter, with one part arguing in terms of exclusive salvation and another in more universal and inclusive terms. God's mercy and love extend to all because of what he finds in their hearts and are not removed because of the clouded conception that often afflicts our minds.

Before further exploring this timeless Christian conundrum, we must examine the historical figure of Jesus. Christians believe that Jesus's birth, some two thousand years ago, marks the coming of the Messiah as foretold by the Old Testament. But who was Christ actually? This question sparks strong feelings and controversies, for opinions vary so widely. Some atheists don't even see sufficient evidence for the historical existence of Jesus. Others may accept he existed but was just a moral person tragically executed. Traditionally, Jews have not accepted him as

1. Rob Bell, *Love Wins: A Book about Heaven, Hell and the Fate of Every Person Who Ever Lived* (New York: HarperOne, 2005), 98.
2. Eric Stetson, *Christian Universalism: God's Good News for All People* (n.p.: Sparkling Bay Books, 2008), 57.

the Messiah, because the world was not transformed afterward in the way they expected. Jesus was not the kingly conqueror, and Israel was not rescued from Rome. Sadly, centuries of anti-Semitism have followed. From the Muslim point of vicw, Jesus was a prophet and brought an authentic revelation. Muslims do not see Jesus as divine, however, and the mainstream Muslim view is that the Qur'an is the final correction of God's message.

Not much is recorded of Jesus's early life. We are told that he was the son of a carpenter, had siblings, and also a miraculous virgin birth. The Gospel of John claims that Jesus is God become man, that God took on flesh and blood, and that he experienced human suffering. Jesus's death and resurrection, according to early Christians, are the ultimate redemptive prices paid for our sins. Forgiveness and eternal life await the faithful. Yet the early years of Jesus's life are shrouded in mystery.

John the Baptist foretold of Jesus's coming. John was baptizing in the wilderness and proclaimed to his followers, "I baptize you with water for repentance, but one who is more powerful than I is coming after me; I am not worthy to carry his sandals. He will baptize you with the Holy Spirit and fire" (Matt 3:11). Jesus will come to gather a following like he is gathering wheat but also will "burn [the chaff] with unquenchable fire" (Matt 3:12). When John did baptize Jesus, it is recorded that a voice came from the heavens and said, "This is my Son, the Beloved, with whom I am well pleased" (Matt 3:17). Jesus's ministry was about to begin, just as John would soon be arrested and executed by Herod.

How do we know these events happened? What evidence exists to support their authenticity? Most scholars of the Bible believe that the Gospels and the other books of the New Testament were written at least forty to sixty years after Jesus's ministry. The Gospels are not eyewitness accounts, and some will accept their veracity more readily than others. What they report is not identical, yet they give us a reasonably consistent picture of who Jesus was and what he did. There are also noncanonical gospels, which were written centuries after the life of Jesus and discovered at Nag Hammadi in Egypt in 1945. The Nag Hammadi gospels do not reproduce the mainstream Bible but fill in perceived gaps in the gospel tradition, including the introduction of various tales of Jesus as a youth. The history and theology of these gospels are sometimes at variance with those of the New Testament and offer a window into later, Gnostic Christian ideas about Jesus.

The New Testament reports that Jesus performed many miracles during his ministry. Many of these had to do with healing, including restoring sight to the blind and curing men of demonic possession, paralysis, and leprosy. He is even said to have raised his friend Lazarus from the dead. Jesus's first recorded miracle was changing water into wine at a wedding party. He is said to have walked on water and to have fed a crowd of many thousands with just a few loaves of bread and a few fishes. We do not see these feats in everyday life, so if true, they are indeed reasons to believe. But are they true? This is a difficult question to answer. But the moral teachings of Jesus can offer guidance even to those who cannot affirm his miracles.

Jesus tells us to love our neighbor as ourselves, but who is one's neighbor? Jesus answered with a parable:

> "A man was going down from Jerusalem to Jericho, and fell into the hands of robbers, who stripped him, beat him, and went away, leaving him half dead. Now by chance a priest was going down that road; and when he saw him, he passed by on the other side. So likewise a Levite, when he came to the place and saw him, passed by on the other side. But a Samaritan while traveling came near him; and when he saw him, he was moved with pity. He went to him and bandaged his wounds, having poured oil and wine on them. Then he put him on his own animal, brought him to an inn, and took care of him. The next day he took out two denarii, gave them to the innkeeper, and said, 'Take care of him; and when I come back, I will repay you whatever more you spend.' Which of these three, do you think, was a neighbor to the man who fell into the hands of the robbers?" He said, "The one who showed him mercy." Jesus said to him, "Go and do likewise." (Luke 10:30–37)

The story is immediate and direct, even a child can grasp it, and as adults we probably realize there are times and places where we should have shown compassion but did not. Even when moral duties are clear, we are often afraid or reluctant to fulfill them.

In a scene in the Gospel of John, a woman is caught for the act of adultery and a group wants to stone her to death. Jesus cleverly and compassionately responds, "Let anyone among you who is without sin be the first to throw a stone at her"

(John 8:7). Caught off guard by this rebuke, the men were unable to stone her. It is an invaluable lesson, for without the capacity to see the shortcomings in ourselves, we are unable to forgive others. Forgiving ourselves and others is indispensable for human life: in families, in romantic relationships, at work, or for reconciliation against past racism, discrimination, or war. Justice is essential, but it must be tempered by mercy and forgiveness.

Jesus may not have healed every disease that needed healing. But he did articulate a way to help us heal ourselves spiritually. So important was the command to love God and to love your neighbor as yourself that the Hindu thinker and reformer Ram Mohan Roy (1772–1833) thought that it was among the most exalted and best of world religions. He argued that the *moral command* of Christianity to love one's neighbor was the real heart of the religion and that belief in the miracles was in fact superfluous. Joshua Marshman argued against Roy that the miracles of Jesus were vitally important to Christianity.[3] Thomas Jefferson, the former president and a contemporary of Roy, was a Deist. He admired Jesus but thought that Christianity contained errors. Jefferson also left the miracles out of his abridged work *The Jefferson Bible*, which he thought distilled the message of Jesus to its essence.[4]

Roy and Jefferson never met, but they were both influenced by a Deistic age that denied the miraculous elements of religion because they did not accord with the world of reason and science, of natural laws like cause and effect. A world ruled by such laws has no room for the miracles described in the New Testament. For Roy and Jefferson, Jesus's message, not his miracles, was real Christianity. They denied the metaphysical and supernatural elements of Christianity like the incarnation, miracles, the Trinity, and the resurrection. But they affirmed its *moral* message. While I share much of the spirit of Roy and Jefferson's belief that moral ends are more important than metaphysical ones, the metaphysical puzzle is not irrelevant. Even the moral teachings of a religion are based in part upon a fuller picture of life and belief. Without such a picture, our actions—moral or not—may not feel meaningfully oriented to a pattern or end. Jesus's miracles, if they were real, do give depth and substance to his ministry.

3. Rammohun Roy, *The English Works* (New York: AMS, 1978), 537–76, 592.
4. Thomas Jefferson, *The Jefferson Bible: The Life and Morals of Jesus of Nazareth* (Radford, VA: Wilder, 2007) entire.

The moral message of Jesus can be controversial. At one point during his ministry, a rich man approached Jesus and asked him what he should do to inherit eternal life. Jesus told him that he should observe the commandments—not to murder, not to commit adultery, not to steal or lie, to honor his father and mother, and to love his neighbor as himself. The rich man claimed he had observed these laws, at which point Jesus responded, "If you wish to be perfect, go, sell your possessions, and give the money to the poor, and you will have treasure in heaven; then come, follow me" (Matt 19:21). The rich man did not feel that he was up to this task, and he went away. Jesus then said, "Truly I tell you, it will be hard for a rich person to enter the kingdom of heaven. Again I tell you, it is easier for a camel to go through the eye of a needle than for someone who is rich to enter the kingdom of God" (Matt 19:23–24). The disciples of Jesus then wondered who could be saved, but Jesus answered them, "For mortals it is impossible, but for God all things are possible" (Matt 19:26).

What does this parable mean? Some interpret it as a call for the rich to divest their wealth as a Christian duty. Jesus tells the rich man to sell his possession *as a prerequisite* to following him. Christian socialism or economic equality might be implied. Many reject this view, however, and argue from other scriptural evidence that a free-market approach is the most desirable economic arrangement from a Christian viewpoint. If the parable is not about money as such, it could also be about idolatry. If the rich man has indeed kept the moral commands but finds this one task difficult to comply with, then perhaps he has made wealth an idol. Idols of all kinds are forbidden in all Abrahamic religions. A third interpretation, suggested clearly at the end of the parable, is that Jesus merely means to show that grace is necessary for salvation. All are sinners, rich and poor, and must rely on God's power and grace to be freed from sin.

Hindus, Jains, and Buddhists also warn against attachment to worldly things. Attachment is literally a snare, a fetter that keeps one locked in a perpetual cycle of reincarnation. Breaking with that attachment and overcoming the fetters of greed and ego are essential steps toward reaching the highest spiritual summit. Rejection of material attachments is a classic case of a moral agreement between world religions, even while indicating metaphysical disagreement. Hindus and Christians, for example, can agree that personal attachments are fetters. Greed for money or power is evil and must be overcome. But the two religions have entirely different fuller pictures of life. Hindus speak of many lives through which we pass to reach the goal, while the Christian context speaks of just one lifetime and then a final judgment. This difference cannot be easily reconciled. There is either one life or many cycles of reincarnation. It is not easy to imagine it being both ways.

Jesus's ministry was composed of at least three major components: signs, miracles, and moral messages. The famous Sermon on the Mount in Matthew 5–7 tells us much of his moral message. It speaks of loving and forgiving; it is where he proclaims the Beatitudes. While some parts of Jesus's ministry were about love and forgiveness, others warned of a final judgment. The many miracles Jesus performed further demonstrate for Christians he was the Son of God, with a divine mission to accomplish here on earth. There were also signs of this special relationship, such as at his Baptism and the transfiguration. During the transfiguration he is shown in blinding white light, accompanied by Moses and Elijah, indicating his prophetic stature. His disciple Peter confessed his belief that Jesus was the Messiah, and Jesus blessed him for his confession. In Matthew 16:17–19, Jesus told Peter that he is the "rock" on which he would "build his church," which Catholics have interpreted as the establishment of the papal office. Protestants suggest it has to do with the character and faith of Peter. Ironically, Peter, who showed such great faith, was also one to deny Jesus three times (as Jesus foretold) after Jesus was arrested. Like the Old Testament figure of David, we see that Peter is a man of faith and principle but also merely a man, subject to fear and temptation.

Jesus did not direct his followers toward armed rebellion or resistance. When Jesus was arrested and one of his disciples drew his sword in defense, Jesus told him to put his sword away, "for all who take the sword will perish by the sword" (Matt 26:52). This instruction is a clear refutation of violence. Jesus goes with his accusers to be tried, convicted, and sentenced to die by crucifixion. But why did this happen? Jesus was healing and preaching moral messages of spiritual uplift. Why was he killed for it?

Jesus's ministry challenged existing religious and political authorities. He had rebuked the Sadducees and the Pharisees and attracted huge crowds. He spoke of the temple coming down and being rebuilt again, which perplexed and alarmed them. When asked whether Jews should pay taxes to Rome, he said, "Give therefore to the emperor the things that are the emperor's, and to God the things that are God's" (Matt 22:21). A few scholars dispute this interpretation and portray Jesus as a revolutionary or a Zealot.[5]

What is clear, however, is that the New Testament asserts that Jesus was arrested, tried by Pontius Pilate, and found to be dangerous enough to warrant execution. He had upset the authorities of Jerusalem and was perceived to be a risk that could no longer be tolerated. But what was the heart of his message that seemed so dangerous? When asked by the Pharisees what the most important commandment is, Jesus responded, "'You shall love the Lord your God with all your heart, and with all your soul, and with all your mind.' This is the greatest and first commandment. And a second is like it: 'You shall love your neighbor as yourself.' On these two commandments hang all the law and the prophets" (Matt 22:37–40). The Bible tells us that Jesus replied to criticism with kindness, that he preached a message of love and forgiveness, and that he offered stern warnings about injustice. His was a tragic and undeserved death, yet for Christians, it is a demonstration of God's ultimate forgiveness. The resurrection of Jesus is a conquest over sin and death. That God should become incarnate in human flesh, suffer, and die is essential for believers but might seem ridiculous to critics. Why would any omnipotent, everlasting God choose that fate?

Of course, not everyone finds this central belief of Christianity plausible, and others criticize many things about Jesus and his ministry. There might be a way to reconcile and explain it, however. How would God express love for the world? Would a loving, caring God tower over us with omnipotent might? Would a good God be a dictator watching over us and reprimanding our behavior at every moment? Such a God would be not a friend but a tyrant. A good God would not deny us the exercise of free will, nor intimidate us with an overbearing presence.

The lack of empirical evidence for religious claims has caused some to dismiss religion out of hand. In short, why believe what you can't physically prove? This lack of empirical evidence may be troubling, but reason can also conclude that a God who is a visible, domineering presence would be intolerable. But the Christian God is loving and forgiving. This God enters into our world, suffers, is rebuked, is crucified, and dies so that our sins could be forgiven. Such a God would be powerful

5. This is a minority view among scholars, but it has been popularized in recent years in Reza Aslan, *Zealot: The Life and Times of Jesus of Nazareth* (New York: Random House, 2013).

by being vulnerable, loving by letting us be free, and forgiving even of the worst things we might do. This is the way I have come to see the Christian idea of God, and I think it is a legitimate and compelling way to view the Christian religion.

Paul, one of the primary missionaries for Jesus and a man who had formerly persecuted Christians, put it quite well when he described the patient, enduring force of love in the world. It seems to me also to speak to the heart of Christ's ministry. Paul wrote, "Love is patient; love is kind; love is not envious or boastful or arrogant or rude. It does not insist on its own way; it is not irritable or resentful; it does not rejoice in wrongdoing, but rejoices in the truth. It bears all things, believes all things, hopes all things, endures all things" (1 Cor 13:4–7). He goes on to say that love never ends and further adds, "And now faith, hope, and love abide, these three; and the greatest of these is love" (1 Cor 13:13).

Love and justice are key themes of Christianity. For if Christ said that we were to love, he also did not abolish the authorities or the law. If we are moved by the spirit of love and justice, we can help make the world a better place; we can stave off the rancor, hate, corruption, and injustice that this world has in abundance. In *Moral Man and Immoral Society*, Reinhold Niebuhr warned that we invariably fail to leap the high moral hurdles we establish for ourselves and our society. The perennial sinfulness of humankind reminds us that while we might try to be Simon Peter, we are often Judas. As such, we are in need of being loved and renewed on a continual basis.

What Jesus said and did have been recorded in the gospels of the New Testament, and we can speculate about how close these portraits are to the real Jesus. The rest is history, or to be more precise, Christian history. There have been many viewpoints on Jesus. Some believed, like the ancient Ebionites, that Jesus was just flesh and blood and not divine at all. Muslims would agree. Islam remembers Jesus as a human prophet, not as divine. On the opposite end of the spectrum, others saw Jesus as entirely divine and spiritual and believe that it would have been anathema to imagine him having a human body. The Gnostics believed this, thinking Jesus was all spirit and appearance and had no flesh-and-blood body. It was not until after the Council of Nicaea in 325 CE, after Rome had gone from persecuting to endorsing Christianity, that the Trinitarian doctrine was finally clarified. Most Christians believe in a triune God, three persons in nature: God as Father, God as Son in Jesus, and God as Holy Spirit.

Saint Augustine (354–430 CE) became one of the most famous defenders of Christianity in the fourth and fifth centuries. Formerly a Manichee, Saint Augustine later changed course, was baptized into the Christian faith, and wrote the *Confessions* about his prior life and ways. His major treatise, *The City of God*, maintained that there was a heavenly city we may wish to try to emulate, but we were more familiar with the earthly city that is embroiled in sinful disobedience of God. Finding justice with peace became a major task in the world as we know it, for we could not be perfect like Jesus, Augustine argued. Try as we might to achieve a more perfect and divine ethic, we would always fall short. We are sinful and need God's grace.

In Rome and the Western church, Latin was the primary language, while Greek was the primary language of the Eastern half of the Roman Empire. Christian theology developed differently in these two languages and regions. Then, in 1054 CE, the Roman Catholic Church in the West and the Orthodox churches in the East separated from one another. After that great breach, Saint Thomas Aquinas (1225–74 CE) became one of the most influential Christian apologists. Aquinas was a thirteenth-century Christian who had become enthralled with Greek philosophy, especially Aristotle. How was it possible that the Greeks, who preceded Christ, had come upon philosophical ideas that seemed so true without Jesus's aid? He believed that a *natural law theology* meant that God's existence and effects could be known on the basis of reason alone. If you naturally reasoned correctly, you could figure out the truth or come near to it, but the Scripture and church teaching was always necessary so that God's full revelation could be known with faith. The Greeks had used their reason well in many instances, so Greco-Roman thought became increasingly integrated with Christian thinking.

Aquinas argued that there were five ways or proofs for God's existence. One could, by reason alone, prove God's existence. The five ways were the following:

1. There must be an unmoved mover, a God who set all in motion.
2. There must be a first cause to all things, and that is what we call God.
3. All beings are contingent on other beings that gave them birth, but there must be a first being that is not contingent, and that is what we call God.
4. There are various levels of perfection in beings, and God is what we think of as most perfect.

5. There appears to be a designer in nature; nature unfolds with such intricacy, seasonality, and regularity, it must have been designed by a creator.

Each of these proofs has been challenged by later philosophers and theologians. While it is true that the arguments are neither final nor refuted, they do have many compelling aspects. What seems to be true and lasting about the five ways is not that they irrefutable arguments but that they suggest a real *possibility* of God existing. Aquinas's arguments have been important to Christians for centuries, Catholic and non-Catholic alike. They are words, the intellectual brick and mortar, that helped build, preserve, and extend the foundations of Christian thinking.

That of course was not the end of the Christian story. Martin Luther, the famous German theologian, protested the selling of indulgences, or exemptions from long terms in purgatory (a place of extended purification in the afterlife on the way to heaven). Luther believed it was through faith alone that one could be redeemed, not through actions, as moral as they may be. Only a good tree bears good fruit, and good, pure actions could only stem from a heart with good faith. Luther's views led to his posting the Ninety-Five Theses at Wittenberg in 1517: theses or ideas that criticized the Catholic Church. Four years later, in 1521 CE, Luther was excommunicated from the Catholic Church.

Faith alone saves, and nothing else, Luther claimed. What does this actually mean? Can it mean that a person can have faith in Jesus and claim to be a Christian yet do all sorts of horrible things and still be saved? Wouldn't an honestly good-hearted Buddhist, Muslim, Jew, or atheist be a better candidate for eternal rewards than such a hypocrite? It does not seem that a genuine faith could be linked with anything else but a genuine moral character. Jesus once warned against false prophets, saying, "You will know them by their fruits. Are grapes gathered from thorns, or figs from thistles? In the same way, every good tree bears good fruit, but the bad tree bears bad fruit. A good tree cannot bear bad fruit, nor can a bad tree bear good fruit. Every tree that does not bear good fruit is cut down and thrown into the fire. Thus you will know them by their fruits" (Matt 7:16–20). It seems logical that a truly good person can have a faith that is equally good. If inside, you are not truly genuine, your acts will soon reflect that. Martin Luther wrote, "Good works do not make a man good, but a good man does good works." Furthermore, he added, "If you have a true faith that Christ is your Savior, then at once you have a gracious God, for faith leads you in and opens up God's heart and will, that you should see pure grace and overflowing love." Yet Luther also made it fairly clear that it was a *Christian* man who was saved, that the works of a non-Christian were not significant: "Unless a man is already a believer and a Christian, his works have no value at all."[6]

Must one be a Christian to be saved? Luther apparently thought so. Elsewhere, he wrote, "Christ never gave any other commandment than that of love, because He intended that commandment to be the test of His disciples and of true believers. For if (good) works and love do not blossom forth, it is not genuine faith, the gospel has not yet gained a foothold, and Christ is not yet rightly known."[7] For Luther, good works could only logically flow from a good Christian character, sustained by a genuine faith, but for many in the modern world, we ask, Can a *genuinely good* Buddhist, Hindu, Muslim, Jew, or atheist also be "saved"? Christian Universalists have argued yes, that with God, all things are truly possible and that no one of sound mind and heart need be left out of God's plan. Christian Universalism, however, is a minority opinion. This remains a controversy, I think, a puzzle to be solved. One must also ask, Is *Christian* salvation the final litmus test? Why not the test from some other faith or perspective? Here the puzzle deepens.

After Luther, other Protestant thinkers and groups broke away from Rome. John Calvin dissented theologically from Catholicism and led the Reformation in Geneva. For reasons having little to do with theology and a lot to do with gaining a marriage annulment, King Henry VIII of England broke with Rome. Unable to divorce his wife, he made the bold gesture of divorcing the Catholic Church, establishing his own Church of England. Unfortunately, European Catholics and Protestants engaged in many bloody confrontations in the following years. The error of this bloody, religious war for political control has contributed to church-state separation today in parts of the West. While Jesus commanded that Christians love and forgive one another, they have frequently fallen into infighting.

If there is one modern Christian who embodied Jesus's saying "Inasmuch as you did *it* to one of the least of these My brethren, you did *it* to Me" (Matt 25:40

6. Roland H. Bainton, *Here I Stand: A Life of Martin Luther* (New York: Meridian, 1995), 178, 50.
7. John Dillenberger, *Martin Luther: Selections from His Writings* (New York: Random House, 1962), 18.

NKJV), one might argue it was Mother Teresa. An ethnic Albanian who became a religious sister, Mother Teresa sailed off to Calcutta and made it her life's work to take care of the poor, sick, needy, and destitute. She took in and cared for the unwanted. Her Missionaries of Charity took off there and today has sisters and apostolates across the world.[8]

Martin Luther King Jr. challenged the social injustice of racism and poverty in America. King fervently believed that the Christian faith should promote a better, more just world. He suggested that "only a 'dry as dust' religion prompts a minister to extol the glories of heaven while ignoring the social conditions that cause men an earthly hell."[9] Learning from the nonviolent strategies of Mohandas Gandhi, King observed, "Nonviolent resistance had emerged as the technique of the movement, while love stood as the regulating ideal. In other words, Christ furnished the spirit and motivation while Gandhi furnished the method."[10]

King was also inspired by Reinhold Niebuhr, the founder of modern Christian realism. Niebuhr believed that the ideals of love and justice in the Christian faith were eternal norms but that injustice was deeply entrenched in the world as we know it. As individuals we might be moral privately, but our societies were governed by sinful and self-interested policies.[11] Niebuhr's realism impressed King, but King also became convinced by Gandhi's nonviolence. King wrote, "I believe this man, more than anybody else in the modern world, caught the spirit of Jesus Christ and lived it more completely in his life. His name was Gandhi, Mohandas K. Gandhi."[12]

There are many more figures who could be named to show the political and social relevance of Christianity and many others who have done harm. No religion lives and walks the earth as an autonomous figure, independent of the life and breath we give to it. Religion forms us and is also deeply embedded in our hearts and minds. As religions change us, so we are capable of changing them for better or worse.

8. Kathryn Spink, *Mother Teresa: A Complete Authorized Biography* (New York: HarperCollins, 1998).
9. King, *Testament of Hope*, 539.
10. King, 17.
11. Reinhold Niebuhr, *Moral Man and Immoral Society* (Louisville, KY: Westminster John Knox, 2001).
12. Martin Luther King Jr., *The Radical King*, ed. Cornel West (Boston: Beacon, 2020), 24.

What Fits?

The heart of the Christian ethic, as Jesus described it himself, is the double love command: "You shall love the Lord your God with all your heart, and with all your soul, and with all your mind.' This is the greatest and first commandment. And a second is like it: 'You shall love your neighbor as yourself.' On these two commandments hang all the law and the prophets" (Matt 22:37–40). The commandments tell us to renounce personal selfishness and seek love and justice. We are constantly tempted by a more selfish human nature to think less of our neighbor, to belittle or neglect them. A strong moral imperative telling us to do otherwise is a corrective to the inherent selfishness we experience as human beings. It may be impossible or even undesirable to love *all neighbors* as equally as ourselves. Freud echoed this criticism and argued the Christian love ethic was untenable.[13] But, from my view, his criticism misses the point. We should not expect to fully realize this imperative, but it always hangs over us as a reason pushing us back toward peace and reconciliation. In short, we must be reminded to love, because we and the world we live in can often be so unloving. It isn't easy.

Criticism of the love ethic is to be expected, even warranted. There are a thousand and one good reasons *not* to love your neighbor as yourself. Perhaps you cannot stand your neighbor's political views, bragging and flaunting of wealth, arrogance, or indifference to the plight of others. Your neighbor may be your boss, whom you cannot stand. In this world-weary life, work can become drudgery; a drab heart is not inspired to love. Time takes its toll on our spirit, and dull work taxes our enthusiasm. But because there are so many reasons not to love, we need a strong reminder to love anyway. A loveless heart makes for a dreary existence.

Selfishness has a seductive wisdom. We look after ourselves because no one is going to look after our interests for us. We pursue the path of wealth so that we can be free of work, drudgery, and poverty. It is easy to be ruled by selfish whims and wishes and be immune to the plight of those around us. But this temptation is deceiving. A sober, moral mind realizes we are all interdependent. Neither man nor woman is a proverbial island. All are dependent upon others for basic economic

13. Sigmund Freud, *Civilization and Its Discontents*, trans. James Strachey (New York: W. W. Norton, 2010), 82.

livelihood, social support, and recognition. The more we feel burdened, oppressed, and overruled by the world around us, the more we are dehumanized. We feel like just a cog in the machine, a part of a whole that is alien to us. Anger and resentment are our natural reactions. To overcome all sources of anger, alienation, and hatred is what the law of love really means. To "love our neighbor" as ourselves is no weak or sentimental calling but is a message that is simultaneously political, economic, social, and moral. To love one's neighbor is political in that it imagines and tries to realize a world in which we are fully capable and eager of loving others by surmounting those thousand and one obstacles that stand in the way of cooperation and solidarity.

Love requires cooperation but also patience, tolerance, and understanding. To understand, we must think, and when we understand, love becomes more possible because our minds are illumined with fresh light. Loving requires puzzle making and sorting out the disordered parts of life until they become better aligned and sensible. Love, in short, and the commandment to love, is no simple or saccharine calling. It is a deep commandment and a struggle to surmount the obstacles of hatred and indifference that can keep us apart. This can happen at the personal or social level. Institutions and civilizations are capable of failing to love even more deeply and irresponsibly than individuals.

But how does one love God? When one cannot see, embrace, or immediately talk face-to-face with God, how does one know and love God? First, the commandment to love God can be thought about in terms of humility. Do not be so vain or arrogant as to believe that you know the answer to everything. Acknowledge that there is a higher, more enduring source of authority outside yourself, one on which your hopes for life depend. By decentering ourselves, our hearts and minds become dedicated to a higher purpose, and that (to borrow from Aquinas) is something religious people call God. Second, we all tend to anthropomorphize God, to render God into human terms. And while this tendency is understandable, God is not a bearded guy sitting on a throne in the clouds. But because it is awkward and uncomfortable for us to think of God impersonally as "It," we bring God closer to our hearts by personalizing God symbolically. God becomes personal and helpful in an often cruel and indifferent world. In this sense, the love of God might be a comforting presence in our lives. Third, one can understand how to love God by following God's commandments. The Ten Commandments, including the prohibitions against lying, murdering, stealing, cheating, being jealous, and committing adultery, show us how to love God in word and deed.

Jesus said the double love command was essential, but the many other things he did and said help spell out how that is to be done. It may be an ethic that we can only hope to emulate and not duplicate but can learn and grow from spiritually and morally. Three things seem to be critical: love, justice, and merciful forgiveness. These are important and interrelated elements. Jesus talks often of love and forgiveness, to forgive not seven times but even more than seventy times. Jesus also speaks of judgment. If you do what is displeasing to God, if you do what is evil, you should take care and try to rectify your behavior. A gospel or moral message that is based purely on infinite love and forgiveness and has no rebuke for bad behavior would really be a misleading gospel. It falsely tells us we can do what we please and there will be no consequences. Forgiveness of past injustices may sometimes be required by love, but forsaking responsibility never is.

What Doesn't Fit?

Christ's identity and messianic role are probably the most controversial things for non-Christians. Jews do not see him as a messiah, though some respect his wisdom. Muslims have seen Jesus as an authoritative prophet but cannot accept the idea of the Trinity. For atheists and skeptics, some doubt Christ ever existed at all, saying that there is a paucity of real historical evidence. There have been theories that Christ's whole story is a fabrication or one borrowed from other mythologies. It should be self-evident that not all accept Christ, or even that there is an afterlife to go to.

Witch burning, Crusades and killing, anti-Semitism, sexism, homophobia, and all manners of discrimination have been practiced in the name of Christianity. None of these is consonant with a religion that pleads for love of one's neighbor as oneself and forgiveness. Taking the worst examples of any religion, one is bound to condemn it, but a balanced view must include positive and negative aspects. The better viewpoints of Jesus ministry will, I believe, continue to have a positive influence in the world.

The controversy over Jesus's identity began early on after his life and has not gone away. Neither has the controversy about salvation. Must one be a Christian to be saved? Or can God's love save those who do not make a profession of faith? Is it the heart, the moral character from which our actions and thoughts spring, that is the most essential? I believe in a Christian faith that knocks down barriers, embraces, and includes. Therefore, I believe that those outside the Christian faith really can be saved and can stand shoulder to shoulder with Christians as spiritual equals. Gandhi taught this message. I believe Dr. King also understood it.

If the point about who is, or is not, saved becomes paramount in Christianity or any other religion, it may be difficult for religions to get along. Putting together a common puzzle and view of life together as one world community is very hard when one tradition insists that it has all the relevant pieces and the others have none. Insisting upon its own, absolute truth, Christianity *or any other religion* that adopts this view may become too adversarial to the world around it. I advocate not abandoning ultimate claims about truth or salvation but not leaning on them too stridently. None of us really knows what, if anything, awaits after death, just as none has been here since earth's beginning. By "being saved" I mean the hope that we can escape the grim fate of death and, short of that great hope, that we can think of one another as spiritual and moral equals. Immediate moral and political problems face us, and we may all serve our part in addressing them. Focusing upon the moral things that we do share, not the metaphysical ones we do not, seems a constructive beginning.

Love, justice, and forgiveness are the core of the Christian tradition. Without the command to love, we too easily collapse into our selfish selves. Without justice, we cannot live in a lawful and peaceful world, with norms and expectations for all of us. Without forgiveness, we cannot accept our human limitations and realize that we may transgress and defy the expectations of love and of justice. Thus these three are essential and do seem to work well with other religions.

5 Islam

Summary of Islam

In the year 610 CE, outside of Mecca in the remote Cave of Hira, Muhammad uttered these words he had received from the angel Gabriel: "Proclaim in the name of the Lord and Cherisher, who created man out of a clot of congealed blood. Proclaim and thy Lord is most bountiful, He who taught the use of the pen. Taught man which he knew not. Nay but man doth transgress all bounds, in that he looks upon himself as self-sufficient. Verily to the Lord is the return of all."[1] Muhammad was terrified and awestruck about what he had experienced. His wife Khadija consoled him. She became his very first follower because she believed that his experience had come from God. Muhammad, though, would not have another revelatory experience for two years. During that time, his own faith and confidence about himself must have been sorely tested. Over the next twenty years, Muhammad would have many revelations, but none of them would be easy. He commented, "Never once did I receive a revelation without thinking my soul had been torn away from me."[2]

The Arabic *Qur'an* means "recitation," and it is a compendium of Muhammad's revelations as he had memorized them. Most religious traditions begin orally before their scriptures are written down. In the case of Islam, this process happened quickly. Muhammad died in the year 632 CE at about the age of sixty-two. The Qur'an was first written down and published by the caliph Uthman in the year 650.[3] So just eighteen years after Muhammad's passing, his direct experiences with Allah were written down. The Qur'an does not read like the Christian Bible. It is not a narrative of events of Muhammad's life. The hadith are the traditions, sayings, and deeds of Muhammad that were written down separately from the Qur'an.

For Muslims, the Qur'an is the primary miracle of Muhammad. Muslims believe he was the greatest and final prophet of the Abrahamic tradition. He was not

1. Qur'an 96:1–8.
2. Barnaby Rogerson, *The Prophet Muhammad: A Biography* (Mahwah, NJ: HiddenSpring, 2003), 92.
3. Barnaby Rogerson, *The Heirs of Muhammad* (New York: Overlook, 2006), 256–59.

divine, and he was not even thought to be able to read. For this reason, Muslims have seen the Qur'an as a miracle from God, because it required God's intercession and speaking to Muhammad. If it is true that Muhammad was not literate, then there is little chance Muhammad could have composed the Qur'an himself. Some scholars have disputed his claim, arguing that a merchant like Muhammad would have been educated to read Arabic.[4] It does seem a reasonable contention, but it is not the mainstream view of Islamic scholars.

If God intended to reach all people, why didn't the same revelation, the same text, appear to every culture and every place? If all people received the same message with the exact same details, wouldn't that be convincing? It does pose us with an immediate philosophical problem, a puzzle we need to sort out. If God were like a loving parent, shouldn't parents teach the same lessons to all their children? As we observed with moral views, there is a lot of overlap but no exact agreement about what religions say. Why didn't everyone get the same Qur'an, the same Bible, or the same Bhagavad Gita, or whichever you affirm to be the true revelation? We will revisit this question soon.

For Muslims, the Qur'an is the correct and final message of God. Islam acknowledges that there have been all sorts of prophetic figures before: Jesus and Moses are acknowledged, but many Muslims believe that their revelations were later altered and not as complete. Muhammad was sent to bring the final word, the correct revelation, and so the Qur'an is revered with a very high authority, just as a Christian fundamentalist would claim for the Bible. When read in Arabic, the Qur'an is said to possess a great beauty and grandeur, the finest of compositions in that language; it is one further reason Muslims feel drawn toward it. We cannot resolve the conflict here but at least state it as part of the story, part of the ongoing puzzle-making process we have in making sense of this world.

Not unlike many prophets, Muhammad had few initial supporters. Moses was a lonely figure and did not feel up to the task that God asked. Many doubted him along the way. Jesus was rejected in his hometown, and many denied his teachings. The prophet Zoroaster did not have a large following for a long time. In retrospect, prophets seem like powerful and towering authority figures. But in their own lifetimes, the way of the prophet might be quite hard and lonely.

4. Reza Aslan, *Not God but God: The Origins, Evolution and Future of Islam* (New York: Random House, 2006), 35–36.

Muhammad's supporters included his wife Khadija and a few early converts, most of whom were family or close to him: Ali, Abu Bakr, and later, Umar and Uthman. It was tough going, however. His uncle Abu Talib supported him and protected him from harm, but Abu Talib never converted to Islam, even on his deathbed. This saddened Muhammad, for it appeared Abu Talib was then destined for hell.[5] And yet what had Abu Talib done that was so wrong? Here again is a troubling point, not far from the one discussed in the last chapter. If Abu Talib was a good man and had done the correct thing, wouldn't he be forgiven for the fog and confusion of his mind, which might easily produce doubts? What is more fundamental to personal redemption—professed belief or our good moral character?

For Islam, on the day of judgment, each person is confronted with their own deeds. The good deeds hopefully outweigh the bad. For example, the Qur'an states, "But those who have faith and work righteousness, they are Companions of the Garden: therein shall they abide (forever)."[6] Elsewhere, the Qur'an also says, "Those who believe, and do deeds of righteousness, and establish regular prayers and regular charity, will have their reward with their Lord: on them shall be no fear, nor shall they grieve."[7] One could interpret this and say (as Luther did for Christianity) that it is *Muslim* faith that is required for the good deeds to matter.

There are very universal Muslims, however, who have maintained that as long as you are a good believer in your own tradition and you do good deeds, you effectively are submitting to God (the word *Islam* means "to submit") and it will be well with you in the hereafter. A Muslim friend of Mohandas Gandhi, a man named Abdul Ghaffar Khan, had this more accepting view, and many more Muslims may support it. Abdul Ghaffar Khan believed Hindus, Sikhs, and many others were Ahl-Kitab, or people of the Holy Book, and could be saved.[8] The Qur'an itself also suggests it may be well with believers who may fall outside Muslim circles: "Believers, Jews, Christians, and Sabeans—whoever believes in God and the Last Day and does what is right—shall be rewarded by their Lord; they have nothing to fear or to regret."[9]

5. Muhammad al-Bukhari, *The Hadith* (self-pub., Amazon Digital Services, 2015), loc. 7974–8159, Kindle.
6. Abdullah Yusuf Ali, trans., *The Qur'an: A Guide and Mercy*, 26th ed. (New York: Tahrike Tarsile Qur'an, 2010), 2:82.
7. Yusuf Ali, 2:277.
8. D. G. Tendulkar, *Abdul Ghaffar Khan* (Bombay: Popular Prakash, 1967), 173–74.
9. Dawood, *Koran*, v. 2:62.

As with Christianity, there are differing opinions in Islam about how to interpret the Qur'an on this matter.

Claims about who is finally saved and who is finally damned get into precarious and incendiary debates. If I presume to take the point of view of knowing who is saved and who is not and what the entire business of heaven and hell or reincarnation is fully and finally about, I really take a God's-eye point of view. This seems to be the most arrogant point of view to take, to be able to speak with divine wisdom about all things and all ends. As a mere human being, I tend to back away from such claims, but it is part again of the puzzle presented by the world's religions.

Muhammad's revelation upset the authorities of his own day, the Quraysh. It upset them for a few clear reasons. The first reason was theological. Muhammad spoke of just one God, Allah, and argued that all other gods were false. In his day, however, the sacred Kaaba of Mecca had some 360 different gods, and each tribe had allegiance to one of them. These clans would make pilgrimages to the shrine in Mecca, and the Quraysh were profiting by collecting fees from traveling pilgrims. If Muhammad's word were really carried out, it would hurt the Quraysh in the pocketbook, which was the second affront to them. A third thing Muhammad believed in was in judgment according to one's deeds, that one would be held accountable in the afterlife on the basis of merit, not on wealth or status. His message demanded greater charity for the poor and care for orphans. This was not the view of the Quraysh, and Muhammad was rocking the boat.

Opposition mounted to Muhammad and his Muslim converts in the year 618 CE. The Quraysh boycotted Muhammad and his Muslims and put them in dire straits. As a consequence, the wealth of one of his Muslim converts, Abu Bakr, was said to have been reduced from forty thousand dirhams to only five or six thousand dirhams.[10] Part of this he used to buy and free slaves who had converted to Islam. Furthermore, after the boycott ended in the year 619 CE, Muhammad suffered two grievous and personal blows: the death of his beloved wife Khadija and also the death of his protector, Abu Talib. Khadija had been his first convert, the one who had consoled him and helped him believe that his first revelation was not just a passing madness. Abu Talib, though he never converted to Islam, kept the tribal

10. Karen Armstrong, *Muhammad: A Biography of the Prophet* (New York: HarperSanFrancisco, 1993), 135; Rogerson in *Heirs of Muhammad* gives the figure of six thousand dirhams, not five thousand, as in Armstrong.

protection of Muhammad intact. When Abu Talib died, Muhammad's life was in danger, and there was even a failed conspiracy to kill him. The faithful Ali donned Muhammad's robes and lay in his home, deceiving the waiting assassins.

In the year 620 CE, Muhammad experienced a deeply profound revelation: his Night Ascent. Either in a dream or perhaps in reality, he was transported with his noble steed to Jerusalem. There he ascended the various levels of heavens and spoke to prophets of the Judeo-Christian tradition: Jesus, Moses, and Abraham. His divine encounter makes Jerusalem the third holiest city of Islam, right after Mecca (the most sacred) and Medina (ranked second). Jerusalem is therefore sacred to Jews, Christians, and Muslims.

In Mecca, however, there was still danger. The few Muslims of Mecca were forced to leave in the year 622 CE. This was the first Hijrah, or the migration from Mecca to the town of Yathrib, which was renamed Medina. This date, 622 CE, also marks the beginning of the Muslim calendar. Medina became the first sanctuary for Muslims, where they had to work hard for their own keep but where Muhammad was accepted as a governing figure. The Quraysh in Mecca, however, still wanted Muhammad dead. He was still considered a threat, and soon, revelations came to Muhammad that granted him permission to fight back. Battles began to ensue: first, the Battle of Badr in the year 624 CE. The Muslims were outnumbered but, in spite of this, won a victory. The very next year, at the Battle of Uhud, the Muslims suffered a defeat, and many male converts were killed, leaving widows without protectors and breadwinners. It was after this battle that a revelation came to Muhammad that Muslims could take up to four wives, so long as they could treat each wife fairly, as a way to protect those who had no other provider.[11] In the context of the times, this was a special dispensation for Muhammad's Muslim followers to take care of widows who were not otherwise able to provide for themselves. Debate still continues, however, among some Muslims whether one wife or four is acceptable.

In refuge in Medina, Muhammad's forces were growing stronger, and he was gaining momentum. The Quraysh made a final assault to try to wipe out Muhammad. An army of ten thousand soldiers besieged Muhammad at Medina. He had seen it coming and was able to make a trench, preparing the town defensively. It proved

11. Dawood, *Koran*, vv. 4:3–4.

successful, and in this climactic Battle of the Trench, the opposing Meccan force ultimately withdrew, unable to penetrate Muhammad's fortifications.

In the aftermath, however, a grisly episode followed. A Jewish tribe, the Banu Qurayza that had made a pact to come to Muhammad's aid had not honored their pledge. Some may have lent support to his enemies. Muhammad allowed an arbitrator to decide the fate of these Jews in a time of war, and Sa'd ibn Mu'adh decreed that some seven hundred males were to be executed and the women and children taken or sold off into slavery. It was not out of line with the standards and practices of the time, but for our time, it is of course greatly controversial. It also runs to a core apprehension many feel about Muhammad.

Muhammad was a prophet who had to wield the sword. Jesus did not wield a sword, nor seemed to feel to be compelled to, and if one looks to Buddha, one finds a much more pacific and contemplative spirit. People wielding weapons instantly strike us with some fear and apprehension. As Gandhi had once said about Islam, "The sword is the emblem of Islam. But Islam was born in an environment where the sword was and still remains the supreme law. The message of Jesus has proved ineffective because the environment was unready to receive it. So, with the message of the Prophet. The sword is too much in evidence among Muslims. It must be sheathed if Islam is to be what it means—peace."[12] And yet in spite of this criticism, Gandhi thought that Hinduism, Islam, and Christianity spoke essentially compatible messages. Gandhi read the Bhagavad Gita, the Qur'an, and the Christian Bible at his prayer meetings, trying to demonstrate their compatibility. One of his best Muslim friends, Abdul Ghaffar Khan, also believed that Muhammad had preferred nonviolence but had only been compelled to take up the sword defensively.

The Qur'an does state that one should take up the sword only in defense: "Fight for the sake of God those that fight against you, but do not attack them first. God does not love aggressors."[13] The verses that follow this are charged with a belligerence against the idolaters, but they also clearly say to stop attacking them if they also stop attacking. There are very widely known *sword verses* in the Qur'an, which give the following command:

12. Fischer, *Essential Gandhi*, 211.
13. Dawood, *Koran*, v. 2:190.

> Proclaim a woeful punishment to the unbelievers, except to those idolaters who have honored their treaties with you in every detail and aided none against you. With these keep faith, until their treaties have run their term. God loves the righteous. When the sacred months are over slay the idolaters whenever you find them. Arrest them, besiege them, and lie in ambush everywhere for them. If they repent and take prayer and render the alms levy, allow them to go their way. God is forgiving and merciful. If an idolater seeks asylum with you, give him protection so that he may hear the Word of God, and then convey him to safety. For the idolaters are ignorant men. God and His apostle repose no trust in idolaters, save those with whom you have made treaties at the Sacred Mosque. So long as they keep faith with you, keep faith with them. God loves the righteous.[14]

The verses clearly command vigorous fighting yet also suggest that one should lay down the sword if treaties are made or repentance is sought. Ultimately, after a long struggle, this is exactly what Muhammad did with his enemies the Quraysh: he laid down his arms and made a peace treaty. This was called the Treaty of Hudaybiyah, and many Muslims at the time considered it to be humiliating. In the treaty, Muhammad did not even require the Quraysh to acknowledge him as a prophet of God; his staunch supporter and friend Umar found this humiliation to be intolerable, but Muhammad told him to keep patient. The treaty happened in the year 628, and just a few years later, in the year 630, Muhammad's forces were strong enough to enter Mecca and to cleanse it of all the other idols. Since then, the Kaaba has been dedicated to one God, Allah. Muslims believe that the Kaaba in Mecca is an ancient shrine going back to Abraham and Ishmael.

Muhammad came back to Mecca and brought the religion of Islam. The act of removing the other idols and rededicating the Kaaba to the one God of Islam was both a religious and a political gesture. It removed polytheism as the ruling religious influence in Arabia and replaced it with a monotheism that politically bound the tribes together in a unity they had not previously known. One was not absolutely required to be a Muslim, though pressure to convert was strong. Muhammad's

14. Dawood, vv. 9:5–7.

efforts were at once intensely religious and political, binding together tribes that had once often been competing or warring rivals.

Jihad

What is *jihad*, what does it mean, and what did Muhammad think about it? *Jihad* does not mean "holy war." The Arabic term means "exertion" or "struggle." This struggle can have a great many manifestations, only one of them being defensive armed force. Generally speaking, a good jihad is to uphold the Muslim tradition and laws. This type of jihad tries to realize a greater spirit of Islamic justice politically, which can put it at odds with other polities. It should not go on the offensive or attack first, however. There have clearly been offensive campaigns and violence done in the name of Islam, but as with Christianity in the past chapter, I do not think these represent the best of the religion.

One tradition of "greater versus lesser jihad" recounts that Muhammad came back from a military campaign one day in which he had defended Muslims against their enemies. He announced that he had come from a state of "lesser to greater jihad." The lesser jihad meant the militant duty to defend the Islamic community. The greater jihad he implied was the duty of becoming a more pious and morally observant Muslim, the personal struggle to submit to God in every way. This distinction stems not from the Qur'an itself but from the hadith or traditions said about Muhammad. According to this tradition, the greater, more important jihad is about social justice.[15] If one accepts this distinction, then Muhammad's view of jihad would be the following:

1. Greater jihad: a moral duty and struggle to uphold social justice
2. Lesser jihad: the military defense of Muslims in danger, under attack

That seems like a fairly defensible ethic and one compatible with other religions, but the real world is not quite as simple as this. Radical militants and terrorists have abused the religion of Islam and not only inverted but also perverted those priorities. They have made the lesser jihad the greater (the inversion), and they

15. John Esposito, *Unholy War: Terror in the Name of Islam* (New York: Oxford University Press, 2002), 28.

have twisted it from defensive to aggressive in nature. The twisted view of militants has been this:

1. Greater jihad (in false distinction): *aggressive* violence toward enemies
2. Lesser jihad: the moral duty and struggle to uphold social justice

Of course, a terrorist thinks they are upholding justice. Both Bin Laden and ISIS have claimed just this. In the mind of mainstream Muslims and other non-Muslims, however, terrorists have seriously misrepresented Islam. I think this confusion is not going to be resolved so simply, or clearly, but I hope the original, more morally justifiable tradition of jihad can be redeemed. This is what Abdul Ghaffar Khan envisioned when he wrote, "This is our jihad, our crusade. Before we can fight the British, we must first end the violence and murder in our own hearts. Remember that overcoming our personal weakness is the greater jihad, the greater crusade. It is what God wants of us."[16] Abdul Ghaffar Khan even assembled a large force of up to a hundred thousand Khudai Khidmatgars. These were nonviolent "servants of God" to aid Gandhi in the cause of liberating India from Great Britain. We should also recall that after Muhammad died, the caliph Abu Bakr gave strict instructions to Muslim troops not to harm noncombatants. Abu Bakr commanded, using his Islamic understanding as a guide to instruct his troops at war, "Do not betray; do not carry grudges; do not deceive; do not mutilate; do not kill children; do not kill the elderly; do not kill women. Do not destroy beehives or burn them, do not cut down fruit-bearing trees; do not slaughters sheep, cattle or camels except for food. You will come upon people who spend their lives in monasteries, leave them to what they have dedicated their lives. . . . Now advance in the Name of God."[17]

Muslim ethics in war would not allow for harm to noncombatants in this view. Nor is any suicide allowed.[18] So the terrorist attacks of 9/11 are far out of line with the spirit of Islam. The Qur'an notes, "On that account: We ordained for the Children of Israel that if any one slew a person—unless it be for murder or spreading mischief in the land—it would be as if he slew the whole people: and if any one

16. Jean Akhtar Cerrina, *Islam's Peaceful Warrior: Abdul Ghaffar Khan* (Bloomington, IN: Xlibris Corporation, 2003), 104.
17. Rogerson, *Heirs of Muhammad*, 162.
18. Bernard Lewis, *The Crisis of Islam: Holy War and Unholy Terror* (New York: Modern Library, 2003), 153.

saved a life, it would be as if he saved the life of the whole people."[19] Life is precious in Islam. It is also preferable to lay down your sword if you have the opportunity. It is what Muhammad did at Hudaybiyah, even without requiring his enemies to acknowledge his prophetic status.

I cannot pretend to render a final interpretation of Islam here. But I can imagine Muhammad looking upon the terrorists and what they have falsely claimed to be Islam with great dismay. I would hope further that the political and religious waters, which have been bloodied and sullied by such acts, would only soon come clean. But that will require further exertion, further jihad, further effort.

Politics

What kind of state does Islam advocate? Monarchy? Theocracy? Democracy? Can non-Muslims abide in an Islamic polity? It might be argued both ways. Some Muslims think in terms of a theocratic state, in which the law of Islam must be the law of the state. Other Muslims have argued that Islam is fully compatible with democracy and has a long tradition to encourage that. Let us take a look at both sides of the issue.

Islam has a long theocratic tradition. Islam is what brought Arabs together from many divided tribes. Muhammad showed a keen and strong interest in the religious conversion of political states. He even wrote a letter to the Muqawqis, the governor of Christian Egypt, asking for his conversion.[20] The removal of the idols from the Kaaba and all the conflict leading up to that had produced a newly organized state in Arabia. Islam was the linchpin. When Muhammad passed away and Abu Bakr became the caliph, or leader of the Muslim community, the "Ridda Wars" were fought against apostates who were seeking to back out of their prior treaty commitments. Without the fervor and purpose of Islam, it is difficult to imagine Arabia coming together and expanding against the powerful Sassanid and Byzantine Empires nearby. Islam is what held the young Arabian state together in the first place.

There is also a strong case to be made for democracy and tolerance in Islam. In Islam, one is not supposed to convert by threat or force. Though that has happened historically, the Qur'an says otherwise: "Let there be no compulsion in

19. Yusuf Ali, *Qur'an*, 5:32.
20. Rogerson, *Prophet Muhammad*, 179.

religion: Truth stands out clear from Error: whoever rejects evil and believes in God has grasped the most trustworthy hand-hold that never breaks. And God hears and knows all things."[21] Muhammad lived among Jews in Medina, and though relations were not always peaceable, he did not force them to convert to Islam. When Islam later expanded into other territories, it required non-Muslims to pay the *jizya*, or "poll tax," but generally speaking, it did not force conversion. The tolerance Muslims offered to non-Muslims was sometimes good, sometimes not so good, according to the nature of the leader in that place and time.

Benazir Bhutto, the former prime minister of Pakistan, has argued that not only is democracy compatible with Islam, but Islam has a long legacy of encouraging it. Bhutto, who was twice the prime minister of Pakistan and tragically assassinated when she came back to run for a third term, had plainly stated her support for democracy: "Democracy removes the oxygen from the air of the extremists. They understand that better than anyone else and deliberately target democratic forces throughout the Islamic world."[22] Bhutto's book *Reconciliation* exemplifies the liberal political view of Islam and democracy. Whether Bhutto was the best leader or the right messenger of this idea, however, is debated.

The democratic question is one that Muslims will have to decide and are trying to decide across the world. John Esposito points out that many clearly have expressed a strong desire for democracy, especially when they may be living under conditions without much political freedom.[23] There are freedoms and advantages of democracy that Muslims in non-Western countries want but also things that they may not want, perhaps seeing too much moral laxity in Western cultural norms. Democracy is not a perfect form of government, but as Churchill noted, it is better than any of the alternatives.

When Muhammad died in the year 632, leadership passed to the caliph Abu Bakr. Abu Bakr lived only two years after Muhammad and fought to keep the integrity of the Muslim state that Muhammad had built. When he died and the caliph Umar took control, Islam expanded beyond the borders of Muhammad's day and took territory by war from the Byzantine (Christian) and Sassanid (largely Zoroastrian) Empires.

21. Yusuf Ali, *Qur'an*, 2:256.
22. Benazir Bhutto, *Reconciliation: Islam, Democracy and the West* (New York: HarperCollins, 2008), 208.
23. John Esposito and Dalia Mogahed, *Who Speaks for Islam? What a Billion Muslims Really Think* (New York: Gallup, 2007), xii, 40–47.

One might ask, If Islam is only supposed to fight defensively, how can the expansion into those rival empires be justified? It could be argued that borders in those days had no international recognition; they were simply drawn where the last war had ended. War was more or less constant, and had Islam not advanced against the Byzantines and Sassanids, then the latter may well have advanced against it. The Byzantines were, in fact, preparing their troops on the borders in reaction to the new unity in Arabia. This may not be a perfect justification, but in terms of what was happening in the day, it makes sense; all empires were moving and threatening each other in a more or less constant game of real-life chess. The new Islamic state had to face that game, and it played its role in it.

Umar reigned as caliph for ten years, from 634 to 644. He was killed by a Persian slave who bore a grudge against him, and then Uthman took control. Uthman ruled for twelve years, from 644 to 656, and there were great accomplishments as well as inner turmoil during his tenure. His most widely recognized accomplishment was having the Qur'an written down and published by the year 650. Many Muslims who had memorized the Qur'an had been killed in combat, and there were some variant versions of qur'anic verses emerging. Uthman and other Muslims did not want the Qur'an to be lost or corrupted, so they collected the authoritative verses and those who had memorized them, producing an official Qur'an. Thus within eighteen years of Muhammad's death, his revelations were written down, a fairly quick timeline compared to most of the world's religions.

Uthman's caliphate began to get into trouble due to the appointments he made for local governors of the new Islamic state. His personal clan group controlled most of the Arabian Peninsula and surrounding areas, and because of this, dissent began to boil. Uthman may only have been appointing persons he felt he could trust to ensure strength and stability, but others apparently did not see it like this. A group of rebel discontents soon ended up on Uthman's doorstep. The rebels were appeased and dismissed, but they soon came back with a letter from the caliph, possibly forged and fraudulent, that gave the order to kill them. Uthman denied all knowledge of the letter, but the damage was done. The rebels forced their way into Uthman's house and killed him before his wife, who was injured trying to protect him. This happened in June of 656.[24]

24. S. E. Al-Djazairi, *The First Caliphs* (n.p.: MSBN Books, 2016), loc. 3178–283, Kindle.

Ali succeeded Uthman, and an emerging Shia faction believed he should have been the first imam after Muhammad. According to the Sunni, the majority of Islam, Muhammad did not designate a clear successor. Sunni believe that Abu Bakr was elected by consensus at the time. The minority "party of Ali"—or the Shia, as they are known—believe that at an oasis between Mecca and Medina, the prophet Muhammad stopped the caravan and gave a clear indication that Ali should be his successor. The Sunni do not recognize this, and the fate of Ali and his children would increasingly divide the emerging factions that would become known as Sunni and Shia.

The fourth caliph, Ali, began his tenure in 656 under hard circumstances. There were rebels who had just killed the prior caliph, and an angry relative in Damascus, named Muawiya, wanted Ali to take vengeance upon the killers. Becoming the caliph, Ali decided not to keep Muawiya on as governor, and a conflict ensued. Coming to confront Muawiya, Ali's troops began to combat him at the Battle of Siffin. After prolonged fighting and negotiations, the battle was ultimately stopped, and arbitrators were appointed to resolve the dispute. The arbitration did not go well for Ali, and one of the arbitrators declared that it was Muawiya, not Ali, who should be caliph. That didn't appear to be part of the arbitration.

In the struggle with Ali, one radical faction emerged and separated itself from Ali's camp. These were known as the Kharijites, or literally, "those who walked out of the camp." They did not trust the way Ali had handled matters. After a bitter and also passionate attempt to reconcile them, there remained a few outside of his allegiance. It was these Kharijites that plotted a coup against the established authorities, including Ali. An attempt was made on the lives of Ali, Muawiya, and Amr, the Islamic governor in Egypt. Two of the attempts failed, but the one against Ali succeeded, and he was murdered in the year 661. Muawiya would finally succeed him, and a new Umayyad dynasty ruled from Damascus until the year 750.[25]

The Umayyads did not take control without a struggle, however. Hussein was the son of Ali and the grandchild of Muhammad and Fatima. Hussein contended for power with Muawiya's son, Yazid. Although seen as heroic and brave, Hussein's bid to become caliph would not be successful. He and his small band of followers were surrounded, cut off from water, and ultimately killed in Karbala, Iraq. Shia mourn

25. Al-Djazairi, loc. 3542–630.

his death and martyrdom to this day. The *Taziyah*, or passion play, is a ritual that commemorates this great loss.

The fighting and struggle within the Islamic religion may have little to do with the religion or its doctrines, and in fact, the Qur'an warns sternly against Muslim fighting with Muslim. When any new power center emerges, as in the case of the new Islamic state, it is likely some may dissent and produce resisting factions. Like the controversy that would emerge between Protestants and Catholics, the struggle between Sunni and Shia is over legitimacy and authority. Shia think Ali was the true successor all along, while Sunni believe that Muhammad did not designate a successor and that Abu Bakr was duly elected as caliph after Muhammad's death. Some doctrinal and ritual differences have emerged between Sunni and Shia in later years, but for the most part, they share the same Qur'an, if not the exact same view of the religion itself.

Another group, composed of Islamic mystics known as the Sufis, believes that they have retained special practices and understandings of the Qur'an. There are many differing Sufi orders, each with nuanced beliefs and practices that make it difficult to paint them with a broad brush. Each Sufi order is organized around an elder Sufi master who passes on his special knowledge to other Sufi mystics. At times, Sufis have likened their rapture with God to intoxication, a controversial claim because Muslims are not supposed to drink alcohol, according to the Qur'an. Sufis have often been the creative, interpretive edge of Islam, but in so doing, they have been really trying to recapture the heart and spirit of Muhammad's core beliefs.

From the seventh to the thirteenth century, Islam grew rapidly and became recognized among the powers of world civilizations. The first Islamic power that ruled from Jordan was the Umayyad dynasty, lasting from the year 661 until 750. It spread far east and into Persia and far west toward Morocco and Spain. The famous "Dome of the Rock," the third holiest shrine in Islam, was built by the Umayyads in Jerusalem. The Umayyads remained a Sunni power for about ninety years. Their power was brought to an end by a rival Abbasid dynasty, which set up its capital in Baghdad. The Abbasids ruled until the year 1258 and occupied an even greater territorial domain than their predecessors. A wealthy, advanced, and highly literate civilization, they also studied Greek philosophy. Renowned philosophers like Avicenna and Averroes emerged. Abbasids also had internal factions and competition, and though they were a Sunni dynasty, there were years in which they would have to compete with and share power with the Shia. The crushing sweep of Mongol conquest put an end to the Abbasid dynasty in 1258, but Islam lived on.

The Ottoman dynasty, centered in Turkey, was one of the last great Islamic powers before the colonial dominance of the West swept over the world. For many years the Ottomans had superior weaponry and a threatening military that penetrated deeper into eastern Europe. The Byzantine Empire had been a holdout for many years but finally fell to Ottoman power when Constantinople was overwhelmed in 1453. The city was renamed Istanbul. The Ottoman advance into Europe nearly took the city of Vienna but was pushed back in 1683. Current tensions between Christians and Muslims are rooted in a past of conflict and war. Time and intention will hopefully build a more peaceful bridge between them in the future.

This history is a sad contradiction, for at the core of both religions, there are many doctrines that suggest peace, not war, should be the governing norm of society. If, however, every religion, creed, or philosophy were to be discredited due to the abuses and injustice falsely done in its name, then hardly any could be said to be legitimate. American democracy, a positive political achievement, was founded alongside the bloodshed of Indigenous peoples and the enslavement of Africans. This should make us not a critic of democracy but a critic of the failure of the way both Indigenous people and Africans were once treated. One might exonerate both Christianity and Islam, for though both have founded great empires with bloodshed, this was due to those in political command, not necessarily the moral dictates of either faith. In fact, reading the scriptures of each religion can yield a good case for rejecting the abuses done in their names.

When the Ottoman Empire collapsed and after World War I, a bold reformer named Mustafa Kemal Ataturk founded the new state of Turkey from its remains. Ataturk was a strong and controversial leader who secularized Turkey and modernized and westernized it at the same time, even changing from the Arabic to the Latin script. If this was not significant enough, Ataturk also abolished the last remaining caliph. In 1924, after nearly 1,300 years since Abu Bakr became the first caliph, this ancient Islamic political and religious institution was shut down. The caliph was given £2,000 and took a train to Switzerland.[26] Although the caliph in Islam is not

26. Andrew Mango, *Ataturk: The Biography of the Founder of Modern Turkey* (New York: Overlook, 2002), 406–7.

quite analogous to the pope in Catholicism, the comparison is not wholly off the mark. Picture an Italian prime minister telling the pope that his services are no longer required and that the Vatican would be closed tomorrow.

Modern Crisis

The crisis of modern Islam, the headlines made by Osama bin Laden and ISIS, are in part due to a severing of the Islamic world from its past and from the power and prosperity it once had. Ataturk is not to blame, but by standards of the Islamic radicals, he could be regarded as part of the problem, not the solution. Western colonial division of what had formerly been the Ottoman Empire as well as the legacy of dictatorship and lack of economic opportunity experienced in many parts of the Muslim world aggravate the situation. In the Gulf States where there is abundant oil, there is economic promise but also not much that we in the West would recognize as democracy.

Many Islamic nations are cut off from the power of their past and have endured stifling political or economic circumstances. Many do not see a lot of promises or opportunities in the modern world. The lack of economic opportunity and the hegemony of Western powers have turned some to a radical and negative interpretation of Islam. Ataturk tried to get past Islam and religion, seeing it as a problem holding Turkey back, but many Muslims have sought to redeem it in the most unwholesome manner. As Karen Armstrong has noted, "Repression of religion can breed fundamentalism, just as inadequate forms of theism can result in a rejection of God."[27]

On September 11, 2001, coordinated terrorist attacks killed nearly three thousand Americans. The world was shocked, and the terrorist tactics of Osama Bin Laden created bloodstains that also soiled the fabric of Islam's history. If the instructions of the Qur'an and Abu Bakr were followed with a benign heart, terrorist violence should not have happened in the first place. That has not stopped groups like ISIS from savagely killing Shia Muslims or beheading defenseless prisoners and posting it on the internet.[28] This is abhorrent, but it is not representative of the spirit of Islam. It is a crass perversion of it. Because of these terrorist acts, however, many in

27. Karen Armstrong, *A History of God* (New York: Alfred A. Knopf, 1993), 362.
28. See Jessica Stern and J. M. Bergère, *Isis: The State of Terror* (New York: Ecco, 2015).

the Christian West still have rejected Islam, perhaps without knowing that Muslims themselves have rejected terrorist acts. One poll showed that over 93 percent of world Muslims condemned the 9/11 attacks.[29]

Murder makes headlines, but the vast majority of Muslims living peaceful lives does not. Headline news can sour our views of the world and its peoples. The violent attacks of 9/11 are emblazoned in our memory, but what is less known is that ninety-five years earlier, on September 11, 1906, Gandhi took an oath of nonviolence to resist South African racism. Many Hindus and Muslims took the oath with him. Decades before Martin Luther King Jr. made nonviolence famous in the United States, Muslims had already joined with Gandhi in South Africa and later in India. This needs to be understood so that we do not fall into sweeping and false mischaracterizations of the Islamic faith.[30]

Abdul Ghaffar Khan (the "Muslim Gandhi") had his nonviolent army of Khudai Khidmatgars take a pledge committing to nonviolence and public service. This included pledges "to serve humanity in the name of God . . . to forgive those who oppress me or treat me with cruelty . . . to practice virtue and refrain from evil . . . good manners and good behavior and . . . to devote at least two hours a day to social work."[31] Extremists have done a grave disservice to their religion. The truer character of Islam is represented by men like Abdul Ghaffar Khan. The better view of Islam is the patient and peaceful one. It does exist; it can be fostered, but it also needs the encouragement of non-Muslims.

What Fits?

Do core Muslim beliefs fit with the essentials of other religions? The short answer is yes. The love of one's neighbor, a form of the Golden Rule, is observed in Islam. Muhammad once said, "None of you is a believer so long as he does not wish for his brother what he wishes for himself!"[32] Furthermore, the Qur'an states, "I ask you only to love your kindred. He that does a good deed shall be repaid many times

29. Esposito and Mogahed, *Who Speaks for Islam?*, 70.
30. Gandhi, *Satyagraha in South Africa*, 95.
31. Eknath Easwaran, *A Man to Match His Mountains: Badshah Khan, Non-violent Soldier of Islam* (Berkeley, CA: Nilgiri Press, 1984), 111.
32. Küng, *Islam*, 657.

over. God is forgiving and bountiful in His rewards."[33] In Muhammad's farewell sermon, he also added a theme of human equality: "All humankind is from Adam and Eve, an Arab has no superiority over a non-Arab, nor a non-Arab any superiority over an Arab: also a white has no superiority over black nor a black and superiority over white except by piety and good action."[34]

Muhammad advocated for women's rights and respect in a time when they had very few rights. He also made a case for social justice and responsibility: "Every one of you is a guardian and responsible for what is in his custody. The ruler is a guardian for his subjects and responsible for them; a husband is a guardian of his family and responsible for it; a lady is the guardian of her husband's house and responsible for it, and a servant is a guardian for his master's property and responsible for it."[35]

In revisiting some of the *global ethics* found in world religion (the Golden Rule, do not lie, do not kill, do not steal, do not commit adultery), one can again find these norms in the Islamic faith. They are not worded in precisely the same way, and they may not be emphasized or interpreted in exactly the same manner. A major thesis of this book is that any good-hearted person with a sound and rational mind can discern the best in their religious traditions. This will give them a spiritual map and a compass, as well as a way to elevate themselves morally. Bad and unsound minds go a different way. Such minds have perverted Islam, and instead of elevating to a higher summit, they've plunged themselves into a dark abyss of moral nihilism.

The Qur'an speaks of striving for righteousness and living peacefully alongside those who do not see eye to eye with you. It declares, "We have ordained a law and assigned a path for each of you. Had God pleased, He could have made you one community: but it is His wish to prove you by that which He has bestowed you. Vie with each other in good works, for to God shall you return and He will resolve your differences for you."[36] This is an interesting passage. It suggests not only positive moral existence but also a reason for the variety of religions and perspectives in the world; God in the Islamic viewpoint, for whatever unforeseen reason, simply intended it. Maybe, by our differences, our understanding is vexed and begs us to come to greater appreciation of our fellow human beings.

33. Dawood, *Koran*, v. 42:23, or p. 341.
34. Rogerson, *Prophet Muhammad*, 208.
35. al-Bukhari, *The Hadith*, loc. 14,339–14,344, 16,882.
36. Dawood, *Koran*, v. 5:49, or p. 85.

It may be that our differences make us more vigorous puzzle makers. If we encounter those who disagree, and disagree profoundly, it makes us more active in mind and spirit, trying to figure things out. With a plurality of religions, we exercise our minds to figure out what is true and what is right, and that makes us better and stronger persons. Without such disagreement, our minds might not be provoked to sort things out, to puzzle. This points to an unexpected conclusion: that if God or whatever sacred source had intended us to be the best of critical thinkers, then one unambiguous, clearly stated rule book or guide would have been insufficient. It would have robbed us of the necessary struggle we need to make to arrive at a higher moral truth by way of exerting our minds. In this way, by the analogy of puzzle making, the diversity and disagreement of the world's religions are better understood.

The heart and mind of the believer, the way they perceive religion, can produce vastly different images and different ways of assembling the puzzle of life. For most Muslims, that is going to be a nonviolent struggle, or jihad, that tries to uphold peace and justice. Insofar as Muslims and others work toward that end, the Islamic religion and many others can be positive ways to move toward a better world. It must be remembered that religions do not live independently of the life we give them, the spirit of our mind and interpretation are crucial for the way they are practiced.

What Doesn't Fit?

As with all the other religions I have studied, there are controversies in Islam. There are things that fit less well with other religions and things that one might outright object to. Take, for instance, the belligerent charge of the "sword verses" we mentioned above. While most Muslims deem defensive violence acceptable, there are parts such as these that raise eyebrows and can trouble the mind. Take also the doctrine of cutting off the hand of the thief: "As for the man or woman who is guilty of theft, cut off their hands to punish them for their crimes. That is the punishment enjoined by God. God is mighty and wise. But whoever repents after committing evil, and mends his ways, shall be pardoned by God. God is forgiving and merciful."[37] It is a harsh penalty if it is applied, and some places in the Muslim

37. Dawood, v. 5:37, or p. 83.

world apply it, while others do not. There is also a question of interpreting this verse. If a thief is in fact repentant, should one still cut off his or her hand? For some Muslims, the answer might be yes, for those who are more moderate and merciful in their interpretation, the answer would be no.

The penalty for adultery in Islam is whipping one hundred lashes.[38] Four witnesses are required to prove it. Obviously, this is harsh by most standards today. There are, however, controversial traditions, or hadith, that report Muhammad authorizing the stoning of adulterers in some cases, and the second caliph Umar was reported to have thought this was acceptable.[39] This is baffling, for in the Qur'an, lashes are very clearly the penalty applied, so why should there be this confusion? Not all of the hadith are reliable, and in the case of this contradiction, the Qur'an should probably be the higher authority.

In terms of women's rights also, in the court of law, a woman's witness is said to be half that of a man's.[40] Additionally, a woman's inheritance is said to be half that of her brother.[41] The latter restriction on inheritance was justified because a woman at that time was not obligated to work to provide for herself. This was the obligation of the men in the family, to work for and provide for the women. As a matter of women's rights, it was progress in the time of Muhammad; the Arabian Peninsula in the time of *jahiliyyah* (pre-Islamic ignorance before Muhammad) did not advocate women's rights. Benazir Bhutto, among others, has tried to argue that Islam offers an ethic of equality for men and women.[42] Be this as it may, the idea of a woman's inheritance and rights in court counting as one-half of those of a man's is not going to square well with what contemporary women's rights advocates. This is another potential source where one tradition may be at loggerheads with another, and again one has to investigate the fuller spirit of Islam to discern whether reconciliation is possible. I think it may be but that it will require further scrutiny and debate.

If the Qur'an is treated as an infallible document, without error, I think it is evident that there will be places that it agrees with other traditions and also places

38. Dawood, vv. 24:2–3, or p. 246.
39. al-Bukhari, *Hadith*; there are numerous places where stoning for adultery is advocated by Muhammad. See al-Bukhari, loc. 13773, 16396, 28955, 33937, 43391.
40. Dawood, *Koran*, v. 2:283, or p. 41.
41. Dawood, v. 4:11, or p. 61.
42. Bhutto, *Reconciliation*, see chap. 2.

where it is strongly at odds with other traditions. There are places people will find it morally inspiring, but as in the case of women's rights, some might find it objectionable. If the spirit of *ijtihad*, or "independent reasoning" (a Muslim philosophical tradition), can be applied to the Qur'an, it might be reinterpreted in many different ways. Theologian Hans Küng has suggested that Muslims of the twenty-first century "need not maintain the . . . perfection, infallibility, and immutability of . . . the Qur'an."[43] Can the Qur'an be challenged? Can any of its verses simply be disagreed with, or abrogated? This is a shocking question to Muslims, as it is a shocking question for any religious believer who elevates a text as having a high, if not total, degree of perfection.

I agree with Küng, Gandhi, and many others about religious texts and traditions. Religions are not necessarily perfect in every regard, in my view, but they may be inspirational. If properly understood and interpreted, they can provide good values for conduct. Gandhi did not think that the tradition of Hinduism was perfect, nor was any other tradition perfect. He condemned the practice of untouchability and said that scripture cannot transcend a reasonable moral truth: "Scriptures cannot transcend Reason and Truth. They are intended to purify Reason and illuminate Truth. . . . It is the spirit that giveth the light. And the spirit of the Vedas is purity, truth, innocence, chastity, simplicity, forgiveness, godliness, and all that makes a man or woman noble and brave."[44] Gandhi believed that the Qur'an, as much as the Bhagavad Gita or the Christian gospel, could serve as a guide to truth but only if one responds to it with reason, a moral mind, and a conscientious heart. The Qur'an can, I think, play a meaningful and positive role in our civilization if reason, a moral mind, and a conscientious heart also play an active role in interpreting and understanding it.

43. Küng, *Islam*, 645.
44. Fischer, *Essential Gandhi*, 135.

6 Zoroastrianism and the Abrahamic Faiths

Summary of Zoroastrianism

Zoroastrianism is a monotheistic religion that dates to the revelations experienced by the prophet Zoroaster, sometime between the sixth and twelfth centuries BCE. Zoroaster was rebelling against polytheism and believed there was one high God called Ahura Mazda, with a devil-like enemy named Ahriman. Ahriman was trying to taint and ruin Ahura Mazda's creation. Human will is still needed in the colossal and cosmic wrestling match between the forces of good, represented by Ahura Mazda, and the forces of evil serving Ahriman. Humans are meant to use their wills to serve the principles of good, and if they do so, there will be rewards both in this world and in the next. Zoroastrianism is not an Abrahamic faith; it does not connect with or recognize the prophet Abraham in any way, but it does have many of the same features as these other monotheistic religions: belief in one high God, a devilish adversary, an idea of heaven and hell, an expectation of the apocalypse, and the resurrection of the dead.

So strikingly similar is the Zoroastrian faith to the religions of Judaism, Christianity, and Islam in theological structure that one might wonder why there are so few Zoroastrians today. With close to four billion Jews, Christians, and Muslims, one might expect there to be a lot of Zoroastrians as well if it is the basic ideas of a religion that decide its appeal. There are, however, only between one hundred and two hundred thousand Zoroastrians alive in the world today. Why so few? Unlike other religions, Zoroastrianism has not had large empires to support it in later years. Other religions have certainly surpassed it, in numeric support, over the centuries.

Structural Similarities of Monotheistic Religions

How does Zoroastrianism relate to the Abrahamic faiths of Judaism, Christianity, and Islam? If Zoroastrianism is as old as some claim, dating back to 6000 BCE, then Zoroastrianism could be seen as a kind of parent or protoreligion that gave rise to the Abrahamic faiths. A date that ancient really does not seem credible, however, as there has been no solid evidence to support it. If Zoroastrianism dates at the earliest to 1500 BCE, then it might be a kind of sibling or cousin to Judaism, whose patriarch Abraham dates back to 1850 BCE. Jews and Zoroastrians became aware of each other and may even have influenced each other when the Jews were taken into the Babylonian captivity. There they had contact with ancient Zoroastrians. Because there is no linkage between Abraham and Zoroaster, and indeed these monotheistic religions developed different names for and ideas about God, their development could also have been more independent. The yearning for unity, the desire to establish one cosmic God, might have simply developed in separate regions at around the same time period.

Some fragments of the Jewish Tanakh bear a striking resemblance to the Persian Code of Hammurabi. As one of the most ancient legal codes known, the Code of Hammurabi was set up before the sun god Shamash and so was believed to have divine sanction. Hammurabi's code reads, "If a man has caused the loss of a gentleman's eye, his eye one shall cause to be lost. If he has shattered a gentleman's limb, one shall shatter his limb." And further "If a man has made the tooth of a man that is his equal to fall out, one shall make his tooth fall out."[1] This is remarkably similar to Leviticus 24:19–20: "Anyone who maims another shall suffer the same injury in return: fracture for fracture, eye for eye, tooth for tooth; the injury inflicted is the injury to be suffered." The law regarding fetal life in the womb and its loss also bears a strong resemblance between these two sources.[2] In many other respects, the laws diverge, but with so exact overlap in these few instances, the Jewish law must have been aware of Hammurabi. The influence of peer cultures in ancient times certainly happened.

1. Hammurabi, *Hammurabi: The Oldest Code of Laws in the World*, transcribed by David Pierce, trans. C. H. W. Johns (Edinburgh: T&T Clark, 1903), 196–97, 201–2.
2. Pierce and Johns, loc. 403; and Exod 21:22.

As it is hard to date Zoroaster and his religion, it is also difficult to say much about him. His name means something like "old camel man," suggesting a trade in livestock. Though he was of a priestly profession, he rejected the polytheist religion of ancestors in favor of monotheism. Like Abraham, he was a prophet who gave birth to a new religion. He received a revelation that told him that Ahura Mazda was the only real God. This message was not well received at first; Zoroaster had very few converts, and no one was interested in his message for about a decade. Like many prophets, he was alone, preaching in the wilderness, without much of an audience. Finally, the scriptures speak of a man named Visthaspa who accepted Zoroaster's religion, and it suddenly found a foothold.

Zoroastrian belief has six stages of creation. Instead of the six days of creation in the Bible, Zoroastrians believe that in the first stage, the sky was made, like a solid dome over the earth and waters, which came about in the second and third stages of creation. In stages four through six, plants, animals, and man were created, and from these, all later plants, animals, and men emerged. Lastly, fire was created, and the world began in time. Fire, water, and earth are all important here and thought to be sacred elements.[3] There was a period of Golden Rule that lasted for a thousand years under the good King Yima. Ahura Mazda's creation was made good, and in its original form, it was fair and pleasant. Like the biblical story, however, there was a devilish adversary named Ahriman. Ahriman's intent was to assault Ahura Mazda's creation and to taint it, and he did just that. The period of Golden Rule under King Yima was lost, and all manner of foul and noxious things were introduced into the world: poisonous snakes and insects, horrible diseases, and natural disasters. In the biblical story, Adam and Eve commit sin and were exiled from the paradise of Eden. In the Zoroastrian tale, there is also a sense of anguish in exile, a good place we have lost to which we need to return.

Zoroastrians believe in an idea of heaven and hell and also in an idea of an apocalypse. The world is a place of cosmic struggle in Zoroastrianism, the forces of good serving Ahura Mazda on the one side and the forces of evil serving Ahriman on the other, trying to ruin all that was good. Ahura Mazda's angelic forces are called the Amesha Spenta, or the Spenta Mainyu. Of these high angels, Vohu Manah was the most important and is said to have led Zoroaster to his original

3. Mary Boyce, *Zoroastrians: Their Religious Beliefs and Practices* (New York: Prentice Hall, 2001), 12.

vision of Ahura Mazda. These forces of good serve the principles of Asha, which stand for good values such as truth and social justice. Against them are arraigned the forces of evil, the angra mainyu who serve Ahriman. Instead of the good, they serve the aptly named Druj (or Drug), the principles of evil that woo and deceive one away from following the straight and narrow path of good. Ethics of "truth, honestly, loyalty, and courage were felt to be proper for mankind."[4] In this cosmic struggle, individual souls are called to serve good, not evil. Zoroastrian scripture speaks of two competing wills and a very real choice that must be made to serve good or evil: "Once those two Wills join battle, a man adopts life or non-life, the way of existence that will be his at the last: that of the wrongful the worst kind, but for the righteous one, best thought."[5]

One can choose to do good, or one can choose to do evil, but the choice has consequences in this world and the world thereafter: "Whoso comes to the righteous one, radiance is his to possess hereafter; (but) a long age of darkness, foul food, cries of woe by way of speech, that is the existence to which, ye wrongful, through your own actions your morality will bring you."[6] If you choose the path of good and justice in Asha, the consequence will ultimately be prosperity, happiness, and the life to come. If you are deceived and choose evil, wooed by the illusion of Druj (Drug), then you will reap the bitter harvest that you sowed. This was a bold, new vision that presented life as a meaningful struggle, a cosmic chess game between good and evil in which every person might serve a function, even if it were that of a pawn.

Zoroastrians believed that after death, one made a journey across the "Chinvat Bridge," or a journey called "crossing the separator," the trip into the next life. If you had been a good person, faithful to the calling of Ahura Mazda, you would step across a wide bridge into the heavens, where a beautiful maiden welcomed you to the afterlife. If, however, you had been not a good person but a faithless and immoral one, the bridge would not be wide; it might turn on its side or become razor thin. Then your journey was like a tightrope walk across a scary abyss. More than likely, you would fall into the limbo of Hamestegan and there await what seemed to be an eternity until the final apocalypse. Zoroastrians were fairly optimistic about

4. See Boyce, 8.
5. Zoroaster, *Hymns of Zoroaster, the Gathas*, ed. M. L. West (New York: I. B. Tauris, 2010), 51.
6. Zoroaster, 65.

the odds of becoming saved at this time, but it did appear that some persons may have been beyond redemption.

The Zoroastrian apocalypse was the final conflict between good and evil. Good would ultimately triumph over evil, and the forces of Ahriman and darkness would be thrown back and defeated. The "Refreshment," called Frashokereti, would follow, and the bones of the dead would take on new flesh. One source reports that those who died as adults would come back at about the age of forty, and those who died as children would come back at the age of fifteen.[7] It is not clear that all Zoroastrians accepted these ages, but the idea of an apocalyptic resurrection of the dead was important to Zoroastrians, and it is a reason they took great precautions in their funeral arrangements.

Since the bones would take on new flesh in the resurrection, cremation was not practiced. Because both water and earth were sacred elements, neither burials at sea nor burials in the ground were practiced either. Therefore, they developed the "Tower of Silence," called the *dakhma*. Here the corpse was exposed to the elements and allowed to decompose naturally until finally there was nothing but dry bones left. The bones could then be interred above the earth in a crypt to await the resurrection. As there are so few Zoroastrians left today, this is not a rite of passing that is much practiced anymore, but it is one of the more unique approaches to death in world religions.

Zoroastrianism was once a flourishing religion commanding loyalty in a widespread area surpassing the borders of ancient Persia. Zoroaster may have been a lonely prophet crying to the wilderness for ten years, but ultimately, people did come to heed his message. After a few friends, relatives, and a sparse number of converts followed him, the religion began to grow. Soon it stretched out from the Bactrian region near central Asia and all the way to the borders of Arabia. Not *everyone* in those borders was a Zoroastrian, but there were several powerful dynasties that embraced and accepted Zoroastrianism.

The Achaemenians, or Median Empire, were one of the first. Dating back to the fifth or sixth century BCE, figures such as Cyrus the Great (ruled 576–530 BCE) and Darius I (ruled 522–486 BCE) presided over Zoroastrians in their kingdom. The religion had grown from a bud to a flower, but soon the invasion of Alexander the Great

7. Solomon Alexander Nigosian, *The Zoroastrian Faith: Tradition and Modern Research* (Montreal: McGill Queen's Press, 1993), 94–95.

swept over the entire region. Zoroastrian priests were killed, and temples were destroyed or vacated. In the Zoroastrian tradition, Alexander has the dubious title of the "accursed" for the damage he did to the kingdom of their faith. This is a title also applied to Ahriman, showing how badly Zoroastrians felt about the Macedonian conqueror. Alexander's conquests were fast and dramatic but not long lived. The empire he left behind began to crumble as the Parthian Empire took hold in Persia. In the third century BCE, the Parthians also accepted the Zoroastrian religion, and its practices were revived. But the Parthians did not last long either. The last Zoroastrian empire to exist was the Sassanid, which existed up until the seventh century CE. By that time, the Sassanids were a mighty force to be reckoned with, having fought wars against the Byzantine Christians to their west.

Judaism, Christianity, and Zoroastrianism came into mutual contact and became acquainted with each other. As monotheistic religions, they all claimed a prophetic, revealed truth. Parts of their values agreed, while other beliefs, ideas, and rituals did not. As Christianity became aligned with Rome and Byzantium in the West, Zoroastrianism still stood as a rival in the East. Jews did not have a kingdom by the time of the seventh century and had been pushed into Diaspora.

Yet another lonely prophet then arose. In the year 610 CE, Muhammad had a revelatory experience in the Cave of Hira. This revelation attempted to settle all the differences among these other "People of the Book." Jews, Christians, and Zoroastrians were referred to as "People of the Book" in Islamic tradition. They are monotheistic religions with a genuine deposit of divine truth. But Muhammad's revelation was said to be the final corrective, the last revelation to earth that would set people on the right path.

When Islam became the religion of the Arabian Peninsula, it consolidated a political power where there hadn't been unified power before. After Islam took hold in Arabia, the religion soon began to pour over the borders and threaten Byzantium in the West and the Sassanid Zoroastrians in the East. The Byzantine Christians would hold out for many centuries. The Sassanids would not. By the year 651, the last Sassanid emperor, Yazdegerd III, was defeated. Unlike Christianity and Islam, which had empires to support and champion their faiths, the Zoroastrians would not after the seventh century. Their numbers diminished. Some Zoroastrians fled to India, where they thought they might be safe. The Zoroastrians that took refuge in India became known as the Parsis, from their Persian roots, and today, the Parsis of India are the largest surviving Zoroastrian community.

In the history of world religions, there have been some that have grown and thrived, spreading over much of the known world. Christianity and Islam are inherently missionary religions that have enjoyed political protection and support in later years. Zoroastrianism did not have the same support, and the number of Zoroastrians has vastly diminished. Today, their beliefs still survive but are not at the front and center of our attention.

What Fits?

The monotheistic faiths discussed so far have some common threads: belief in one God; belief in a struggle between good and evil; a belief in the afterlife, the soul, and a day of judgment or apocalypse that will occasion a resurrection of the dead. The morphological unity between the Abrahamic faiths of Judaism, Christianity, and Islam should be expected. Beyond these theological similarities, each of these monotheistic faiths advances a similar moral message of justice, mercy, and redemption. If they share values and beliefs, is it possible that they simply offer up different names for the same God? Like language, is the meaning the same but its form and structure varied across the globe?

One cannot help but notice a deep similarity in the monotheistic faiths, and this gives room for optimism. Perhaps our sensibility of divine truth is real, a sacred heart to our universe; we have just come to picture it and express it differently. Conceptions, general ethics, and spiritual directions can overlap, true. If we do not get too hung up on particulars, general ideas can unite us. To be honest, however, one must note also some sharp divergence.

What Doesn't Fit?

There is an important unity in these religions, but the differences between them are deep. Even within the Abrahamic faiths, many Christians do not feel that the God they pray to is the same as the Muslim Allah. The perceived rift is so deep between them that they do not feel like they belong together. Jews and Christians share part of the Bible but are very divided about its meaning, order, and the arrival of the Messiah. Zoroastrians do not share a scriptural tradition with the Abrahamic faiths. The Avesta is the "Bible" of Zoroastrianism.

This, once again, prompts the most vexing question about monotheism: If God intended to reach human beings, wouldn't God have given one clear and perfect message *just once*? Yet upon reading various revelatory texts, we find they not only are not all the same but also have some profound differences! We should expect a God that is truly universal would preside equally, fairly, and justly over a *humanity* that is equal. If God is a parent to us all, why did God not treat us all equally? Why would God reveal truth to just one part of the world and yet not to others? Is it true that either one of these traditions is *the truth*, in which case it appears God acted partially, or is there a truth that might transcend or encompass them?

A perfectly communicated, received, and preserved revelatory experience should be God's clear words given to humanity. If evolution is a fact, couldn't revelatory texts have told us about it? If the big bang happened, why is it not clearly and unambiguously written? Modern minds have much to doubt in these texts, as they leave out scientific truths we have come to accept. They demand empirical evidence for revelation's claims and modern morality in revelation's ethics. A flawless revelatory text would be clear and intelligible and offer a straightforward path that *all of us*, regardless of our race, caste, or background, could follow, *right*?

These are modern assumptions about universal human rights, and though they are, I think, good assumptions, we have to step back a moment and think. The universal ethics, such as the Golden Rule to "love they neighbor as you love yourself" and to care for the poor and the needy, can be seen as a dialectical extension of religious values themselves. Our modern belief in universal human rights is indebted not to a noble political philosophy that came out of a cultural vacuum but in some measure to the religious beliefs that supported it. Nevertheless, strict traditionalism presents complicated and significant problems for the understanding of religion. It is possible that God spoke truly to *one and only one* religious tradition and that this could have been the Jews, Christians, Muslims, Zoroastrians, Mormons, Sikhs, or Hindus, or any other tradition. Buddhism, though not monotheistic, might also be the true faith. If sacred truth was imparted to one and only one tradition, then the rest of us are left out in an arbitrary manner that erodes the fabric of common bonds essential to our modern, interdependent, and interconnected world.

Final Reflections

I have grown to appreciate a more open-minded Universalism. When I see good spiritual ideas scattered in a wide variety of religions (and snares in many of them as well), I do not feel satisfied with the notion that truth can be found *only here* and *never there*. God does not play favorites. And even if there is no God, as Buddhism and Jainism suggest, there is still an element of compassion and benevolence essential to both these traditions. No religious tradition has a monopoly on compassion. I think one can affirm one religion and also learn a great deal from others. Even a secular humanist perspective appreciates the values of religion (without arguing that they are necessarily true). Religions may be correct about offering many good morals but wrong about the final map of truth, in the completely secular view. The doubt of atheism, the skepticism of ancient doctrines, has turned some people away from the idea that there is an inherent or deep truth in religion.

The secular mindset should not be so severely restricted, however. Not all people who would call themselves secular are atheists. A secular person can accept the moral truths of religion while being agnostic about its metaphysical claims. I wholeheartedly accept secularism's broadened view, but I still look to reconnect with something larger. Like a bell rung long ago, the echoes of our ancestors have not died out and are heard by many. In the modern world, however, these echoes can also be drowned out by a lot of other noise.

Looking into this past, I see our religious history like a great bed of fire, ash, and embers. Some things are still true, as burning today as it was to our ancestors. To love one's neighbor, to embrace goodness, compassion, and humility: these things are still true. There is a legacy in religion that we still need to pass on, but we are not always so adept at discerning this legacy.

There are also ashen pits and dead coals from the past of religion, things that burned brightly years ago but are dead to us now. Slavery, oppression, misogyny, racism, war and killing, and all manner of discrimination vile and unacceptable have been given religious sanctification at some points in history. Others of those same faith communities may have steadfastly rejected them, but we still battle with their legacy to this very day.

My view is the view of the puzzler. God, or what is sacred, certainly could have passed the whole and entire truth to only one part of the world and left it up to them to share it with the rest of us. But that is not the way I have come to see it. We all have been given a *good and sufficient* glimpse of a much deeper truth, but the whole picture in its full clarity still eludes us. By puzzling and piecing together meaning and value, our minds and our hearts are required to do more work, to put things together, make them whole, render them sensible. As with literal puzzles, this will often be a confounding and confusing process. We *think* we have the right puzzle piece, but it does not seem to fit. So we rethink, we reevaluate, and in short, we *puzzle*.

Though my belief is in a universal truth that encompasses many religions, my primary identity is that of a Christian. I intend no slight on the perspectives of others. The traditionalist view is still a common one and will be for a long time to come. The strength and preservation of religions are in part due to this traditionalist approach, which gives its heart and strength to just one religion. If the traditionalist keeps an open heart and open mind, this view of religion can continue to benefit us all.

The secular humanist perspective is also commendable. A secular mind looks broadly and is influenced by modern social sciences, such as psychology, and hard sciences, like biology, astronomy, and physics. Science has given us the internet and the iPhone and put men and women into space. To deny its accomplishments and remained unmoved by them is impossible, and the secular mind wants to be present in the midst of all of this.

The Universalist looks for something betwixt and between these two perspectives. Confronted by the achievements of the scientific present and the mysteries of the past, the Universalist finds truth not confined exclusively in the covers of one book or in the confines of one tradition but rather in the complete puzzle of life that is presented to us in the variety of world religions and philosophies. The Universalist has not really jettisoned one religious view but in fact is probably still deeply connected to one religion but just feels a bond and a unity with many others as well.

The complexities and adversities of the modern world need a moral response. Religions of the world are in a good position to offer it. To do this, they need to be engaged and active in the world, working cooperatively and internationally to make it a better place. It is easier to do this when they see some good and legitimacy in one another, as the Universalist clearly affirms. A mature and strong character is a prerequisite to surviving and thriving. Religions, if properly conceived, can develop this character and help keep us and this project we call civilization on track. Religions all speak of a sacred duty. Let us not forget that duty to the moment we are in.

7 Hinduism

Summary of Hinduism

Hinduism is one of the oldest religions of our civilization, but its exact age cannot be determined. The mists of time conceal much about origins, but scholars believe that Hinduism is at least three and a half millennia old. It is possibly linked to the ancient Indus valley civilization, also called the Harappan civilization. Harappa and Mohenjo-daro were two ancient Indus cities that existed between 2500 and 1700 BCE on what today is the border of India and Pakistan. One of Harappa's religious icons, Pashupati, might be a prototype of Hindu gods like Shiva.[1] This civilization flourished, trading with ancient Sumer for many years. At the end of its days, Harappa deteriorated, and many locations may have been abandoned because of a shifting climate and agriculture. As the Harappan civilization disappeared, the Aryans of central Asia invaded.

The Aryans brought with them a society that was divided up into three castes: warriors, priests, and workers. Aryan culture and their deities are associated with ancient Hinduism. Dating to at least 1500 BCE, the Aryans may have given shape to the caste system of Hinduism. Cows were sacred to the Aryans, and they used them as currency for the Brahmin priests. The Aryans also drank an intoxicating beverage known as soma.[2] As they entered India, they crossed the Indus River, and the modern word *Hindu* is a derivative of the Persian *Sindhu* for those people who live across the Indus River valley.[3] Another name for Hinduism is *sanatana dharma*, or "eternal religion."[4]

The oldest Hindu texts, called the Vedas, go back to about 1400 BCE. These venerable writings are called *sruti*, those scriptures that were heard by ancient

1. Mark Muesse, *The Hindu Traditions* (Minneapolis: Fortress, 2011), 15–26. See also Thomas Trautmann, *India: Brief History of a Civilization* (New York: Oxford University Press, 2016), chap. 2.
2. Stanley Wolpert, *A New History of India*, 7th ed. (New York: Oxford University Press, 2004), 18–22, 26, 29–30.
3. Muesse, *Hindu Traditions*, 1–3.
4. Fred Clothey, *Religion in India: A Historical Introduction* (New York: Routledge, 2006), 177.

Indian sages. They are a sacred connection to the world of divinity. Hindus also have many other scriptures, such as the Upanishads that scholars date between 900 and 400 BCE. *Upanishad* means something like "sitting beneath," to gain wisdom by sitting near a venerable guru.[5] The Upanishads are a collection of texts emphasizing spiritual themes we can still relate to today. From the *Taittiriya Upanishad*, "Speak the truth. Do your duty. Do not neglect the study of the scriptures. Do not cut the thread of progeny. Swerve not from truth. Deviate not from the apt or good. Revere greatness. . . . Whatever you give to others, give with love and respect. Gifts must be given in abundance, with joy, humility and compassion."[6]

One of the most widely known texts, the Bhagavad Gita, actually comes from a later period, from texts called *smriti*, or "remembered" by the sages. The classic moral codes of the Laws of Manu belong to this latter period. Though the Laws of Manu were believed to be from a wise king and spelled out the moral law for humanity, it is the Bhagavad Gita that is closest to the Hindu heart today.[7]

Technically, Hinduism is polytheist, or at least it appears to be so. It has innumerable gods and goddesses in its pantheon. Some of these gods and goddesses, such as Shiva, Vishnu, Parvati, and Lakshmi have a wide following across India. Saivites (devotees of Shiva) and Vaishnavites (devotees of Vishnu) are common. The textbook answer to the question, "Is Hinduism polytheistic?" would undeniably appear to be yes, but it is a bit more complicated than this. Many Hindus remain devoted to one god, such as Shiva, Kali, or Ganesh. They see this as their closest, most accessible connection to God and may think of themselves as monotheists. But all of the different gods and goddesses can be viewed as the expression of one divine essence called Brahman. It is not necessary that one is the best or most important but that all are in some way a part of Brahman.

In a way, the Hindu pantheon of gods might be thought to be waves, emanations from a divine ocean. One wave comes rolling in, and it crests and takes shape, rising in stature as it approaches the beach. This is the wave called Vishnu, and it crashes upon the shore, and its waters recede into the common essence of

5. Christopher Partridge and Tim Dowley, eds., *Introduction to World Religions*, 2nd ed. (Minneapolis: Fortress, 2013), 175.
6. Swami Prabhavananda and Frederick Manchester, *The Upanishads: Breath of the Eternal—the Principal Texts Selected and Translated from the Original Sanskrit* (New York: Mentor Classic, 1958), 54.
7. Wendy Doniger and Brian K Smith, *The Laws of Manu* (New York: Penguin Classics, 1991), xviii.

Brahman. The next wave that comes right after that is the divine emanation known as Shiva, and the one after that is Parvati, and Lakshmi follows after. All the waves collapse into the sacred essence known as Brahman, a divine oceanic presence. Hindus believe that the underlying God without defining attributes can be known as Nirguna Brahman, the God beyond our senses. But the divine as manifested in the individual waves with characteristics might be known as Saguna Brahman.[8] Hence, Saguna Brahman may be a wave, but Nirguna Brahman the greater ocean.

The Hindu soul, called the atman, is as one droplet of this great ocean. The droplet is conscious that it has become separated from its parent, estranged from the divine presence. It is a condition known as *avidya*, or the ignorance of the divine reality inside the self, and is a central part of the spiritual problem for Hindus. We are estranged from the very divinity inside us: that one drop yearns to reconnect with the great ocean, yearns to be again a part of God. There may be many lifetimes of spiritual and moral learning needed before ignorance can be overcome. While we pass through those lives, we enter the world here and now, the realm of sensual attachments called samsara. There is some good in samsara, the worldly here and now, but it does not compare with the infinite bliss beyond. As the *Chandogya Upanishad* says, "In the finite there is no happiness. The infinite alone is happiness."[9] If we see beyond this life to the truth, ignorance will not prevail: "Truth alone triumphs, not falsehood."[10] This is the classic cycle of Hindu reincarnation. We go around and around in a reincarnating cycle, our souls like a drop of water that needs to be reconnected with a great ocean, until we become enlightened and attain *moksha*: oneness with the divine.

Hinduism has a few different creation stories. The *Rig Veda* speaks of an omnipotent creator: "The All-Maker is vast in mind and vast in strength. He is the one who forms, who sets in order, and who is the highest image."[11] Brahma is known for being the creator God, but there is another narrative about Brahma being born from Vishnu's navel.[12] Another story tells of creation from a kind of golden cosmic egg named Hiranyagarbha. In another story the gods were spawned of mother

8. David Kinsley, *Hindu Goddesses: Visions of the Divine Feminine in the Hindu Religious Tradition* (Los Angeles: University of California Press, 1988), 136.
9. Sri Chimnoy, *Commentaries on the Vedas, the Upanishads, and the Bhagavad Gita* (New York: Aum, 1996), 66.
10. Chimnoy, 5.
11. Wendy Doniger O'Flaherty, trans., *The Rig Veda* (New York: Penguin, 1981), 36.
12. Muesse, *Hindu Traditions*, 44–46.

goddess Aditi. Probably the most frequently cited text about creation is this pensive excerpt from the *Rig Veda*:

> There was neither non-existence nor existence then; there was neither the realm of space nor the sky which is beyond. What stirred? Where? In whose protection? Was there water, bottomlessly deep? There was neither death nor immortality then. There was no distinguishing sign of night nor of day. That one breathed, windless, by its own impulse. Other than that, there was nothing beyond. . . . Who really knows? Who will proclaim it? Whence was it produced? Whence is this creation? The gods came afterwards, with the creation of this universe. Who then knows whence it has arisen? Whence this creation has arisen—perhaps it formed itself, or perhaps it did not—the one who looks down on it, in the highest heaven, only he knows—or perhaps he does not know.[13]

This last excerpt is appealing but ambiguous. It tells of a mysterious world beyond the full explanation of myth and religion. Imagine yourself sitting on a beach, back on the cool sand, eyes set on the stars above, some twinkling very bright, others soft and dim. The wind sweeps across your face, the crashing of the waves on the shore comforts you and helps you relax. In this moment the complexities and problems of life are swept away with the tide. You contemplate the heavens in their immense size and cannot possibly fathom them, except with the crutch of knowing numbers that are very large. Clearly, however, there is a sense that there is something grander, more elusive, that has yet to be understood.

The ancient Vedic passage above reflects that tone of thought. The modern mind knows of countless creation stories from the past and asks the obvious question: Have we been imaginatively inventing them for lack of a better way to explain the cosmos? It may well be true that there is a spark of creative fiction in religion and in myth. Much of what we know from the past may be our own hope-filled imaginations, yet it might also be a bit presumptuous to reduce them to just that. I prefer the view of myth described by J. R. R. Tolkien. Tolkien saw myth not as lies but as inspirational sparks that imply a higher truth: "You call a star a star . . .

13. O'Flaherty, *Rig Veda*, 25–26.

and just as speech is invention about objects and ideas, so myth is invention about truth. We have come from God and inevitably the myths woven by us, though they contain error, will also reflect a splintered fragment of the true light, the eternal truth that is with God."[14]

"But is religion really true?" This the giant question. There are at least three possible answers. If religion is merely born of our mind's imagination, manufacturing myths and purposes for ourselves, then the secular atheist is correct. If, however, there is a sliver of truth, suggestive but incomplete, then the more liberal or Universalist religious view is proper. God or the sacred spoke to our ancestors and may speak to us now, but imperfectly, by means not fully understood. And, of course, God or the sacred could be speaking to us in unambiguous terms from just one singular tradition, and the others are simply in error. But which is truth, and what is fantasy? As puzzlers, we receive information about the world around us; each piece of data is hard to assemble and make fit with the others.

Creation and Caste

Hindu concepts of creation also have myths that explain the origins of the ancient caste system. The *Rig Veda* describes how caste emerged from an ancestral deity named Purusha. From various parts of Purusha came the Hindu castes: "His mouth became the Brahmin, his arms were made into the Warrior, his thighs the People, and from his feet the Servants were born."[15] Castes have been a dominant social hierarchy in Hinduism for ages and probably developed since the time of the ancient Aryans.

Caste denotes social belonging and hierarchy. You are born into a caste and remain in it. At the top of the caste system are the Brahmins, the priests who are supposed to be the spokesmen for the divine wisdom. They attend to the rituals of the temple. At the next level are the Kshatriyas, the warriors and administrators, the ruling force of law in society. The Kshatriyas came from the arms of Purusha, but in the world, they are the strength of rules and law. Nominally, they were supposed to listen to the Brahmins, but undoubtedly, the king was the one with true power. Below the Kshatriyas are the midcaste professional artisans and workers,

14. Humphrey Carpenter, J. R. R. *Tolkien: A Biography* (New York: Houghton Mifflin, 200), 151.
15. O'Flaherty, *Rig Veda*, 31.

those with some craft or skill, whether it is weaving, pottery making, building, or selling produce. The middle-caste professionals, the Vaishyas, are the supporting thighs of Purusha. These three castes compose the privileged "twice-born," those who wear the sacred thread and are allowed to read the sacred scriptures.

Below the Vaishyas are the Shudras, who are the servants and working peasant class of society. They are perceived to be the feet of Purusha. Then there are the outcastes, the untouchables. They are treated as the lowest of the low, below the pale of caste, and are traditionally marginalized. They live apart from others, doing the most menial of chores and getting the worst treatment. It is a form of social slavery and oppression, a blight on Hinduism, according to Gandhi. Today, the caste discrimination has been outlawed. But that does not mean it does not exist, just that it is not supposed to exist. Everyone familiar with the disease of racism and discrimination knows that even given strong social medicine, it is difficult to eradicate it from the body.

The Laws of Manu spell out the imperative to treat the untouchables poorly. For example, the Laws of Manu state, "But the dwellings of the Fierce Untouchables and Dog-cookers should be outside the village; they must use discarded bowls, and dogs and donkeys should be their wealth. Their clothing should be the clothes of the dead, and their food should be in broken dishes; their ornaments should be made of black iron and they should wander constantly."[16]

Ironically, the Laws of Manu also give a form of the Golden Rule, for the benevolent treatment of all others: "Whoever sees the self through the self in all living beings achieves equanimity towards all of them and reaches the supreme condition, ultimate reality."[17] By seeing the self in others, it might seem logical to lead to the Golden Rule of reciprocal good treatment: do unto others as you would have them do unto you. Gandhi, known as the Mahatma, or "great soul," for his selfless devotion to others, saw this rule concretely expressed in the Bhagavad Gita: "They live in wisdom who see themselves in all and all in them, who have renounced every selfish desire and sense craving tormenting the heart. Neither agitated by grief nor hankering after pleasure, they live free from lust and fear and anger. Established in meditation, they are truly wise. Fettered no more by selfish attachments, they are

16. Doniger and Smith, *Laws of Manu*, 242.
17. Doniger and Smith, 290.

neither elated by good fortune nor depressed by bad. Such are the seers."[18] Gandhi believed that by relinquishing selfish attachments, you could reach a common love for all human beings, and this included the untouchables. His reforms challenged Hindu conventions in many ways.

The Gods

Hindu deities developed and grew in number. The gods of the ancient Vedas are not always the same as those that are so widely revered today. Agni was a god of fire and cremation who kindled the stars in the skies. He may date back to the ancient Aryans. Indra was the warlike god who was also important to the warrior Aryans. Both Indra and Yama, the god who presided over the dead, remain part of the Hindu pantheon but are less widely revered than Shiva or Vishnu.

There is a trinity of deities, the creator Brahma, the preserver Vishnu, and the destroyer Shiva. Brahma, sometimes known as Prajapati, the four-headed creator, is not the only deity associated with creation. In one account, it is said that Vishnu gave birth to him and that he came out looking in all directions with a head facing each way.[19] Another tale relates that Brahma had sprouted a head in the direction of the attractive goddess Sarasvati to follow her wherever she went. When, finally, she leaped above him and a head sprouted in that direction, Shiva cut that head off to end his obsession.[20] Brahma, as the creator, is not as widely revered as his counterparts Shiva and Vishnu.

Vishnu is a four-armed, generally blue-skinned preserver god. Vishnu is believed to have become incarnated some nine times (with a tenth yet to come) in order to protect and preserve the world. In his first incarnation as Matsya the fish, he rescued the great ancestral Manu from an impending flood. Manu was advised to build a large boat, and Matsya helped tow it to a dry mountaintop. The similarity between the biblical and Babylonian flood stories is interesting. Where did these flood stories come from? Were they related? In his fifth incarnation as the dwarf Vamana, Vishnu faced the great demon Bali. Confronting Bali, he asked

18. Eknath Easwaran, trans., *The Bhagavad Gita* (Berkeley, CA: Nilgiri Press, 2007), chap. 2:55–57, or p. 95–96.
19. Muesse, *Hindu Traditions*, 45–46.
20. Hillary P. Rodrigues, *Introducing Hinduism* (New York: Routledge, 2006), 191.

to own all of the earth that he could cover in just three steps. Not impressed with Vamana's small size, Bali allowed it. So Vamana grew to his true enormous size as Vishnu and in three steps strode across the whole of existence, crushing Bali into the underworld with the final step.[21]

Vishnu's most famous incarnations were as Rama and Krishna. His incarnation as Rama is told in the beloved Hindu classic the *Ramayana*. In it, Vishnu becomes incarnate as the handsome warrior-king Rama. He falls in love with the wonderful Sita, and their marriage is destined to make them a happy king and queen. But through rivalry and jealousy, they are banished to the forest together with Rama's faithful friend Lakshmana. In the forest, Sita is abducted by the demon-king Ravana, who wishes to make her his bride. Remaining faithful to Rama, she refuses. Rama and Lakshmana try to rescue Sita with the aid of a remarkable monkey-warrior named Hanuman. Ultimately, they find Ravana's secret fortress, lay siege to it, and destroy it. In combat, Rama defeats Ravana and wins back Sita. That would seem to make for a happy ending, but Sita's chastity is called into question by those in the kingdom. Undergoing an ordeal by fire, she passes the test, and she is shown to be pure. The *Ramayana* is one of the favorite Hindu epics.[22]

The other celebrated incarnation of Vishnu is as Krishna. This tale is a part of the epic war of the *Mahabharata*. In this book, the Pandava brothers have been cheated out of the kingdom of Kurukshetra by their rivals the Kauravas. The "cheating" took place in a game of dice that seemed rigged, because the Kauravas always won, leading to the Pandavas surrendering their kingdom and going into exile. The Kauravas tried to kill their rivals, and ultimately, the two forces were aligned for battle. The great Pandava brother Arjuna was needed to fight the Kauravas' champion warrior, Karna. Arjuna, as one of the best Pandava warriors, must help the eldest brother regain his just claim on the kingdom. Arjuna, however, had a moment of despair as he faced former friends on the battlefield. The horror and senselessness of war gripped him, and Arjuna protested his duty to fight. Here is where Krishna, his charioteer, who is really the incarnation of Vishnu, will become instrumental to the Pandava victory.[23]

21. Rodrigues, 200–202.
22. For a good shortened version, see R. K. Narayan, *The Ramayana—a Shortened Modern Prose Version of the Indian Epic* (New York: Penguin, 2006).
23. For a good English version, see William Buck, *The Mahabharata* (Berkeley: University of California Press, 1981).

The Bhagavad Gita can be seen as an elaboration upon or an insertion into the text of the *Mahabharata*. The Gita, as it is often abbreviated, is the tale of Arjuna's painful confrontation with his duty to fight and the response of his charioteer, Krishna, to call him to action. Arjuna doesn't know the divine identity of Krishna, but soon he will come to find out. Krishna tells him to do his caste duty, to fight on the battlefield, for this is his calling as a Kshatriya, a warrior who embraces the call of justice. Arjuna should not think of the grisly fate that awaits them as a final bitter end, for the soul wears many different human bodies in its transmigrations across time: "As one abandons worn-out clothes and acquires new one, so when the body is worn out a new one is acquired by the Self, who lives within."[24] Hence the Gita might be interpreted as a call to action and fighting, for it takes place on a battlefield, and the consequence of it is that Arjuna does go and fight. The Pandavas, the "good guys," defeat their rivals, the Kauravas. It is a classic tale of war, tragedy, and justice.

The Gita, however, has more the tone of a sermon on morality and duty than a call to arms and killing. Although set on a battlefield, it is a moral calling to selfless action, to a renunciation of selfish desires, pointing toward altruistic behavior. Gandhi believed that the Gita, properly understood, should lead not to violence but to selfless action. For Gandhi, the Gita's battlefield was not a physical one but an allegorical battle of the forces of good and evil that are also raging within us. Krishna tells this to Arjuna: "Fulfill all your duties; action is better than inaction. Even to maintain your body, Arjuna, you are obliged to act. Selfish action imprisons the world. Act selflessly, without any thought of personal profit. At the beginning, mankind and the obligation of selfless service were created together. Through selfless service, you will always be fruitful and find the fulfillment of your desires."[25]

Gandhi also thought the heart of the Gita was that "they live in wisdom who see themselves in all and all in them, who have renounced every selfish desire and sense craving tormenting the heart." One could not be trapped in selfishness by such laws, for "they are forever free who renounce all selfish desires and break away from the ego-cage of 'I,' 'me,' and 'mine' to be united with the Lord. This is the supreme state. Attain this, and pass from death to immortality."[26]

24. Easwaran, *Bhagavad Gita*, 88–92.
25. Easwaran, 105.
26. Easwaran, 95, 97.

Arjuna struggled to accept his calling, and the discourse unfolds until Krishna unveils his godly self, in its myriad forms and bewildering complexity. He tells him at one point, "Behold, Arjuna, a million divine forms, with an infinite variety of color and shape. Behold the gods of the natural world, and many more wonders never revealed before."[27] There are many more points of spiritual wisdom discussed in the Gita, so much so that one does indeed feel that they have left an ordinary battlefield entirely and are on an entirely new and exalted spiritual plane. It is the wisdom of God, according to the Gita.

Shiva is known as the god of destruction. But Shiva's destruction is not random or evil. For Hindus, death brings new beginnings and new life. In order to escape the cycle of reincarnation, one must overcome enough ignorance, or *avidya*, and gain enough wisdom, or *jnana*. Reaching this supreme truth inside, one attains *moksha*. As the Gita had instructed, "The Lord does not partake in the good and evil deeds of any person; judgment is clouded when wisdom is obscured by ignorance."[28] Shiva may help burn away the lustful attachment, help sever the fetters of illusion. This theme of coming to terms with oneself pervades Hinduism and can be found in numerous texts, such as the Isha Upanishad: "He who sees all beings in the Self, and the Self in all beings, hates none. To the illumined soul, the Self is all. For him who sees everywhere oneness, how can there be delusion or grief?"[29] The Gita reiterates, "Those who possess this wisdom have equal regard for all. They see the same Self in a spiritual aspirant and an outcaste, in an elephant, a cow, and a dog."[30] Shiva is also known as an ascetic, one who tames the senses. His union with his wife Parvati can be most sensual, however. Shiva's destructive powers offer a new beginning, culminating in the final union with God. The dancing Shiva is rich in spiritual imagery, capturing both the pull of samsara, or the realm of sensual attachment, as well as the soul's final liberation in *moksha*.[31]

Shiva's spouse is Parvati, and there is an alluring sexual as well as ascetic tension between them. Parvati's name means "she who dwells in the mountains."[32] She had to seduce Shiva because only Shiva's offspring could defeat a near-invincible

27. Easwaran, 194.
28. Easwaran, 129.
29. Prabhavananda and Manchester, *Upanishads*, 27.
30. Easwaran, *Bhagavad Gita*, 130.
31. Diana Eck, *Darsan: Seeing the Divine Image of India*, 3rd ed. (New York: Columbia University Press, 1998), 41.
32. Kinsley, *Hindu Goddesses*, 41.

demon named Taraka. Shiva was a champion ascetic, able to refrain from sexual appetites, so how was Parvati going to do this? Parvati begins to woo Shiva by showing him that she also is a champion ascetic. The austerities called *tapas* that she performs actually build up a latent energy, and she wins Shiva's attention. From their union, the god Karttikeya is born, who will be able to slay the demon Taraka.[33]

There is also a fascinating tale of the elephant-headed Ganesha, their son who is the god presiding over good fortune and removing obstacles. Ganesha is a widely popular deity across India. One of the stories tells how Parvati created Ganesha from her own power and set him to watch the door and let no one in while she bathed. Coming home, Ganesha did not allow Shiva to enter, and in a fit of anger, Shiva lopped off his head. Parvati, horrified at Ganesha's beheading, made Shiva restore his head with that of the first animal convenient. That animal happened to be an elephant. That is one story of how Ganesha acquired his elephant head.[34]

Ardhanarishvara is a deity that is half-male and half-female. This deity reflects the divine support for both genders. David Kinsley writes that "without its female half, or female nature, the godhead of Shiva is incomplete and is unable to proceed with creation."[35] This may be a refreshing, more gender-balanced view of God. It would indeed be nice if all religions of the world had such an egalitarian model for gender relations. Sadly, this does not seem to be the case, even in Hinduism. Many religions of the world have oftentimes subordinated women rather than given them a role of gender equality. Women's equality in religion was not always granted but something later earned by great efforts. Ardhanarishvara is a welcome and imaginative balance of genders, a departure from more male-privileged norms.

Sri-Lakshmi is a goddess of prosperity and Vishnu's wife. Royally seated atop a lotus blossom, Lakshmi is depicted with four arms and presides over wealth and good fortune. As Vishnu's wife, she is an exemplar of devotion and said to have become incarnate as Sita in the *Ramayana*.[36] Like Ardhanarishvara above, she can even be seen to be interdependent with Vishnu. Ten qualities are often associated with her: food, royal power, universal sovereignty, noble rank, power, holy luster, kingdom, fortune, bounteousness, and beauty.

33. Kinsley, 41–43.
34. Stephen Huyler, *Meeting God: Elements of Hindu Devotion* (New Haven, CT: Yale University Press, 199), 195–200. See also Kinsley, *Hindu Goddesses*, 44.
35. Kinsley, *Hindu Goddesses*, 50.
36. Rodrigues, *Introducing Hinduism*, 208–9.

Sometimes the goddess can be so exalted, she can be seen to be supreme. *Mahadevi* is this notion of the great goddess.[37] Durga is one such goddess. She is an invincible demon slayer depicted with ten arms and a different weapon in each arm. Riding atop a lion steed, she rushes to defeat the buffalo demon Mahisha. Mahisha was so powerful that the other male gods could not defeat him. Durga, whose name means "she who is formidable," had to be summoned by the gods to face the demon Mahisha, as she alone could vanquish him. Overwhelming and slaying Mahisha, Durga saved the world from his peril.

Kali is also a demon-slaying goddess prominent in the Kolkata-Bengal region of northeast India. Associated with tantric rituals and sexual courtship with Shiva, she is said to be a "mother goddess" despite her very fearsome appearance. Often wearing a garland of skulls and having fangs dripping blood, her skin is black and her hands grip weapons to defeat the demon Raktabija.[38] As a figure very much associated with death, she is the more menacing counterpart to Shiva. If Shiva's destruction is sometimes thought to be necessary and auspicious, Kali's devastation and wrath can be terrifying: "If mother goddesses give life, Kali feeds on life. What they give, she takes away."[39]

Sri Ramakrishna (1836–86), who was inspired by many religions, including Christianity and Islam, was also a devotee of Kali.[40] Ramakrishna's pupil, Swami Vivekananda (1863–1902), came to the United States and helped make Hinduism better known in the West. Coming to the Parliament of the World's Religions in 1893, he was a compelling voice for the Hindu tradition.[41]

Though there are countless other deities in Hinduism, the last we will discuss is Sarasvati. Sarasvati was a river goddess but has come to be associated with learning and wisdom. Quite the opposite of the menacing Kali, she is depicted in white brilliance. Light is the source of sight and also symbolic of wisdom. *Sattva* is associated with light in Hinduism and also called one of the three *gunas*, or "qualities." Sarasvati's brilliance is tied up with this quality of knowledge, and her symbol is the swan.[42] The Bhagavad Gita also makes clear the other two major *gunas*. Passionate

37. Rodrigues, 211–12; Kinsley, *Hindu Goddesses*, 20, 133.
38. Rodrigues, *Introducing Hinduism*, 209–12.
39. Kinsley, *Hindu Goddesses*, 126.
40. Rodrigues, *Introducing Hinduism*, 285.
41. Clothey, *Religion in India*, 179–80. See also Muesse, *Hindu Traditions*, 3–4.
42. Kinsley, *Hindu Goddesses*, 62–63.

feelings and emotions come from the *guna* called *rajas*, and ignorant, dull minds come from *tamas*. Sloth, darkness, ignorance, and insensitivity come from *tamas*.[43] The Gita offers a line of brief summary: "From sattva comes understanding; from rajas, greed. But the outcome of tamas is confusion, infatuation, and ignorance."[44] Here we have a spiritual psychology of good and evil.

Wisdom, Truth, and Goodness

The wisdom of India is not well known in the West. While we fondly cite Plato or Aristotle, we do not always realize their equals or counterparts in India. For example, Socrates said, "For a human being a life without examination is actually not worth living."[45] The Hindu Upanishads say, "Truth alone succeeds, not untruth." Recall also they also tell us, "Speak the truth. Do your duty. Do not neglect the study of the scriptures. Do not cut the thread of progeny. Swerve not from truth. Deviate not from the apt or good."[46] Socrates, as reflected in the writings of Plato, thought that since the unexamined life was not worth living, the philosopher's duty was to prepare the soul to live a good life and make one ready for death.[47] Hindus already understood that the divine law of Brahman, of God, was linked up with following the law: "(Brahman) created the most excellent Law. There is nothing higher than the Law. The Law is the truth. Therefore, it is said that if a man speaks the truth, he declares the Law and if he declares the Law he speaks the Truth. The Law and the truth are one."[48] Socrates believed in a soul that does not die with the body but transmigrates or reincarnates in another, but Hindus of India already believed this. Indeed, truth is the ultimate goal, as the *Rig Veda* expressed: "The vessels of Truth carry men of good deeds across the ocean of ignorance."[49] The quality of wisdom, the *sattva* guna associated with Sarasvati, was also supreme in Plato's writings: "The only true coin, I hazard, for which all these things should be exchanged is

43. Easwaran, *Bhagavad Gita*.
44. Easwaran, 226.
45. Plato, *The Last Days of Socrates*, ed. Christopher Rowe (New York: Penguin, 2010), 57.
46. Prabhavananda and Manchester, *Upanishads*, 47, 54.
47. Plato, *Last Days of Socrates*, 124–25.
48. Prabhavananda and Manchester, *Upanishads*, 81.
49. Chimnoy, *Commentaries*, 25.

wisdom. It's when everything is bought and sold for this, or rather in the company of this, that there'll truly be courage, moderation, justice, all true virtue."[50]

In the world's religious and philosophical wisdom, one can find essential moral messages of agreement: do the right thing, seek truth, and obey the Golden Rule. The heart of the Universalist view of religion is that humans can find and do what is right. Furthermore, this expression of what is right may already have been stated clearly in their own culture. To find what is right and good in religions takes a keen eye, a discerning mind, and a compassionate heart. Neither agreement nor right understanding will ever automatically spring forth from every tradition; it has to be encountered, discerned, and discovered. I believe it is a great hope to the puzzle of life, which challenges all perspectives to look beyond their immediate horizons and also to see what they have in common.

But Is It True?

The Hindu gods and goddesses are wonderfully complex, but are they *real*? Charles Darwin expressed incredulity with ancient biblical Scriptures, comparing them to the fantastic stories of Hinduism. Darwin relates his skepticism:

> But I had gradually come by this time, to see that the Old Testament from its manifestly false history of the world, with the Tower of Babel, the rainbow as a sign, etc. etc., and from its attributing to God the feelings of a vengeful tyrant, was no more to be trusted than the sacred books of the Hindoos, or the beliefs of any barbarian. The question then continually rose before my mind and would not be banished,—is it credible that if God were not to make a revelation to the Hindoos, would he permit it to be connected with the belief in Vishnu, Shiva, &c., as Christianity is connected with the Old Testament. This appeared to me to be utterly incredible.[51]

Can the modern mind, living by the creeds of science, accept some of the more fantastic stories of religion? Could Noah have built an ark? Could Moses have parted

50. Plato, *Last Days of Socrates*, 102.
51. Charles Darwin, *The Autobiography of Charles Darwin*, ed. Nora Barlow (New York: W. W. Norton, 1958), 71.

the Red Sea? Did Jesus really rise from the dead? Did Muhammad really experience a revelation from God in the Cave of Hira? Can the wild tales of Hinduism with their multiarmed gods and goddesses be accepted? At the believing mind's nadir, religion seems like no more than surreal myths from the past. At its zenith, religion tells us that we matter and that the universe is not heartless. Whether Freud, Socrates, Jesus, or Krishna is correct, I cannot prove with the precision of math, but I cast my lot with hope and not despair.

Hindus also have long been aware of the fantastic nature of the divine. Ram Mohan Roy (1772–1833) was something of a Hindu Universalist. Roy believed that the "double love" commandment was one of the most exalted in world religions. I have tried to argue that this also serves as an essential "moral magnetic north," a common moral direction for world religions. What I haven't said about Roy is that he rejected the idols of Hinduism. Roy was attuned to an abstract, invisible concept of God, like that of Deism or Islam. God was beyond imagination, and the wild Hindu deities were just convenient images for the masses. Roy wrote, "It will also appear evident that in the Vedas, although they tolerate idolatry as the last provision for those who are totally incapable of raising their minds to the contemplation of the invisible God of nature, yet repeatedly urge the relinquishment of the rites of idol worship, and the adoption of a purer system of religion on the express grounds that the observance of idolatrous rites can never be productive of eternal beatitude."[52]

Roy did not have much patience with many conventional aspects of the Hindu religion. Critics of Roy's Deism might say that he was a reductionist, boiling away religion to just moral and rational precepts, with few supernatural elements remaining. Roy admitted that the purpose of religion is to ensure a better moral and civil society: "Religion cannot be equated to blind adherence to tradition or to unquestioning subservience to authority. In it there is no place for prophets and miracles. But is there anything on which religion may rest? Yes, the simple faith of man on which is based all moral precepts calculated to maintain an orderly government of society."[53]

52. Bruce Carlisle Robertson, *Raja Rammohun Ray: The Father of Modern India* (Oxford: Oxford University Press, 1995), 141–42.
53. Minni Thakur, *Raja Rammohun Roy: His Social, Political and Economic Ideas* (New Delhi: Deep & Deep, 1987), 58.

Arguably, Roy did believe in more than this. There *was* an actual God, some creator above and beyond. Roy founded an interfaith church named the Brahmo Samaj, a radical idea for his day. Roy preferred the Hindu faith that he grew up with but invited the perspectives of other religions as well. The founding of the Brahmo Samaj was a reflection of Roy's own eclectic norms: "By establishing it, he had given a concrete expression to his ideal of a non-sectarian universal religious body on a specifically Hindu basis. The doctrine of self-knowledge inculcated by the *Upanishads*, the social message of Buddhism, the emphatic monotheism of Islam, the simple piety of the saint of the medieval Indian *bhakti*-movement, the ethical teachings of Jesus Christ, each had at different times helped to shape this universal outlook."[54]

Roy was a puzzle builder of a more universal type. He saw religion as an expression of something sacred, though imperfect and muddied by the limitation of culture and human minds. Like a diamond in the rough, religion came with small flaws that needed to be chiseled out and worked upon in order to discern its deeper, lasting nature. Gandhi would later have much the same view that Roy had. Hindu tradition can be open to new interpretations and new ideas, to absorbing them into its very complex folds.

If religion could be reduced to *just* moral precepts, such as the Golden Rule, then it would be simple humanism. It would be indistinguishable from secular philosophy. Offering no *felt belief*, no hope that the beliefs it professed were in any way true, it loses its religious heart. To be vital, religion must have a *felt belief*, a plausible conviction that what it says may actually be true. It may not be literally true, or true in every fact or detail, but it must in some way capture an indispensable truth.

Roy's criticism of Hindu conventions included the practice of suttee, or "widow burning." The rite of suttee might be the tragedy of Hinduism that witch burning has been elsewhere: a superstition with no moral or rational basis. Roy wished to eradicate it. While suttee was not universally practiced, that it was practiced at all was bad enough. Roy could not tolerate that some Hindu women, upon the death of their husbands, would be condemned to a cruel and arbitrary death. Roy wrote about suttee,

54. Sophia Dobson Collet, *The Life and Letters of Rammohun Roy*, ed. Dilip Kumar Biswas and Prabhat Chandra Ganguli (Calcutta: Brahmo Mission, 1962), 248.

> Eye-witnesses that cases have frequently occurred when women have been induced by the persuasions of their next heirs, interested in their destruction, to burn themselves on the funeral pile of their husbands; that others who have been induced by fear to retract a resolution rashly expressed in their first moments of grief, of burning with their deceased husbands, have been forced upon the pile and there bound down with ropes, and pressed with green bamboos until consumed with flames; that some, after flying from the flame, have been carried back by their relations and burnt to death. All these instances, your petitioners humbly submit are murders according to every Sastra, as well as to the common sense of all nations.[55]

Roy may have witnessed his brother's widow die by suttee sometime between 1811 or 1812.[56] For sixteen years Roy fought suttee, until the governor-general Lord William Bentinck banned it in 1829. Roy argued that suttee was not only murder but also not a legitimate Hindu practice. With time and perseverance, suttee was extinguished, but not without considerable opposition. When Roy submitted a petition with signatures to abolish suttee, a counterpetition was submitted by some to actually keep the institution legal.[57]

The practice of things like suttee can make religion difficult to defend. Self-professed Christians have burned witches, Muslims have practiced honor killings, and all manner of absurd and unjust things have been done in the name of religion. But although things are often done in the *name of religion*, they are not done in the best spirit or even the correct interpretation of what is good. Reason and compassion are necessary for moral integrity. A good heart and critical mind are imperative to keep the compass of religion guided to its magnetic north.

The most famous Hindu of modern times, Gandhi—known as the Mahatma, or "great soul"—understood this truth. When confronted by the injustice of untouchability, Gandhi rejected it, saying, "Untouchability is not a sanction of religion . . . scriptures cannot transcend Reason and Truth. They are intended to purify Reason and illuminate Truth. . . . It is the spirit that giveth the light. And the spirit of the

55. Collet, 87.
56. Collet, 33.
57. Roy, *English Works*, 475.

Vedas is purity, truth, innocence, chastity, simplicity, forgiveness, godliness, and all that makes a man or woman noble and brave."[58]

Gandhi was born on October 2, 1869, in Porbandar, India, in the northwestern province of Gujarat. He was married at age thirteen, and though his marriage seemed a fairly good one, he later rejected this "childhood marriage" as a practice that should not be continued. After his father died in 1885, he set sail for England in 1888 to get his education in law. Leaving India behind was controversial, and members of his own caste threatened to ostracize him, but he went anyway. To appease his concerned mother, who was worried he might lose his Indian roots, he took three vows from a Jain monk (even though his family was Hindu). He vowed not to drink wine, eat meat, or get involved with any women. In this way, he would remain faithful to both his wife and the Hindu culture of his birth.

Gandhi was not particularly religious in his youth. Reading the Laws of Manu inclined him toward atheism. And while he was not an atheist, neither was he passionate about religion when he set sail for England. When he arrived in England, he was asked about his own Hindu traditions. Not knowing much about them, he began to read the Bhagavad Gita. It began a spiritual love affair that would last a lifetime. He wrote of the Gita, "The book (the Gita) struck me as one of priceless worth. The impression has ever since been growing on me with the result that I regard it today as the book *par excellence* for the knowledge of Truth."[59] He read the Gita as a spiritual battlefield that commanded nonviolence.

Nonviolent confrontation became the only way in which he felt political conflicts could be resolved. He wrote at the end of his autobiography, "My uniform experience has convinced me that there is no other God than Truth. And if every page of these chapters does not proclaim to the reader that the only means for the realization of Truth is Ahimsa [non-violence], I shall deem all my labor in writing these pages to have been in vain."[60] He showed that nonviolence can make a difference. His nonviolence was not, however, born in India; it first came to life in South Africa.

When Gandhi returned from England, he spent a few years unsuccessfully as a lawyer. Speaking in court and conducting cases were not his strengths, but

58. Fischer, *Essential Gandhi*, 135.
59. Mohandas K. Gandhi, *Gandhi, an Autobiography: The Story of My Experiments with Truth*, trans. Mahadev Desai from Gujarati (Boston: Beacon, 1993), 67.
60. Gandhi, 503–4.

negotiation and drafting legal work were. Soon a Muslim law firm in South Africa made him a job offer to help with a case. He intended to go for a year and earn £105.[61] Not meaning to become a Mahatma, he encountered racism there for the first time. He was thrown forcibly from a train for being an Indian sitting in a first-class train car for whites. He was angry and humiliated as he sat on the train platform in Pretoria, South Africa. He considered what to do and determined that he had to resist. It was not, however, going to be a violent rebellion; that was wholly against his inner conviction. He proposed to strike a nonviolent blow to the conscience of his oppressor and get him to change his ways. This nonviolent method of civil disobedience he called satyagraha, derived from the Sanskrit *satya*, meaning "truth," and *agraha*, meaning "the pursuit of."[62] Standing firm in the pursuit of truth, satyagraha delivered a nonviolent blow to the conscience of the oppressor by forcing him to witness the error of his ways. His intended stay of only a few years turned into a twenty-one-year campaign of civil disobedience.

In 1915, at the age of forty-five, Gandhi returned to India. World War I had broken out, and he was recruited to support the effort of the British in the War. He abhorred all violence but could be pragmatic about the issue: "I do believe that where there is a choice only between cowardice and violence, I would advise violence."[63] He believed there was always a better option, however: "But I believe non-violence is infinitely superior to violence, forgiveness is more manly than punishment."[64] He helped India through nonviolent campaigns to win her independence from British colonialism.

For thirty-two years Gandhi labored and struggled. He was arrested many times, as were thousands of others. He insisted that British rule of India must come to an end. It did come to an end, but not exactly in the way he wanted or hoped. He intended an India that was united and free, where Hindus and Muslims could live alongside one another. His former ally, Muhammad Ali Jinnah, ultimately could not accept his view of a united India. Jinnah insisted India be divided in two to protect its Muslim minority. When India became free from Great Britain, it was partitioned into India and Pakistan.

61. Gandhi, 102.
62. Fischer, *Essential Gandhi*, 86–87.
63. Fischer, 153.
64. Fischer, 157.

Gandhi had hoped to unite Hindus and Muslims as brothers. Near the time of partition, however, there were estimates that over half a million people were killed in violence and rioting.[65] He did his heroic best to stop the violence. He fasted against it, warning that he would not eat until the violence subsided, even if that meant his death. Stubbornly, the masses began to come around, and violence slowly abated. He wanted nothing more than for Hindu to stop killing Muslim and for Muslim to stop killing Hindu. As he had observed before, "Should we not remember that many Hindus and Muslims own the same ancestors and the same blood runs through their veins? Do people become enemies because they change their religion? Is the God of the Muslim different from the God of the Hindu? Religions are different roads converging to the same point. What does it matter that we take different roads so long as we reach the same goal? Wherein is the cause for quarreling?"[66]

Gandhi read from the Bhagavad Gita, the Qur'an, and the Christian Bible at his prayer meetings. He passionately believed in the unity of persons and the equality of their religions. This egalitarian outlook seems noble and fair, possessed of a vision that there is something that unites us all. This Universalism is a vision I have shared and tried to make work here. It is not, however, easy. He championed a nonviolent cause, believing Hindu could be united with Muslim. He was assassinated on January 30, 1948, by a Hindu, Nathuram Vinayak Godse, who rejected Gandhi's views. Gandhi's martyrdom, though, elevated his cause. Years later, Martin Luther King Jr. would be inspired by Gandhi and use nonviolence to challenge racism in America. Sadly, both men who dedicated their lives to nonviolence met a violent end.

Gandhi was not perfect, nor did he think his religion was perfect. He admitted the flaws of religion: "[All] religions are more or less true. All proceed from the same God but are all imperfect because they come down to us through imperfect human instrumentality. . . . [No] propaganda can be allowed which reviles other religions. . . . The best way of dealing with such propaganda is to publicly condemn it."[67] A Universalist can best argue for the compatibility of religions because they do not think they are absolutely true in every detail. The edges of puzzle pieces may better fit when not so rigidly conceived by the mind; unwanted false pieces might even be discarded. Each religion needs only to be true enough to be a guide, for its

65. Khan, *Great Partition*, 6.
66. Fischer, *Essential Gandhi*, 12.
67. Fischer, 213.

spiritual compass to point to a moral magnetic north. If indeed, as Roy suggested, the double love command was a good place to start, Gandhi would have agreed. Each religion expresses a form of the Golden Rule in its own way.

What Fits?

Hinduism offers to the world many moral lessons. Gandhi tried to teach us nonviolence and the comparative equality of religions, something I've dubbed "Universalism" in this book. General George C. Marshall said that "Mahatma Gandhi was the spokesman for the conscience of all mankind."[68] Jawaharlal Nehru, Gandhi's close friend and the first prime minister of a free India, eulogized Gandhi: "'The light has gone out of our lives and there is darkness everywhere and I do not quite know what to tell you and how to say it. Our beloved leader, Bapu, as we call him, the father of our nation, is no more . . .' but then Nehru corrected himself, for this was no ordinary light, but a light that 'will illumine this country for many more years, and a thousand years later that light will still be seen in this country.'"[69]

Gandhi found his own light in the Bhagavad Gita. The Gita commanded selflessness and dedication, a way to free oneself from the cycle of reincarnation. Hinduism tells us that the divine spark is within. The Hindu greeting namaste, or "the divine in me salutes the divine in you," acknowledges this key belief. Hinduism does not share Christianity's notion of original sin, although it recognizes in humanity something trenchant and resistant to moral change. Hindu philosophy might call it *avidya* (ignorance) or perhaps the guna of *tamas*, which is laziness, resisting illumination and wisdom. Yet for Hindus it is possible to overcome selfish attachments, with many years of practice and many cycles of reincarnation. The soul, or atman, finally escapes the bonds of this-worldly attachment. We can reach *moksha*, that wonderful point where the drop of water of the soul reunites with the great oceanic essence of God called Brahman. These ideas, though unique to Hinduism, may well resonate with other faiths.

68. Fisher, *Mahatma Gandhi*, 17–18.
69. Fischer, *Essential Gandhi*, 368–69.

What Doesn't Fit?

Reincarnation flies in the face of many other faiths that believe in just one life for the soul. Souls either reincarnate or do not. One cannot logically posit both. The Abrahamic faiths as well as Zoroastrianism look to a resurrection of the dead, a world in which we take on new bodies after a final apocalyptic battle with evil. In Hinduism, however, there is no idea of resurrection at the end of time. The concept of time also is different. For the Abrahamic faith, time is a linear concept, from a point of creation, to the point here and now, to a final judgment day. Hinduism thinks of time in great cycles, or yugas, that repeat themselves. The best, most moral time is Satya Yuga, the age of truth in which we are nearest to God. It is also said to be the longest age. Next come the ages of Treta Yuga and Dvapara Yuga, transitional times that are good but not perfect. These latter two ages are less connected with God's wisdom, until you get to the present age called Kali Yuga, which is said to be the most depraved. As time is cyclic, however, the dark clouds of Kali Yuga will pass, and a better time of Satya Yuga will come again. These are wonderful ideas, but are they true? What is the truth of religion? If religion offers the world a moral compass and a hope for the future, it may have done the job it needs to accomplish. But this job, of finding hope and direction for our civilization and giving voice to it, is never finished.

The Universalist mindset, believing that no religion is perfect but that a great many inspire us, can better make the puzzle pieces of life fit together. If we discard pieces that are false or unwanted and reimagine awkward pieces that do not seem to fit, the very shape of the pieces might shift until their edges better conjoin. It may seem a dangerous business, to reimagine and reinvent religion, but in some ways, we are doing it all the time. We attempt to build an idea, an image, a way of making sense, and though there is always a hole, always some unexplained part, each day our images and ideas are revised, our efforts are renewed, and tomorrow, things may make better sense than they did yesterday.

8 Buddhism

Summary of Buddhism

Buddhism begins with four straightforward ideas. These ideas are the four noble truths of life:

1. All life is suffering.
2. The cause of suffering is *tanha* (clinging, craving attachment).
3. Suffering will cease when tanha has ceased.
4. The way to end suffering is the eightfold path.

The four noble truths of Buddhism state that life is incomplete and must involve suffering. The cause of that suffering is rooted in our inability to accept the transitory and imperfect condition of life. When we adjust to that imperfection through the eightfold path, we move closer to the goal of enlightenment, often called nirvana by Buddhists.[1]

These truths have their origin in the teachings of the Buddha, who lived in the North India–Nepal region sometime in the fifth or sixth century BCE. His birth name was Siddhartha Gautama. Siddhartha was a prince who stood to inherit his father's kingdom.[2] Before he was born, a prophecy said that Siddhartha would become either (1) a *cakravartin*, a universal king, or (2) the founder of a new religion, or dharma, having become moved by the world's suffering. According to the prophecy, "He will abandon the kingdom in his indifference to worldly pleasures; he will obtain the Truth (tattva) through diligent effort; he will shine forth, like the sun of knowledge, to expel the darkness of delusion in the world."[3]

1. Karen Armstrong, *Buddha* (New York: Penguin, 2004), 82.
2. Charles S. Prebish and Damien Keown, *Introducing Buddhism*, 2nd ed. (New York: Routledge, 2010), 26–30.
3. Theodore de Bary, *The Buddhist Tradition in India, China, and Japan* (New York: Random House, 1972), 60.

When Siddhartha was born, his mother was reported to have had a vision of a white elephant entering her side. The infant Siddhartha, according to legend, stood up and declared that this was his last rebirth.[4] He took seven steps and said, "I am the highest in the world; I am the best in the world; I am the foremost in the world. This is my last birth; now there is no renewed existence for me."[5] This story presents the young Buddha's exalted status, presciently knowing his place and destiny. Siddhartha's father, Suddhodana, wanted to make sure that his son succeeded him as king. Eagerly, he pampered the young Siddhartha so an exposure to pain and suffering would not turn him toward religion. Siddhartha married a woman named Yasodhara and had a son called Rahula. Siddhartha might well have chosen the palace life and followed in the footsteps of his father, but it was not to be. Soon the callings and questions of his inner conscience would lead him away.

Siddhartha experienced four sights, on four successive days, as his chariot rider Channa took him out to see life beyond the palace. The story goes that on the first day of his chariot ride, Siddhartha saw a wrinkled, vulnerable old man. The man had lost the vibrancy of youth, which caused Siddhartha to reflect on the fleeting nature of youth and its pleasures. On the second day of the chariot ride, Siddhartha witnessed a man afflicted by disease. Siddhartha had taken his health for granted but realized in that moment that anyone might lose it. On the third day of the chariot ride, Siddhartha witnessed a funeral procession, and this drove his questions deeper. All mortals die. On the final day of the chariot ride, Siddhartha witnessed a Hindu ascetic, a man searching for release from the infirmities and insecurities of life. Perhaps this was inspiration. Troubled and deeply moved by what he had witnessed, he secluded himself in the palace.[6] Siddhartha now understood the truth. Palace life seemed meaningless now, like a role that someone else was meant to play.

His father, King Suddhodana, saw this and tried to cheer him up. Calling in his favorite dancing girls, the king threw a party for Siddhartha. The attractive dancing girls came in and began to perform, but Siddhartha's heart had already been transformed. Instead of seeing the girls as they were in their youthful, alluring form, he saw them as they inevitably would be in their old age, as old and withered hags.

4. Prebish and Keown, *Introducing Buddhism*, 26–30.
5. Bodhi, *In the Buddha's Words*, 53.
6. Armstrong, *Buddha*, 33–34.

The four sights around the palace had deeply disturbed him, and palace luxuries no longer meant anything. Siddhartha realized he had to move beyond the confines of his comfortable home in order to deal with his inner torment. While the palace was sleeping, he stole upstairs to have one last look at his wife and child before he left. He did not wake them. Perhaps he could not face that painful separation, but in doing so, he was deserting them without a word.

One can sympathize with Siddhartha's despair over his royal destiny while at the same time criticize his decision to abandon his family. His struggle is evidence of his humanity, that he could be torn by passions and make a morally suspect decision. He was not yet the Buddha, not yet the morally exalted and awakened one that was supposed to be free of pain and suffering.

Siddhartha left, remembering his last sight from his travels around the palace: a Hindu ascetic, a renunciate who was seeking final spiritual liberation. He knew that there must be a wise guru, a teacher who could give him the spiritual answers he craved. Siddhartha tried several schools of Hindu philosophy and meditation and one by one found them unavailing. He joined the school of Alara Kalama, who taught that life was filled with illusion and ignorance and that his meditation would be able to take him beyond that. There was an absolute spirit, and there was a material world, but our ignorance, or *avidya*, prevented us from connecting with that spirit. Siddhartha learned and tried the meditative disciplines of Alara Kalama, but they did not work for him. He left that group and tried another but soon became disappointed again. He had mastered different yogas and practiced in different Hindu schools, but none of them satisfied his questions.[7]

Finally, Siddhartha fell in with a group of five ascetic *bhikkus*, or monks, who were practicing the austerities of self-mortification. They would abstain from worldly pleasures, check physical appetites, even try to control basic hunger. Siddhartha perfected such methods, becoming so good at refraining from eating that he began to resemble a walking skeleton. He found himself in no better state, however, and came later to believe that severe austerities were foolish. He later said, "Ignorant people practice austerities; those who seek pleasures gratify their senses. As neither method leads people to liberation, those two extremes are utterly wrong; they are not the right ways."[8] Siddhartha had become proficient in various

7. Armstrong, 61–62.
8. de Bary, *Buddhist Tradition*, 71.

meditative yogas and had denied his appetites to the point of near starvation but was no closer to enlightenment.

But Siddhartha did not give up. He remembered the art of meditation that he had long practiced. He found a rose apple tree, sat down beneath it, and entered a deep meditative trance. It is said that on three successive watches, he came nearer to enlightenment. On the first watch, he saw all his past lives and their struggles pass before him. As his trance deepened, he encountered on the second watch the coming and passing of lives all around him. Life came to be, grew, waned, and ceased, then new life took its place. Finally, on the third watch, he understood the four noble truths of Buddhism. He had become awakened; he had become a Buddha.[9] Mara, a demon-like personification of evil, then appeared to him, trying to thwart his enlightenment. Tempted with worldly powers and luxuries that he had once enjoyed, Siddhartha shook them off, and Mara's plans were foiled.

The Pali Canon records these four noble truths that he discovered. They have been repeated in countless formulations. They are, once again, the following:

1. All life is suffering.
2. The cause of suffering is *tanha* (clinging, craving attachment).
3. Suffering will cease when tanha has ceased.
4. The way to end suffering is the eightfold path.

These truths suggest that a lot of our suffering is self-produced. We crave and cling to things for comfort, pretending that they are going to be permanently satisfying, when the truth is that they are not. All things are ephemeral, have fleeting existence. They come and they go. To pretend that things have a permanence is to insist upon the reality of an illusion. Give up clinging to that illusion and believing that it is real, and you will advance yourself dramatically to the goal of enlightenment: nirvana (or *nibbana*). Nirvana is the extinguishing of all egoistic attachments, after which comes tranquility.

After becoming awakened, a curious thing happened to Siddhartha. He had just been released from the fetters of worldly woes, but he almost despaired at the thought of trying to teach the four noble truths to others. The lessons were

9. Prebish and Keown, *Introducing Buddhism*, 34–37.

too hard to follow. What purpose was there in learning such a dharma, or "duty," if it was too hard to pass on to others? Strangely enough, the Hindu god Brahma becomes alarmed that the Buddha would refrain from teaching this religion. So Brahma intervened, imploring the Buddha to teach what he has learned for the benefit of others. Buddha relented. Over the next forty years, he became known as one of India's greatest moral and spiritual gurus, or "teachers."[10]

What is a Hindu god doing in the Buddhist tradition? Buddhism does not generally acknowledge the idea of God. Buddhism's doctrines deny the existence of the external soul and challenge the importance and reality of the Hindu deities. Though Buddhist texts and traditions make occasional references to deities, it remains that Buddhism does not regard deities to be of the greatest importance. The most important thing is liberating one's mind from suffering. One might argue that Brahma appears as a gesture that Hindus should embrace Buddhism.

When Buddha left the place of his enlightenment, now called Bodh Gaya in Bihar, India, he set out to find people to teach. Buddha met the five ascetics with whom he had previously practiced austerities. They had ridiculed him for abandoning their practices, but now as he hailed them, they saw a numinous glow, as if his inner peace was a tangible aura that surrounded Buddha. At a place called the Deer Park, the Buddha instructed them on the four noble truths:

> Now this, monks, is the noble truth of suffering: birth is suffering, aging is suffering, illness is suffering, death is suffering; union with what is displeasing is suffering; separation from what is pleasing is suffering; not to get what one wants is suffering; in brief, the five aggregates subject to clinging are suffering. Now this, monks, is the noble truth of the origin of suffering: it is this craving that leads to renewed existence, accompanied by delight and lust, seeking delight here and there; that is, craving for sensual pleasures, craving for existence, craving for extermination. Now this monks is the noble truth of the cessation of suffering: it is the remainderless fading away and cessation of the same craving, the giving up and relinquishing of it, freedom from it, nonattachment. Now this, monks, is the noble truth of the way leading to the cessation of suffering: it is this Noble

10. Prebish and Keown, 57.

> Eightfold Path; that is right view, [right intention, right speech, right action, right livelihood, right effort, right mindfulness,] right concentration.[11]

The four noble truths say that we cause ourselves pain by pretending to find final bliss in an impermanent and ever-changing world. We should not grasp for these fleeting things.

What the Buddha had learned from the four sights—the old man, the sick man, the dead man, and the ascetic—is that we all must suffer loss at some time in our lives. The things we cherish we will also lose. Buddhism says we are in denial about these truths. What the Buddha saw is that we must accept the transitory nature of things. We must face the reality of suffering and its causes before we can be freed from it.

The idea of abandoning "desire" can be misleading. It may sound like Buddha wants you to become an emotionless automaton without any love. But this is not so. Buddhism deems some emotions to be good. Compassion, in particular, is emphasized in all sects and schools of Buddhism. So it is not that Buddha wants you to abandon all emotion, but rather he wants you to be freed from their domination. That is not easy.

What did the Buddha actually achieve? Perhaps what the Buddha experienced was simply a state of deep tranquility in which he experienced emotions but as on the surface of his being. In the depth of his mind, he felt tranquil, at ease. The emotions and trauma of this world were perceived but could not disturb his inner depths. Perhaps that is what is nirvana was like.

How does one attain such a remarkable disposition? The last noble truth says there is a way forward and that this way is the eightfold path. These are parts of a whole, not steps to be taken in a particular order. Taken comprehensively, the eightfold path is supposed to complete your journey toward nirvana. The eightfold path consists of right understanding, thought, mindfulness, action, livelihood, speech, effort, and concentration. What do they mean?

The *right understanding* means that you must have a full appreciation of the four noble truths, accepting Buddhism fully before you embark on its path. If you do not accept the formulation of the four noble truths as the essential problem

11. Bodhi, *In the Buddha's Words*, 75–76.

of life, if you do not take solace in the life and lessons of the Buddha, or the Buddhist community (called the *sangha*), then you are not ready for Buddhism. It is a question of the mind's alignment. If a plane is not lined up for takeoff, it does not do so. So too the mind must be aligned with the ideas of Buddhism in order to follow them.

If your mind is aligned, then the *right thoughts* are going to be important. Having thoughts that are ensnared by worldly delights is clear evidence that more work needs to be done. The mind should feel clear and unfettered, and thoughts should be free from clinging desires. To desire wealth, status, or fame is a sure sign of *tanha*, the clinging, craving attachment that needs to be surmounted. Proper thoughts should be accompanied by the correct *mindfulness*. Mindfulness is being present in the moment, not drawn back to what you did or did not do in the past, and not worrying about something in the future.

Right mindfulness and *right thoughts* may be difficult to achieve. We must often think about our past and our future. We need to reflect upon the past, and we need also to anticipate the future. Without this we cannot plan or adjust the course of our lives. Part of this planning and adjustment may require us to relive parts of our past mentally and reevaluate something we either did or did not do well. In this way we may change the rudder of our present and veer into a new future. What I think Buddhism has in mind is that these adjustments for thinking about our past and future take place so that we have the capacity to be present in the moment rather than captive to the past and the future.

The *right action* of Buddhism includes the five precepts of Buddhist morality. All of them, with the exception of the ban on intoxicants, are common to the major religions of the world. These are the five precepts of right moral action:

1. Tell the truth; do not lie.
2. Support life; do not kill.
3. Do not steal.
4. Do not commit unchaste acts, such as adultery.
5. Do not use intoxicants.

The fourth precept, chaste acts, would simply mean fidelity to one's partner for a lay Buddhist, but for a monk, it might involve complete celibacy.

Deeply connected to the practices of *right action* are those of *right livelihood*. For a Buddhist, you cannot make a living in a way that is going to cause injury to another person. This means not selling weapons, poisons, or anything harmful. There is also a strong vegetarian ethos in Buddhism and a commitment not to harm livestock. In this way human and animal life must be respected. This is the ideal, the norm, though I am sure you could probably find deviations from it. Overall of course, *right action* and *right livelihood* constitute a serious moral life for Buddhists. One cannot find enlightenment at the expense of others.

A monastic commitment is not necessary for all Buddhists. Just as one can be a Christian and not a priest, one can be a lay Buddhist. In the past I was critical of monasticism, which seemed to be an irresponsible retreat from the world. But as an adult, I realize that the constant bustle and hustle of the world do make it hard to pursue the interior life of reflection, and I appreciate the monastic life and effort more seriously now.

The *right speech* is also important. As with other religious traditions, Buddhists are not supposed to lie. This is quite logical. We do not want to defraud our friend or neighbor with false information. We need to work together on reliable information. We also cannot do this when we use speech injuriously or harmfully. Buddhism cautions that speech is a gateway to discerning what is inside the mind. A mouth that is constantly full of profanity probably reflects some inward agitation that needs to be settled. The complete absence of speech, the moment of silence where you can be truly reflective, is also essential to Buddhism. We live in a world of constant and furious distractions. Before the invention of lights, our ancestors were, in a way, lucky. They had to flow with the natural cycle of the world, and at night they slept peacefully; at best they might read or talk by candlelight. Then lights were invented, and we violated the natural cycle of the day; we stayed up to all hours. Now we have gadgets that connect our minds to all corners of a world full of distractions. The vipassana, or "insight meditation," retreat that is often practiced in Southeast Asia is one where you remove all diversions—phones, papers, books, the internet. There is no talking, no reading, no distraction of any kind. There might be things understood, sources of attachment, or tanha, that you did not anticipate. Prolonged moments of silence are in some measure the peaceful gateway through which Buddhists must pass. Tuning in to one's inner voice requires, for a short time a least, tuning out the external noise of the world.

The last two elements of the eightfold path are the *right effort* and the *right concentration*. Simply put, you must have the right level of energy put into Buddhism; you must make an honest effort and actually concentrate on it. If you are not at all entering any sort of meditative state, not focusing your will and your mind to do so, you will not attain Buddhism's ends. One might be lazy, half-hearted, or easily dissuaded and not make the effort. If this is the case, the concentrated discipline of meditation will never happen; you will not accomplish your end. Concentration might be called the actual discipline of meditation, of directing your will toward nirvana, and effort is the regularity and zeal with which you do this.

A key question is, When does one know that enlightenment has been reached? Nirvana is the "blowing out," the extinction of desires, but how do we know we have achieved it? This is difficult to say because it is an inward spiritual journey that no outward observation may easily measure. For Buddhists the inward voyage to nirvana has no concrete landmark. The spiritual journey to nirvana is one less certain to plot out. Take a few excerpts from Buddhism, and you might get a sense:

> As a mother cares for her son, her only son, all her days, so towards all things living a man's mind should be all-embracing, friendliness for the whole world.[12]

> Never in the world is hate appeased by hatred. It is appealed by love—this is an eternal law.[13]

> Hard it is to train the mind, which goes where it likes and does what it wants. But a trained mind brings health and happiness. The wise can direct their thoughts, subtle and elusive, wherever they choose: a trained mind brings health and happiness. Those who can direct thoughts, which are unsubstantial and wander so aimlessly, are freed from the bonds of Mara.[14]

If you focus your mind and carry a benevolent attitude toward all about you regularly, it might be a sign that you are close to nirvana. Can anyone really *get*

12. de Bary, *Buddhist Tradition*, 38.
13. de Bary, 38–39.
14. Eknath Easwaran, *The Dhammapada* (Berkeley, CA: Nilgiri Press, 2010), 115.

there, one might ask? This has no certain answer, and sometimes also I share in that skepticism. Though it may seem like an evasion, let me answer a question with a question: Can anyone do the things Buddha or Jesus or Muhammad or Moses are said to have done? Maybe not, yet we have sacred texts telling us that the way is open. And as long as a road is open, though its ultimate destination may be uncertain, there will be people who will walk it. If some of these curious investigators come back with good news, even if the destination was not reached, there will be others who follow them on this path.

Like many religions of India, Buddhism believes in reincarnation. After many cycles of life, you might become aware of the Buddhist wisdom and have only seven reincarnations left. If so, you have become a "stream enterer." Then you might soon become a "once returner" with one reincarnation left and finally a "nonreturner." When you have become a "nonreturner," it is claimed that you have attained the nirvana of this world, the conquest of all inner suffering. Then there is only the final release of death. But what is that? Even to me, after many years of study, this is not entirely clear. It is blissful release, but I would not exactly call it a *heaven*, though some might make that analogy. Imagine a candle burning brightly. The candle's flame is like the burning of samsara, the burning of our attachments to this world. When we attain nirvana, literally the "blowing out," there is a puff of curling smoke tranquilly and freely coiling above the candle; it is released. Nirvana is like this smoke: the extinguishing of attachments to this world. It is tranquility and bliss.

Even the Buddha's words do not seem to give us a full notion of it: "Where there is neither earth nor water, light nor air, neither infinity or space; it is not infinity of reason but nor is it an absolute void . . . it is neither this world or another world; it is both sun and moon."[15] The Buddhist philosopher Nagarjuna used the word *shunyata* to describe it, which seemed to indicate the complete negation of things that we know of this world. Nirvana could not be put into any words or concepts, but it was the stripping away and negating of them that could lead the way to it. Buddhism does not believe in a creator God, so the idea of such a God is of no real importance to liberation, or nirvana. Buddhism also rejects the idea of an eternal soul. The Hindu atman as an everlasting soul was denied and even thought to be a

15. Armstrong, *Buddha*, 181.

form of attachment. Furthermore, the idea of a permanent self, the Cartesian ego of "I think therefore I am," is also denied. What then is left?

This is why it is a bit perilous to say that nirvana is like heaven, because it denies the God concept, the soul concept, even the self-concept that most "heaven-based" religions affirm. Nirvana seems to be something else that is still blissful and good. A final release from the burdens of this world, whatever reincarnates in human beings is forever freed and at rest.

How can Buddhism get away with denying God, the soul, and the self? This is not easy. Gods find their way into the story of Buddhism, as with the tale about Brahma above, but they do not have a paramount importance. For some this may be a great liberation. For others it is a great weakness. If there is no God but something sacred is affirmed, then what is it? What created this world, and why? Buddhism says the answer is either unknowable or not important to disclose. While Buddhism operates on a deep time frame that may be compatible with ideas of evolution, its lack of a creator God will strike some as jarring and unsatisfactory.

What about the denial of a permanent soul? Christianity, Islam, Hinduism, and other religions affirm that there is an eternal soul. Mustn't Buddhism also accept the soul if it believes in reincarnation? What is there to reincarnate if there is no soul? The karma, or "spiritual energy," of Buddhism is conceived differently. Like a match passing flame to an unlit match, in an endless cycle, so life imparts karma to newborn life. Energy is transmitted, like the heat and light of a lit match, and some sort of karma, like a "spiritual momentum" of consciousness, is imparted to new life. It is less permanent and distinct than a soul. One might also imagine ripples or disturbances on an otherwise smooth pond. The ripples are the karma, the transmission of attachment and reincarnation, but when the attachment runs out, the ripples abate, and the pond is glassy smooth again. As long as there continues to be some wind or agitation, however, there will be ripples or waves. The Dalai Lama has referred to the reincarnating essence as *suchness*, and some Buddhists used the term *pudgala* to describe it, although even this notion of a "subtly changing self" (pudgala) has been controversial.

Why is there *really* no self? Buddhism claims we are ephemeral beings, coming and going and passing in time. We are made of five aggregates: (1) material form, (2) feelings and sensations, (3) perceptions, (4) mental formulations, and (5) consciousness. We experience stimuli and interact with our environment, receive a sensation from our nose or fingertip, which becomes a perception, a part of the assembled formulations of our mind, which then becomes part of our consciousness.[16] In the sum total of consciousness resides some spiritual *karma* or momentum of the "subtle self." It is not a permanent, Buddhists reckon, because it is under constant influence and support. Like a rock thrown in a pond, creating ripples in the water, a breeze causing the same ripples over a pond, or a lit match passing energy to an unlit match, there is a passing spark; there is *something* that accounts for reincarnation, the push and pull on our minds. Our morality flows with it. It is just something so subtle and transitory it defies permanence. We are, according to Buddhism, constantly conditioned and dependent beings. There is nothing in us that is not dependent upon some other phenomena, nothing that is isolated and eternally unchanged. Therefore, they argue, there is no *permanent and distinct* self.

To give a further illustration, after Alexander the Great failed to conquer India, there were Greek kingdoms left behind. One of those kingdoms was that of King Menander, and he was puzzled by this Buddhist doctrine of no self. King Menander asked the Buddhist monk Nagasena to explain the idea of "no self," for the king surely felt like he had a real self. The king's image was emblazoned on the coins of his kingdom. To explain the idea of five aggregates and no self, Nagasena pointed to a wooden chariot that belonged to the king. It was made also of five basic parts: chariot walls, a platform to stand on, a yoke to be pulled by, an axel to spin, and wheels on which to ride. The chariot was there, had existence, but it was not always a chariot, nor would it always be. Once it had been a tree, and then it was cut up for wood and made into a chariot. The tree had come from the soil, sunshine, water, and a seed that was planted in earth, but later, the wooden chariot would fall apart, rot, and rejoin the soil of the earth. Therefore, it too was impermanent, just a fleeting form in time.[17] So the human self has a dependent origin in other things, arising and falling, coming to be and passing. The idea of permanence as we see it is, from the Buddhist point of view, a misleading illusion of our minds. The attachment to that illusion too needs to be broken for us to attain nirvana.

Vietnamese Buddhist Thich Nhat Hanh explains a related idea he calls *interbeing*. All life interpenetrates and is dependent upon and mingled with other life. There is nothing left in isolation. Nothing is really separated. Hanh writes, "We inter-are with

16. Prebish and Keown, *Introducing Buddhism*, 55–57.
17. Prebish and Keown, 88–89.

our ancestors, our descendants, and the whole cosmos. We don't have a separate self, we are never really born and we never really die. We are interconnected with all life, and we are always in transformation."[18] He continues, "If you are a poet, you will see clearly that there is a cloud floating in this sheet of paper. Without a cloud, there will be no rain; without rain, the trees cannot grow; and without trees, we cannot make paper. The cloud is essential for the paper to exist. If the cloud is not there, the sheet of paper cannot be here either. So we can say that the cloud and the paper inter-are."[19]

In the monotheistic idea of heaven, separate and distinct souls go to meet their maker in judgment. In Buddhism, there is no absolute separation, and whatever release we go to might be like a blissful connection with totality.

Thich Nhat Hanh also believes that religions are very interdependent. By studying the core and heart of another religion, as strange as it may initially seem, we come close to the heart of our own religion. For example, Buddhism and Christianity seem very different. Christ is God incarnate, the Messiah come to free souls from sin and offer a chance at the kingdom of heaven. For Buddhism, there is no God to incarnate; it is bodhisattvas and not messiahs that are key, and there are no distinct souls to enter a heaven. Yet Hanh argues, "The more I got in touch with Christianity and Judaism the better I could understand Buddhism."[20] Although Buddha and Christ are different figures, Hanh sees an essential compatibility in their teachings:

> When Jesus said "I am the way" he meant that to have a true relationship with God, you must practice His way. In the Acts of the Apostles, the early Christians always spoke of their faith as "the Way." To me, "I am the way" is better than "I know the way." The way is not an asphalt road. But we must distinguish between the "I" spoken by Jesus and the "I" that people usually think of. The "I" in his statement is *life* itself. His life, which is the way. If you do not really look at His life, you cannot see the way. If you only satisfy yourself with practicing a name, even the *name* of Jesus, it is not practicing the life of Jesus. We must practice living deeply, loving

18. Thich Nhat Hanh, *The Art of Living* (New York: HarperOne, 2017), loc. 762.
19. Thich Nhat Hanh, *Peace Is Every Step* (New York: Bantam Books, 1991), 95.
20. Thich Nhat Hanh, *At Home in the World: Stories and Essential Teachings from a Monk's Life* (Berkeley: Parallax, 2016), 134.

> and acting with charity if we wish to truly honor Jesus. The way is Jesus Himself and not just some idea of Him.[21]

The Dalai Lama of Tibet has seen a similar thing, looking at compassion as central to Buddhism and also to religion itself. The Dalai Lama has written, "I believe that this suffering is caused by ignorance, and that people inflict pain on others in pursuit of their own happiness or satisfaction. Yet true happiness comes from a sense of inner peace and contentment, which in turn must be achieved through cultivation of altruism, of love, of compassion, and through the elimination of anger, selfishness and greed."[22]

There is an art of interpreting religions to surmount the obstacles that appear to separate them. It is an art I have been trying to learn and teach for much of my life. Thich Nhat Hanh writes, "Interbeing is an important characteristic of all the Buddha's teachings. When you touch one, you touch all."[23] The affirmation of Universalism, the equality and compatibility of religion that Mohandas Gandhi, the Dalai Lama, and Thich Nhat Hanh would all affirm, is probably not a full statement about religions as such. Universalism is partly about religions, but it is also a statement about our shared humanity. Universalism affirms a common humanity that binds us, values that can be the compasses and maps of a shared moral and spiritual life.

Let's return for the moment to the unfinished story of the Buddha. What happened to him? The Buddha eventually returned home and reunited with his family. He met with his father, King Suddhodana; his wife, Yasodhara; and his son, Rahula. Some accounts say that he converted all three to Buddhism, but others are less certain about the conversion of his wife. Buddha attained many converts in the four decades of his teaching. He outlived some of his more promising students. Ananda, a very faithful student of the Buddha, would outlive him but was deeply grieved by his passing. In the small town of Pava, Buddha dined with the smith Cunda, suffering some kind of food poisoning. He did not blame Cunda. He survived for a while longer but died at Kusinara.[24] Although Ananda deeply mourned as his master lay dying, the Buddha tried to encourage him: "Let the Dhamma and the

21. Thich Nhat Hanh, *Living Buddha, Living Christ* (New York: Riverhead Books, 1995), 56.
22. Dalai Lama, *Freedom in Exile: The Autobiography of the Dalai Lama* (New York: HarperOne, 1991), 270.
23. Thich Nhat Hanh, *The Heart of the Buddha's Teaching* (New York: Broadway Books, 1998), 45.
24. Armstrong, *Buddha*, 132, 180–85.

Discipline that I have taught you be your Teacher when I am gone." And furthermore, "All individual things pass away. Seek our liberation with diligence." Buddha told him, "As a flame blown out by the wind, goes to rest and cannot be defined, so the enlightened man freed from selfishness goes to rest and cannot be defined. Gone beyond all images—gone beyond the power of words."[25]

After his death, the Buddha's religion flourished and spread. Two of the major schools are known as Hinayana and Mahayana Buddhism. Hinayana Buddhism means "lesser raft" because it is believed we are like individuals in a solitary canoe, paddling across the stream of samsara, trying to reach the goal of enlightenment. The monastic effort of the Arhat, or enlightened being, is highly valued. *Hinayana* may be a somewhat biased term for it, as adherents themselves refer to it as *Theravada* Buddhism, which means "way of the elders." Theravada Buddhism embraces the scriptures first compiled in Sri Lanka and called the Pali Canon. It is a collection of the oldest and most authoritative texts in Buddhism.

The other major school of thinking, Mahayana, or Buddhism of the "greater raft," believes their enlightened beings will bring others across the stream of samsara *together*, as you might imagine a group of people clinging to a larger raft. The person guiding the raft is called a bodhisattva, one who has compassion for others and their enlightenment. A bodhisattva may literally come back to the world, delay an escape into enlightened nirvana, so that others can be shown the way. Many schools of Buddhism derive from the Mahayana school.

Zen Buddhism of Japan is one of the most well-known schools. Emphasizing the *zazen*, or seated meditation method, it seeks to purge the mind of tanha and approach satori, another name for nirvana. Zen as a school of Buddhism was originally known as Chan Buddhism in China, from which it initially came. The great Chan patriarch was Bodhidharma, a fifth- or sixth-century CE Buddhist monk who imported the religion to China from India. Since leaving India, Buddhism has sprouted and developed, but oddly enough, in India, the country of its birth, it began to go into decline beginning in the ninth century CE.

25. Armstrong, 187.

What Fits?

The classic picture of Buddhism is of monks or nuns, seated in meditation, pursuing their own enlightenment. It's a tranquil picture, but it might also seem to others sheltered, even selfish. Why should a Buddhist walk away from social responsibilities to deal with inner emotional problems? Has this religion, in emulating the life of its founder Siddhartha, only walked away from the world and its problems? Buddhists may disagree about this. There are increasing awareness and emphasis on what has been called *socially engaged Buddhism*, a Buddhism that does not withdraw from the world's problems.

Thich Nhat Hanh explains his situation during the Vietnam War: "When I was in Vietnam, so many of our villages were being bombed. Along with my monastic brothers and sisters, I had to decide what to do. Should we continue to practice in our monasteries, or should we leave the meditation halls in order to help the people who were suffering under the bombs? After careful reflection we decided to do both—to go out and help people and to do so in mindfulness. We called it Engaged Buddhism. Mindfulness must be engaged."[26]

Others have also championed a socially engaged Buddhism. The Dalai Lama won the Nobel Peace Prize in 1989 for his plan to restore autonomy to Tibet, which had been annexed by Communist China. The Dalai Lama recognized that religion must take responsibility for things done in the world. One must stand up to injustice and offer a better alternative. The Dalai Lama has stated, "My feeling is simply this. If in this present atmosphere, in which everything depends on money and power, and there is not much concern about the real value of love, if we human beings now lose the value of justice, of compassion, of honesty, then in the future we will face more difficulty; more suffering will come."[27]

Furthermore, the Dalai Lama has said that Buddhism's moral answer is compassion: "I call this kind of love that I am describing: religion. This sort of compassion is the real essence of religion. On this level there is hardly any difference between Buddhism, Christianity, or any other faith. All religions place emphasis on bettering

26. Hanh, *Peace Is Every Step*, 91.
27. John F. Avedon, *In Exile from the Land of Snows* (New York: Harper Perennial, 1997), 366.

human beings, on improving man. Brotherhood, love—these things all religions have in common."[28]

B. R. Ambedkar (1891–1956), a famous Buddhist, began his life as an untouchable of India, discriminated against and spurned by caste Hindus. Even after he attained a PhD education, he was discriminated against when he came back to India. He nevertheless made a few major accomplishments. The first, becoming a part of Jawaharlal Nehru's cabinet, Ambedkar helped write the Constitution of India, including the amendment that abolished legal discrimination against untouchables. Ambedkar knew, however, that it would take more than the stroke of a pen; he had lost confidence in the capacity to reform Hinduism. Consequently, he vowed to convert to another religion before he died, which he did, embracing Buddhism. As a religion that spurned caste inequality, Ambedkar thought Buddhism was the most true and rational religion. He and his wife converted just shortly before he died in 1956.

Buddhism does not seem like a political religion, but Ambedkar wished it to be. Aung San Suu Kyi, the Nobel Peace Prize winner in 1991 and leader of Myanmar, has come under sharp criticism for the military's killing of Rohingya Muslims (she does not control the military, actually). She nonetheless points to ten duties of a Buddhist king, which might well be used under any political system:

1. Liberality: He contributes toward people's welfare, provides for their needs.
2. Morality: He holds with five Buddhist precepts: don't kill, steal, lie, commit adultery, or take intoxicants. His example reflects on the kingdom and its administrators.
3. Self-sacrifice, generosity: He entails selfless public service to the people. A good ruler "sublimates his needs as an individual to the service of the nation."
4. Integrity: He upholds the truth. Kyi writes, "Those who govern should be wholly bound by the truth in thought, word and deed."
5. Kindness: He loves and cares for citizens.
6. Austerity: He has simple habits.

28. Avedon, 365.

7. Nonanger: He has a good temper.
8. Nonviolence: He refrains from injury, killing. Kyi writes, "Violence is totally contrary to the teachings of Buddhism. The good ruler vanquishes ill will with loving kindness, wickedness with virtue, parsimony with liberality, and falsehood with truth."
9. Forbearance: He has forgiveness.
10. Nonopposition: He does not oppose people's will: a Buddhist "endorsement of democracy."[29]

Kyi won the Nobel Prize for Peace in 1991 but has become a controversial figure in recent years. Whether Kyi can recapture her integrity remains uncertain at the time of this writing, but it is hoped that she can and that justice will be done in Rakhine state.

Some may think Buddhism is a pessimistic religion, emphasizing inevitable suffering. Others may view it as a realistic religion for the same reason. It has eschewed reliance on ideas of God or the soul and tried to focus on the relief of suffering and the transformation of human hearts here and now. Buddhism affirms an ancient and cyclical idea of life and has not placed as much reliance on God or the supernatural. This also appeals to some but not all. Buddhism has many things that are positive about it and compatible with aspects of other world religions: to accomplish real change and to ease the suffering of human life.

What Doesn't Fit?

There are obviously some points where Buddhism does not fit with other religions. The idea of "no God, no soul, and no self" would alienate almost everyone of a Western religious view, including the Abrahamic faiths of Judaism, Christianity, and Islam. "I am the Lord your God," declares Judaism, and "There is no God but God, and Muhammad is his prophet," says Islam. If God does not exist, whom do Christians, Muslims, and Jews pray to? What becomes of the exalted status of Jesus, Muhammad, or Moses? There is a large gap in understanding between the various faiths of the world and an uncertainty about how to fill it or how to speak

29. Aung San Suu Kyi, *Freedom from Fear—and Other Writings* (New York: Penguin, 2010), 160–61.

across this gulf. No model or thinking about religion yet reconciles them to each other, but the gap remains with the challenge of filling it. Universalism is a humble attempt, but it succeeds more in affirming a common moral humanity than a perfect idea to unite religions.

Buddhism has also been called the "middle way" between the extremes of luxury and asceticism. Some Jains may take issue here, as the great Tirthankaras were in fact champions of self-renunciation. Buddhism and Sikhism, however, do not embrace extremes of self-mortification. Buddhism also rejects the extremes of wealth and luxury. For Buddha, and religions of India in general, there is some good in this realm of samsara, the here and now in which we find ourselves, but the ultimate good is found beyond. For Buddhism, the ultimate peace is found in a state of nirvana, in a final release from the cycle of suffering in this life. Buddhist simplicity and renunciation don't square with a very consumer, materialistic world. Which way is better?

Howsoever we piece the puzzles of religion together, there are difficulties. If we meaningfully try to assemble them all and add a modern scientific view of life, there are gaps in the picture that will remain and pieces that just do not conjoin. If we assume we have all the pieces necessary, we may be making false assumptions that other religions or viewpoints are not meaningful. I cannot resolve the picture of all these contrasting worldviews fully for you, for it is honestly difficult for me to conceive it myself. What I can advise is that the greater you stretch your mind and extend your views to include others, the more possible peace and harmony seem evident in our future. This seems a first step toward a Universalist viewpoint, that all our religions matter and have something to contribute.

9 Jainism

Summary of Jainism

Imagine that this is how your life played out: you were successful, you started a business, you worked hard to support your business and grew rich. In the process, however, you neglected to love your family, you cheated on your partner, and your circle of friends was constantly shrinking. Yours was a long life, but in the last few decades, you realized that you were too zealous in pursuing material wealth. You failed to learn the lesson of *aparigraha*. In Jainism, the principle of aparigraha means not being possessed by your possessions, not being ensnared by worldly attachments. When you died with your lesson not learned, you were forced by the weight of your worldly attachments to come back and learn it again.

In the next life, you were more moderate about accumulating wealth, but you were angry about your marginalized place in society. You had the means to eke out a living, but they were always more meager than those of the next person. You still had not learned the lesson of aparigraha, and soon you found your partner cheating on you (perhaps this was due to a karmic neglect of her in a past life). Becoming angry, you divorced, took to drinking, and became an alcoholic. You became abusive toward those around you. You got involved in fights and harbored ill will toward your fellow human beings. You failed to learn the lesson of ahimsa, or "nonviolence," which instructs us not to be belligerent in heart or deed.[1] Your soul, which the Jains call the *jiva*, was burdened and thus made to come back again.

In your third life, you moderated your pursuit of wealth, tempered your thoughts, and calmed your anger. But you did not strive to understand the lives of the Muslims, Sikhs, or Hindus around you. You built yourself into a castle of self-certainty. You could not bridge the cultural gap from your own perspective to that of your

1. Paul Dundas, *The Jains*, 2nd ed. (New York: Routledge, 2002), 162–63.

neighbor. For the Jains, you failed to learn the lesson of *anekantavada*, the idea that legitimacy might be found in a number of different perspectives. Once again, you were made to return to the weary world to learn yet another spiritual and moral lesson.

The ideas of ahimsa and aparigraha can be found in many of the religions of India. Many lifetimes of reincarnation may be needed to deepen the spiritual self and prepare it for emancipation from the world. The idea of anekantavada, the doctrine of the relativity of viewpoints, is more unique to Jainism, but the tolerance it implies is well known in other religions of India. The sixth-century Jain scholar Haribhadra developed anekantavada, meaning "main pointedness," suggesting a relativity in points of view on truth. The admission of many points or perspectives introduced an idea called *syavada*, or the "doctrine of may be." One of the humblest admissions we can make is our inability to know the absolute truth.[2] Not having this certainty, it is reasonable to suppose that true spiritual learning takes human beings a long time. Thus many lives are lived; lessons are learned or failed in a long race to be freed from worldly woes. Jainism believes your soul can escape life's fetters, and if you learn ahimsa, aparigraha, and anekantavada, you are well on your way to your soul's enlightenment.

Jainism is an ancient religion of India, but how ancient is it? Many scholars date Jainism from the time of Mahavira, a person born around the sixth century BCE. Jains know Mahavira as the last of twenty-four great "ford makers," or Tirthankaras. A Tirthankara is one who has shown a way across a spiritual river, from the near banks of the "this-worldly" to the far banks of the "otherworldly" and spiritual. He has shown how to escape from the cycle of reincarnation. One of the moral lessons Mahavira taught from the *Acharanga Sutra* might be seen as a form of the Golden Rule: "He who knows what is bad for himself knows what is bad for others, and he who knows what is bad for others knows what is bad for himself. One whose mind is at peace and who is free from passions does not desire to live at the expense of others. He who understands the nature of sin against earth, water, air, fire, plants, and animals is a true sage and understands karma. For, all these elements are truly alive (possess soul energy) and those who harm them harm themselves by bonding their souls firmly with

2. Dundas, 228–32.

non-liberating karma."[3] This is bolder than the "do unto others as you would have them do unto you" maxim that we think of as the Golden Rule. It confers a spiritual and moral weight upon all the living elements and calls upon Jains to respect the web of life. If this were taken as a central maxim, it would make Jainism an eco-friendly religion.

There were, according to the Jains, twenty-three "ford makers," or Tirthankaras, before Mahavira. Parsva, who immediately preceded Mahavira, had taught the fourfold restraint of "abstention from violence, lying, taking what has not been given, and possession."[4] In a previous life, Jains believed Parsva had saved a snake from a Brahmin's sacrificial fire. In the next life, when Parsva was deep in meditation, he was attacked with fire and rock by that same Brahmin, now incarnate as a demon. The grateful snake, however, rose over Parsva and protected him with the great hood of his cobra body.[5] In a simple illustration of karma, spiritual cause and consequence, Jains also show their spiritual competition with the Hindu Brahmins.

Periodically, the Tirthankaras came and showed the way to enlightenment, renewing the dharma, or "religious duty," for Jains. The first of these was Rikhava (or Rishabha), whose life was said to date to 6500 BCE. Historians cannot independently confirm Rikhava's existence, but for Jains he was of legendary size (literally a giant) and a founder of Jain civilization, religion, and culture.[6] Jains see Rikhava as the founder of civilization itself, as the first ford maker, who taught humanity basic social skills, food preparation, the kindling of fire, agriculture, writing, and organizing institutions such as marriage.[7] The Tirthankaras are central to the Jain temple, where statues of them are attended to by the temple dweller, called a *caityavasi*.

Jains do not have a central creator God figure. Instead, Jains look to the Tirthankaras for spiritual guidance. In the absence of the Tirthankaras, there exist many spiritual leaders, sometimes called *arhats* (one who is worthy) or *acharyas* (teachers). The Tirthankaras have laid down the doctrines necessary for Jains to follow to become enlightened and escape the cycle of reincarnation. The ardent and devoted Jain will take vows that will result in great austerities and extreme self-renunciation, spurning all attachments to clothes, possessions, and basic appetites. To become a

3. Vastupal Parikh, *Jainism and the New Spirituality* (Toronto: Peace, 2002), 10.
4. Dundas, *Jains*, 32.
5. Dundas, 32–33.
6. Parikh, *Jainism and the New Spirituality*, 164–65.
7. Dundas, *Jains*, 20.

monk, a Jain plucks out and removes their hair. In solitude the Jain monk becomes acutely aware and can try to stop the karma that leads to rebirth.[8] These are some of the same practices that the Buddha tried and found them wanting. He rejected the extremes of asceticism and instead chose the "middle way."

A lay Jain makes a commitment to the principles of the faith but observes them with less rigor than a monk. A lay Jain may have fewer possessions but will not abandon them all. A lay Jain will keep sexuality within marriage, while an ascetic Jain monk would give up sex altogether. For the lay Jain, the goal is to come closer to escaping reincarnation, or *kevala* (Hindus have named it *moksha*). The lay Jain might be comfortable with moderate progress and get to kevala in another few lifetimes, but the renunciate Jain monk wants *this* to be the last reincarnation and will try to achieve kevala. Both are respectable paths, but great honor is given to the sacrifice of the monks. Jains are those who wish to become Jinas, or persons who have conquered the attachments to reincarnation.

The Jain idea of the soul is called the *jiva*, and it is spiritual essence that yearns to escape the cycle of reincarnation. It cannot escape the cycle, however, because the light jiva is bonded by a heavier *ajiva*, or ensnaring spiritual shackle that keeps the soul here and now. Like spiritual fetters or shackles, the heavier ajiva prevent the lighter jiva from escaping to the end of kevala.[9] The bonding of the light souls to the passions of this world is called Kashaya, and includes such things as anger, greed, or pride. *Bandha*, or the "binding connection," is another name for this.[10] The end is the same: a light soul caught in a heavy world wanting to escape to kevala, a place of enlightened bliss.

Like Jacob Marley in Charles Dickens's *A Christmas Carol*, who wears the chains of greed—long heavy fetters—that he made in life, a Jain who has not learned aparigraha is bound by worldly attachment. Christians would say that he served mammon (wealth) rather than God. But while Marley's soul wanted freedom for its fetters in order to be with God, a Jain's soul desires freedom from worldly entanglements (the ajiva) in order to be free of reincarnation and embraced in omniscient bliss.

8. Dundas, 42–43.
9. Parikh, *Jainism and the New Spirituality*, 8–9.
10. Long, *Jainism*, 96.

Figure 9.1 *Symbol of Jainism*

Figure 9.1 visualizes the Jain idea of the spiritual cosmos. The top of the diagram where the curving bowl shape cups a single dot is the highest place of Jain heaven, the place of spiritual release called kevala. The soul at this point has attained a kind of omniscient bliss. The Jains have called this topmost plane the *paramatman*.[11] It is a hard place to get to but the place where all souls must strive to go. The three dots below represent *insight*, *knowledge*, and *conduct*. If you have the right insight, knowledge, and conduct, you can escape reincarnation and attain kevala.

As long as one is heavily bonded to the world, they go around in the cycle of reincarnations, fettered to some aspect of worldly reality or attachment, delighted in part by worldly pleasures but also desiring nothing more than to escape their limitations. The swastika-shaped part of the diagram represents this world of

11. Dundas, *Jains*, 110–11.

reincarnation, and the four spokes represent the types of animate life that can exist: heavenly, human, animal, and hell beings. Ironically, for the Jains, one might become a heavenly being but not yet be enlightened. A further development, a fuller awareness, is needed to escape altogether. One might also reincarnate in a plane of hell, undergoing torture and torment, but this is not a place of permanent punishment. Planes of hell are places to burn off bad karma, bad accretions to the soul that have ensnared it and misdirected it. Jains, Hindus, Buddhists, and Sikhs all seek release from attachment and the bliss of enlightenment. But they may disagree with one another about which path is the right one to follow.

One striking difference between the religions of India and the Abrahamic faiths is the model of enlightenment, or "salvation" from the world. Christianity and Islam emphasize that each person has only one lifetime and a judgment that comes at its end. Who gets saved and how can be debated, but generally speaking, for Christians and Muslims, a life faithfully lived faces judgment with confidence. Yet it seems a scary and infinite precipice awaits at the end of life. One can fall into damnation, into the fiery pits of hell, if one is bad and unworthy. One might also enter paradise if one is good or perhaps experience a redemptive time in purgatory first. In any case, it is a short life we have on earth and a long punishment or reward that looms thereafter. That puts a lot of pressure on a person in this life to "get it right" the first time and be worthy of redemption. In the Indian faiths, one can get to the reward called moksha, nirvana, or kevala, but it may take many lifetimes to learn the necessary spiritual lessons before the end is attained. It is possible, but it is hard. You have the time you need to accomplish it, but you must find the will and the purpose to set yourself to it. Jains do not have the model of an overseeing God judging your choices. In Jainism there is kind of a self-imposed judgment—your karma is the riverbed of your soul's reincarnation; wherever the river flows with force, that is the channel you cut out for your future.

In Jainism a prerequisite for attaining the highest level of spirituality includes extremes of asceticism. The ascetic renounces all material pleasures, all attachments to the world. The ascetic Jain monk will join a community that has vowed to abolish all attachments and reach the highest goal of renunciation. The Buddha had practiced such austerities until he had become so famished you could see the individual bones of his rib cage. He turned away from these austerities, saying they were of no use to him. Jainism, however, has continued to embrace the ascetic renunciation of all attachments—so much so that even the Digambara Jain monk will give up the clothes on his back so as not to be attached to them.

The most extreme Jain practice may be the rite of *sallekhana*, fasting unto death. Whereas many people outside of the Jain tradition will see this as suicide by starvation, some Jains have seen it as a legitimate step for the monk who has let go of all possessiveness. Being released from every bond of attachment, if it is deemed the circumstances are right, the rare Jain monk may be allowed to let go of even the attachment to food. One ceases to worry, even to eat, and soon passes away. It is intensely controversial and not universally practiced. A restricted number of Jain ascetics would practice this rite, and the lay Jain would not practice it at all.[12]

Should this practice be condoned or criticized? No religion is free from criticism, and it is self-evident that this practice is not going to be agreeable to all the world's religions. If a Universalist mindset believes there is a common ethic that can be found in religion, it realizes some norms are not easily found or shared by all. Some religions are going to hold up ideas as essential that other religions might wish to discard. To find the truth in one's own tradition and one's own heart and mind is imperative. Texts and traditions might be held aloft not so much for their own perfection but as mirrors to discern truth.

Hard-core monastic asceticism is not a choice for everyone. Not all Jains choose it but may be supportive of those who do. No Jain would undertake the rigors of monasticism without the belief in freeing the soul for kevala. While the conviction of many believers in a great variety of faiths may be half-hearted, tempered with secularism, merely going through the motions and rites of their religion, it is not so with monastics. Like monks of other traditions, Jain monks feel the faith deep in their hearts, souls, and minds. Otherwise, they would not be prepared to commit to the renunciations demanded by monastic life. For the deep believer of any faith, this stuff is *very real, lived*, and *actual*. William James said such faith was "living, forced, and momentous."[13] For the hard-core believer, it becomes as real as physics and chemistry.

Because convictions can be so deeply heartfelt and interpretations of beliefs vary, there are factions in all religions. Jainism also has divided into two main camps: the Svetambaras, who are known as the "white clad" for the white garments their

12. Long, *Jainism*, 98.
13. James, *Will to Believe*, 3.

monks don, and the Digambaras, or "sky-clad" monks who are completely nude. The two factions may have divided, according to Jain legend, because the monk Bhadrabahu led a part of the Jain community away to escape an impending crisis. When Bhadrabahu and his fellow Jains returned after the crisis was over, they did not recognize the beliefs or practices of the Svetambaras who had been left behind. The Digambaras believed the Jain canon had been lost and that the Svetambaras had not retained it. The Svetambaras argued that they had stayed true to the faith and its practices.[14]

The Digambara Jains believed that only complete abandonment of one's possessions could lead one to enlightenment. Hence only one who was completely nude was really embracing the idea of aparigraha. In the third and fourth centuries, Jains debated whether deliverance of the soul was possible for women. Could women also practice monastic nudity? Prabhachandra, in the eleventh century, concluded that monasticism could not be extended to women and adopted the perspective that only males could escape reincarnation. Curiously, however, Prabhachandra also believed that women could not go to the deepest plane of hell, that this kind of depravity was a mark only of men's souls.[15] Since only males could make the final abandonment and reach kevala, an unequal gender standard exists for Digambaras but not for all Jains.

The Svetambaras did not concur. They articulated a more gender-egalitarian standard for Jains. They even insisted that the nineteenth Tirthankara, Malli, was a woman. Previously a king named Malli, who had reneged on a pledge to commit austerities, Malli was reborn as a woman who was committed to fulfilling those obligations.[16] For the "white-clad" Svetambaras, to achieve aparigraha it is not necessary to abandon absolutely all things, including clothing. Both male and female monastics are recognized and are allowed to wear white clothing. The *muhapatti*, or white mouth shield, is worn so as not to cause the slightest of injury, even to the point of not inhaling insects. Svetambaras have espoused a more gender-egalitarian perspective on women's enlightenment, and nudity is not a prerequisite for the soul's liberation.

14. Dundas, *Jains*, 47.
15. Dundas, 56–57.
16. Dundas, 56.

All Jains, monastic or lay, are required to take oaths in order to practice their religion. They differ in the degree of strictness with which the oaths will be observed. These vows are the following:

1. Nonviolence (*ahimsa*): for the Jain monk, a more total abstention on killing living things; for all Jains, a commitment to a largely vegetarian diet and minimizing *himsa*, or violence, in thought and deed
2. Truthfulness (*satya*): being honest and forthright
3. Not stealing (*asteya*): working for one's living as a lay Jain; refraining from theft for all Jains
4. Celibacy (*brahmacharya*): for monks, complete abstention from sex; for lay Jains, faithfulness to one's partner
5. Nonpossession (*aparigraha*): for monks, abandonment of all possessions for Digambaras or nearly all for Svetmabaras; for lay Jains, keeping possessions to a simple minimum[17]

One can recognize in these vows some of the universal norms that are found in all religious traditions: don't kill, don't lie, don't steal, don't commit adultery, and be cautious about possessions. If human beings observed these norms most of the time, we would live in a stable and tranquil world. It is abundantly clear, however, that most of us fail to observe these basic moral precepts *totally* across the whole of our lives. We are all, in our own ways, committed to and simultaneously disobeying laws we know are good for us. In that light, religion is a constant reminder to fulfill these basic duties.

Jainism may be alluring to some and repelling to others. It might be tempting to laugh at or trivialize the naked Jain monk: poor, powerless, naked, and too meek to kill a fly. Such a Jain might seem marginal and irrelevant. Contempt comes easily when differences seem deep, but no religion can be understood by belittling or looking only at its most extreme elements. A more nuanced view of Jainism is far more compelling. In a world with nuclear bombs and bacterial and chemical weapons ready to unleash death, we are in a position to destroy our civilization in a single conflagration. In such a world, the strict call to nonviolence, as the Jains

17. Long, *Jainism*, 102.

teach, could be an aid to avoiding such disaster. Christianity, Judaism, Hinduism, Islam, and other religions also have resources in them to contribute toward nonviolence and peace.

In a heavily populated world threatened by pollution and global warming, the idea of limiting one's possessions is also wise. To err on the side of caution, to embrace a simpler, cleaner, more ecologically sustainable standard of living, is fully compatible with the idea of aparigraha. It would be foolish to think that the planet's resources are unlimited, and as such, responsible development, moderation, and aparigraha might curb the consumerism that puts the planet at risk.

The doctrine of anekantavada, of recognizing multiple viewpoints, is essential in a multicultural and globalized world. The Buddhist parable of the blind men and the elephant describes it well. If one's vision is not complete, the same object could be perceived and understood in different ways. By embracing a plurality of viewpoints, anekantavada wards off the kind of fanatic certainty that leads to terrorism and other forms of religious violence. Not only is any concept of anekantavada lost upon the fanatic, but so may be the idea of ahimsa. Bad religion and bad ideas abound. Better ones might stave off extremes.

What Fits?

Jainism has essential moral teachings, good principles of living, that can be a boon to civilization. The ideas of nonpossession, of humility in viewpoint, and of nonviolence—all of which are reflected in other faiths as well—are embraced in Jainism with a special passion. One should be cautioned against ridiculing a religion that is so totally preoccupied with nonviolence, because those same moral resources might be helpful in preventing deadly, large-scale violence. If we were less violent, more truthful and respectful, less adamant and righteous, among other things, civilization would be far better than it is.

Religions have a compatible set of basic moral principles when you strip them down to simple ideas. The problem is, once you strip them down just to those basic ideas, they lose a great deal of their motivational force. To believe with great vigor that these things really matter, that they are truly sacred and consequential, is the thing religions can offer us. Emotions, the core workhorses of our spiritual lives, can be wild and untamed, and religion has a way of harnessing and motivating the emotional side of us. We need moral commands and a host of myths, narratives, and ideas of emotional significance to give those commands force and vigor. Strip Jainism, or any religion, to its basic principles and it is more easily understood and more compatible with other faiths, but without the trappings of traditions, religions become weaker and are robbed of their full breadth and meaning. Rare is the person who can capture the heartfelt meaning of something, without some ritual or cyclic means of reinforcing that value. Religion and all institutionalized beliefs may be flawed, but if you strip away at them, you also jeopardize the social reinforcement they give to our ethics.

Human beings do not like to be controlled. We often choose not to listen to the guidance of others' advice. We are not robots. And religion is not a programming language. But because the subject of religion is *us*, we can hope that the human race has a *transcendental* element, whether it be a soul or some sacred essence shared in common by all. There is a choice, a decision, something that transcends our human flesh, that ghost in the machine capable of free choice. We cannot know for sure, but it is the great hope and gamble of all religions that this is true.

What Doesn't Fit?

Some of the extremes of Jainism—ascetic renunciation, *sallekhana* (fasting to death), and refusal to harm even insects—stand out. They are not consonant with the norms and values of other religions. Furthermore, the lack of an idea of the centrality of God may also alienate believers of other faiths. Faiths, as they encounter each other, invariably encounter consensus and strong disagreement.

The naked Jain Digambara, bereft of all possessions, or the Svetambara monk, who is also penniless, runs completely contrary to the consumer mindset of modern civilization. Instead of living a frugal, simple, nonviolent life, contemporary civilization prizes buying and selling, having and owning. Greater gadgets, larger homes, and faster automobiles, phones, computers, and services make our lives more convenient but also more frenetic and distracted. As Madonna sang when I was a kid, we are indeed living in a material world. Material civilization is here to stay. It is not easy to turn away from its forces. But the naked Jain monk has broken with that world utterly. The video games, movies, and secular distractions we are immersed in are constant distractions from the spiritual and religious forces that are far older. If we listen to the voices and messages of religion, we may be able to remain afloat in today's ocean of materialism. Perhaps we might even glimpse dry land. Jains, among the other world religions, remind us that materialism may not be the final end.

10 Sikhism

Summary of Sikhism

On a beautiful, bright day with puffy clouds in the distant horizons, you look up and see a spectacular sight. Out of a tranquil man-made pool of water rises a large rectangular golden building. Its golden leaf gleams brilliantly in the sunlight, and a single walkway allows access across the water. It has doors on four sides, symbolizing an openness to all castes: Brahmin, Kshatriya, Vaishya, and Shudra, or priest, warrior, artisan, and worker. "There is neither Hindu nor Muslim" was the proclamation of the founder. And when the temple was built in honor of his religion, care was taken that all would be invited to this new faith. Not far off, a communal kitchen puts out meals for anyone who wishes to come to eat them. For the moment, the brilliant glare of the sun reflecting on the golden building captivates you as men wearing turbans gracefully congregate underneath and around it. Where is this place that you have found yourself? You are in Amritsar, India. The temple is the Harimandir, the sacred center for the Sikh faith.

Sikhism and the Ten Gurus

Sikhism emerged in the fifteenth or sixteenth century on the border of what is today India and Pakistan, a place called the Punjab, or "land of five rivers." The central founding figure was Guru Nanak, one of ten important gurus, or religious teachers. At the time of Guru Nanak, Hinduism and Islam were the two most common religions in India. Contrary to popular opinion, Islam had not come just by the sword and conquest, but traders and missionaries also had been responsible for many Muslim converts.[1] Which faith would Nanak choose? Hinduism or Islam? He ended up choosing neither. Instead, he chose a third path, a new Sikh vision. The

1. Richard Maxwell Eaton, *Rise of Islam and the Bengal Frontier, 1204–1760* (Berkeley: University of California Press, 1993), chap. 5.

Sikhs recorded their own scripture in a distinctive *Gurmukhi* script. Initially, this sacred scripture was called the Adi Granth, then finally, the Guru Granth Sahib.

Guru Nanak (1469–1539) lived in Punjab beginning in the fifteenth century. Islam was making a home in India by the rule of mighty kings and the inspiration of Sufi mystics. Nanak was a lower tier (subcaste) Kshatriya and worked as a revenue collector for ten years. He married a woman named Sulakhni and had two children, Sri Chand and Lakhmi Das. Seeking employment, he migrated to Sultanpur. He was not content with the established religious or political order of the day, a protest shared by the *sants* such as Ramananda and Kabir.[2] There was something that Hinduism and Islam both captured and yet both missed, which left many spiritual seekers wanting a fresh alternative. Guru Nanak left Sultanpur in the year 1500 at about age thirty-one to go on a spiritual quest. He did not return until around the age of fifty-five in the year 1524. Restlessly seeking after God, he would eventually find him.[3]

Guru Nanak did not adhere to conventional dictates of Hinduism or Islam. While in the companion of Muslims, he had slept with his feet toward the Kaaba of Mecca. This was thought to be an affront by the Muslims he was with. Guru Nanak replied, "Then kindly turn my feet towards some places where God is not."[4] Orthodox Islam was not for him. He also challenged the caste inequality of Hindus, saying, "We are not high or low, or the middling; we have taken refuge in God, and we are His people."[5] Guru Nanak spoke highly of women's importance as well: "Of woman are we born, of woman conceived, to woman engaged, to woman married. Woman we befriend, by woman is the civilization continued. When woman dies, woman is sought for; it is by woman that order is maintained. Then why call her evil from whom great men are born? From woman is woman born, and without woman, none would exist. The eternal Lord is the only one, O Nanak, who depends not on woman."[6] While equality of women in all cultures, and probably all religions, needs to be improved, many Sikhs have tried to emphasize women's equality with men.[7]

2. J. S Grewal, *The Sikhs of the Punjab* (New York: Cambridge University Press, 1998), 27.
3. Grewal, chaps. 1 and 2.
4. Mary Pat Fisher, *Living Religions*, 7th ed. (Upper Saddle River, NJ: Prentice Hall, 2008), 436.
5. Grewal, *Sikhs of the Punjab*, 40.
6. Patwant Singh, *The Sikhs* (New York: Doubleday, 1999), 27.
7. Gurinder Singh Mann, *Sikhism* (Upper Saddle River, NJ: Prentice Hall, 2004), 102–5.

Guru Nanak settled in Kartarpur, India, where he began teaching *sikhya* (students).[8] One day, while immersed in a river in the Punjab and having drunk a sacred nectar, or *amrit*, he received his revelation and pronounced, "There is no Hindu, there is no Muslim."[9] By denying aspects of each tradition, he was embracing a religion that transcended and included them both. Those who were truly reverential, Nanak noted, were not bound by the trappings of their religion: "Let compassion be your mosque. Let faith by your prayer mat, let honest living be your Koran."[10]

Sikh doctrine steers a course between Hinduism and Islam, affirming elements of each while challenging others. With Muslims, Sikhs recognize the high unity of God. Sikhs refer to it as Ek Onkar. God is one, ever present, and eternal. God does not become incarnate, so the avatars of Vishnu central to Hinduism are not generally recognized. God does not take human form but speaks through the guru's words. Hindus and Sikhs share a belief in reincarnation. Sikhs believe we pass through a series of lives before the pride in our own heart withers and our true devotion to God increases.

The curtailing of pride is accompanied by reflection upon God's true name, which is Nam Simaran. Without reflection on God's eternal reality, all becomes vanity. Nanak said, "They who have treasured God's Name in their hearts bear the marks of his grace on their brows. For grace is the means to obtaining the Name; all other is bluster and wind."[11] To recognize God's centrality is vital for the soul's release and attaining divine truth (*sach khand*). Obscuring the way to God are common illusions, such as pride, lust, covetousness, attachment, and anger.[12]

The idea of God's supreme unity and everlasting reality is the Mul Mantar, the affirmation of the Sikh faith in one God, expressed in a daily prayer called the Japji. The Japji begins like this: "There is one Supreme Being, the Eternal Reality. He is the Creator, without fear and devoid of enmity. He is immortal, never incarnated, self-existent, known by grace through the Guru. The Eternal One, from the beginning,

8. Grewal, *Sikhs of the Punjab*, 6–8, 39–40. Patwant Singh reports his overall travels took twenty-eight years. See Singh, *Sikhs*, 24.
9. Singh, *Sikhs*, 18.
10. Singh, 20.
11. W. H. McLeod, *Textual Sources for the Study of Sikhism* (Chicago: University of Chicago Press, 1999), 42.
12. Grewal, *Sikhs of the Punjab*, 37.

through all time, present now, the Everlasting reality."[13] The Mul Mantar idea is that God is one, God is eternal, God is understood by the Sikh gurus.

Guru Nanak did not pass his authority to either of his sons but instead chose Guru Angad as the second Sikh teacher. The faithfulness and integrity of Angad impressed him. Guru Angad warned of *haumai*, which might be translated as "self-centeredness" or "pride"; pride does not give due credit to God, from whom all blessings come. Guru Nanak's son, however, Sri Chand refused Angad's legitimacy. Sri Chand began his own ascetic order called the Udasis, embracing austere practices that mainstream Sikhs eschewed. The Udasi order created by Sri Chand thrived but would never become the core of the faith as later Sikhs recognized it.[14]

Guru Nanak died in 1539, and three years later, the third Mughal Akbar was born. As a leader of the Muslim Empire in India, Akbar showed much more tolerance toward non-Muslims than did his predecessors. He opened an interfaith court of dialogue and abolished the *jizya*, or the tax upon non-Muslims. Sharp distinctions between Muslims and non-Muslims were softened. Akbar offered land and sanctuary to the Sikhs, allowing them to thrive just as their religion was blooming. When Akbar died, his son Jahangir did not take an interest in the religious policies of his father. Akbar's great-grandson Aurangzeb (1618–1707) even reversed Akbar's reforms. Aurangzeb oppressed and attacked the Sikhs, fought with the tenth guru of Sikhism, and reinstated the jizya. When Pakistan and India divided in 1947, the Punjab divided at the border. Amritsar, the Sikhs' sacred city, was on the Indian side of the border. Sikhs received no sanctuary state of their own during the partitioning, which would have ramifications in the years to come.

The words of the gurus created a spiritual community that partly embraced and partly repudiated ideas of Hindus and Muslims. The Gurbani, or the first ten gurus' sacred words, was believed to offer core instructions for a living faith. Under the next two gurus, Amar Das (1484–1574) and Ram Das (1534–81), the Sikh community became increasingly distinct from its Hindu and Muslim neighbors. Amritsar was its central city, though the golden temple, or Harimandir, had not yet been built. The Sikhs emphasized caste equality, challenging the age-old stratifications and iniquities that they saw in the Hindu system. Taking on the privileges of the Brahmin caste, the third guru, Amar Das, said, "Let no man be proud of his caste. For

13. McLeod, *Textual Sources*, 86.
14. Grewal, *Sikhs of the Punjab*, 42, 46–48, 62, 75; Singh, *Sikhs*, 29.

the man who has God in his heart, He, no other, is the true Brahmin."[15] Further, he added, "Though they say there are four castes, One God created all men, all men are molded of the same clay."[16]

Challenging worldly hierarchies, oftentimes based on unfair and arbitrary distributions of power, has been done by many religions. It could be argued it is a universal element shared by most of the major, well-known religions. Jesus challenged the authorities of his day, commanding a rich man to sell all he had and to serve the poor.[17] The Qur'an teaches Muslims to do good to orphans and widows.[18] The laws and instructions given to Moses reported, "If there is among you anyone in need, a member of your community in any of your towns within the land that the Lord your God is giving you, do not be hard-hearted or tight-fisted toward your needy neighbor."[19] Mohandas Gandhi also famously rejected the caste inequalities of Hinduism and said, "I cannot picture to myself a time when no man shall be richer than another. But I do picture to myself a time when the rich will spurn to enrich themselves at the expense of the poor and the poor will cease to envy the rich. Even in a most perfect world we shall fail to avoid inequalities, but we can and must avoid strife and bitterness."[20] Of course, religious traditions have not always challenged inequity or iniquity and instead at times fostered them.

In the time of the fourth guru, Ram Das, the bathing pool in the holy city of Amritsar was constructed.[21] In Hinduism, *amrit* was a nectar that was prized by the gods, and in Sikhism, it became part of ritual anointing and bathing. Important transformations occurred during the time of the fifth guru, Arjan (1563–1606), who is arguably the most pivotal guru after Nanak. He built the holy golden temple of the Sikhs, the Harimandir. With doors on all four sides, signifying its openness to all four castes, it stands amid the sacred pool in Amritsar. Guru Arjan composed the first version of the Sikh bible, called the Adi Granth, and was the single largest contributor to its verses.[22] One source reports that during his time as guru,

15. Singh, *Sikhs*, 30.
16. Singh, 30–31.
17. Luke 18: 8–30.
18. Qur'an 2:24–25.
19. Deut 15:7.
20. Fischer, *Essential Gandhi*, 231.
21. Grewal, *Sikhs of the Punjab*, 50–54.
22. Grewal, 46–56.

he contributed 2,218 hymns to the holy scripture.[23] While many religions affirm a single revelation coming from one man at one time, such as Jesus, Muhammad, or Zoroaster, Sikhism is distinctive in believing that God spoke or acted through a succession of ten gurus before their scriptures were completed.

Guru Arjan experienced the turmoil of Mughal transition. The third Mughal, Jalal-ud-din Akbar (ruled 1556–1605), who had been very supportive of the Sikhs, passed away in 1605 and was succeeded by the fourth Mughal, Nur-ud-din Jahangir (ruled 1605–27). Jahangir was not interested in the policies of his father. He was not tolerant toward the Sikh community and began to oppress them. In the times of Jahangir, there was no clear separation of church and state. A Muslim ruler upheld the kingdom and the faith, and any challenge to his religion could also be perceived as a challenge to his rule. Simple proclamations like the Sikh idea that "God is neither Hindu nor Muslim" could be perceived as an attack on the theological authority of the Qur'an and the rule of the Muslims. The tolerant policies of Akbar were forgotten, and though the Qur'an is opposed to conversion by force, the policies of Jahangir were forcefully directed against the fifth guru, Arjan. He was instructed to expurgate, or remove, the offensive passages from the Sikh bible. When Arjan refused, he was tortured and killed, becoming the first martyr of the Sikh community.[24]

Guru Hargobind, the sixth guru, was a departure from his predecessors. He loved hunting and organized the Sikh's militarily for the defense of their religion. Establishing the doctrine of *miri piri*, which was an equal division of time between religious and spiritual matters, the sixth guru constructed the Akal Takht, or the "Almighty's Throne," as a place of political administration. He further developed the Sikh holy temple called the *gurdwara*.

Hargobind also spent time in prison after being perceived as a threat by Jahangir. Legend says that after many years of imprisonment, he was allowed to leave with as many princes and prisoners as could grab hold of his robe. Having a long robe made specially for his release, it is said fifty-two prisoners came out with Hargobind. The ascent of the fifth Mughal, Shah Jahan, made things more difficult for

23. Pashaura Singh, *The Guru Granth Sahib: Canon, Meaning, and Authority* (New York: Oxford University Press, 2000), 11.
24. Singh, *Sikhs*, 39.

Hargobind, and again he had to defend the Sikh community. It is important to note that this was the policy of the latter Mughal emperors, not a requirement of Islam.[25]

Figure 10.1 *Khanda: symbol of Sikhism*

The Sikhs may appear to have a militant faith, but they have been compelled to defend their community. The Khanda, the religious emblem of the Sikhs, reflects the doctrine of Degh Tegh Fateh, or "cauldron, sword, and victory."[26] With a double-edged sword and cauldron, it represents not just the duty to defend the Sikhs from aggression but also the obligation to feed the needy with the communal meal (*langar*). Begun by Guru Nanak, the *langar* is a vegetarian meal offered to all regardless of caste or faith. Serving to feed the hungry and bring the religious community together, the langar accomplishes religious and practical social ends. The *kirpan*, a short sword or dagger carried by the Sikhs, is to remember the need to defend the community. In Sikhism, the doctrine of *dharamyudh*, which might mean something like "just war" or "holy war," is an obligation to *defend* the community when outside forces threaten it. Offensive violence is not condoned.[27]

25. See Singh, 39–41; Singh, *Guru Granth Sahib*, 207, 249; Grewal, *Sikhs of the Punjab*, 64–66, 244.
26. Mann, *Sikhism*, 48.
27. Mann, 83.

By the time of Hargobind, the lineage of the gurus had become hereditary. The seventh guru, Har Rai (1630–61), refused the summons of the emperor, given the legacy of the execution of the fifth guru and imprisonment of the sixth. The eighth guru, Har Krishan (1656–64), held the position only for a few years and died as a child due to smallpox. The ninth guru of Sikhism was Tegh Bahadur (1621–75). He was also martyred, killed at the hand of a Mughal ruler. He led the community during the time of Aurangzeb, who was the great-grandson of the more tolerant Mughal Akbar. Aurangzeb reinstated the tax on non-Muslims that had been abolished by Akbar. Aurangzeb was oppressive to both Hindus and Sikhs, and Tegh Bahadur defied the Mughal's attempts to cow them. Tegh Bahadur wrote, "The truly enlightened ones are those who neither incite fear in others nor fear anyone themselves."[28] When Tegh Bahadur was taken into custody, he witnessed two of his companions killed before his eyes for refusing to convert to Islam. When Tegh Bahadur also refused to bow to Aurangzeb, he also was decapitated.[29] Now the Sikhs had lost two leaders at the hands of the Mughals.

The tenth and last guru, Gobind Singh (1666–1708), was only nine years old when he received the severed head of his father, Tegh Bahadur. The grisly attempt to intimidate the young boy failed, and as he grew into manhood, he organized the Sikhs militarily. In later adulthood he asked a stunned assembly of Sikhs if any one of them was so devoted that he was willing to give his head for his religion. The audience was hushed, but in a few moments, a volunteer raised his hand and came forth. Entering into a tent with Gobind Singh, the tenth guru reemerged alone with a bloodied sword. He then asked the audience for the head of another volunteer, and another stepped forth. Again, the guru entered the tent with the man and reemerged with a bloodied sword. This test was repeated until five volunteers of differing caste backgrounds had offered to give their heads in devotion to their religion.

After the fifth volunteer was supposedly finished off, all five of the men reemerged from the tent in perfect health wearing the typical adornments of the Sikhs: the comb that secured the unshorn hair in a turban, the undergarment, the bracelet, and the short sword. Accounts of what happened that day vary, but many report that the guru was testing the courage of his followers. When he went into the tent, he dipped his sword in the blood of an animal to create the illusion of their death.

28. Singh, *Sikhs*, 46.
29. Grewal, *Sikhs of the Punjab*, 69–72; Singh, *Sikhs*, 44–46.

Some even say he miraculously revived them. In any case, when the five reemerged, they were the first of the Khalsa, the Sikh community so pure and dedicated to their faith that they would give their life for it. It is a fascinating and controversial story.[30]

When Guru Gobind Singh initiated the five members of the Khalsa, he anointed them with a ritual *amrit* and required of them five symbols that define the Sikh community. Collectively, they have been called the "five Ks" and include the *kesh*, *kanga*, *kaccha*, *kara*, and *kirpan*. The *kesh* is the unshorn hair that expresses devotion to God. It is kept in place by a *kanga*, or "comb," and wrapped up with a turban. Although Sikhs wear turbans, not everyone who wears a turban is a Sikh; Muslims and Hindus also have worn the turban. The *kaccha* are the short breeches worn by Sikh men and are symbolic of restraint and continence. The *kara* is the steel bracelet worn on the sword arm for protection, and the *kirpan* is the dagger that is carried for the defense of the religion. Together, these five Ks make up the ritual dress of the Sikhs.

Gobind Singh was the last of the ten gurus. He finalized the organization of the Sikh bible, the Guru Granth Sahib (Adi Granth). Before he died, he left his authority to the finished text rather than a successor. Collectively, the inspired words of the gurus (called Gurbani) compose the core of the Sikh bible. Editing, finalizing, and publishing of the work would continue after his death into the time of the Maharaja Ranjit Singh (1780–1839). Gobind Singh also wrote his own work called the Dasam Granth (Book of the Tenth Master[31]), a holy work to the Sikhs but subsidiary to the Adi Granth. Excerpts from the Dasam Granth can be as pluralistic and inclusive as the Guru Nanak had been. One of Gobind Singh's writings reads,

> Recognize all mankind as one,
> Whether Hindus or Muslims,
> The same Lord is the creator,
> And nourisher of all:
> Recognize no distinctions between them.
> The monastery and the mosque are the same,
> So is Hindu worship and Muslim prayer.
> Men are all one![32]

30. Mann, *Sikhism*, 39–40; Singh, *Sikhs*, 55–56.
31. Grewal, *Sikhs of the Punjab*, 76.
32. Singh, *Sikhs*, 49–50.

But Gobind Singh also lived a military career in defense of the religion. This martial spirit comes out in his writings as well:

> You are the subduer of kingdoms,
> The destroyer of evil armies.
> You adorn the brave on the battlefield,
> Your arm is unbreakable, your brightness dazzling,
> Your radiance is like the sun's.
> You bestow happiness on the good,
> You terrify the evil, you scatter sinners.
> I seek your protection.
> Hail! Hail to the world's creator,
> I cherish you, the savior of creation,
> Hail to you O Sword![33]

These two excerpts capture some of the mixed experiences of the Sikhs. The former emphasizes the universal inclusion and brotherhood of all humankind into their religion. The latter quote reflects their need to take up the sword, having experienced firsthand persecution and the martyrdom of their gurus.

Finding a home and residence in the city of Anandpur, Gobind Singh defended the city against the Mughal threat of his time. The guru paid dearly and personally for defending the Sikhs. As the Mughals assaulted Anandpur, Guru Gobind Singh's wife Mata Sundri, his mother, and two of his sons were separated from him. His wife escaped, but Wazir Khan ordered the death of his mother and two young sons, and his elder sons were also killed in combat.[34] The great Mughal Aurangzeb, who was so desperate to subdue Gobind Singh, died in 1707. Gobind Singh outlived his rival by scarcely a year.

In 1708 assassins were sent to try to kill Gobind Singh. While the assassins were killed, Gobind Singh himself was mortally wounded in the attempt and would die shortly later. Some sects of Sikhism maintain an ongoing line of gurus, and one sect believes that Gobind Singh did not die on that day but lived on for many more years.

33. Singh, 48.
34. Grewal, *Sikhs of the Punjab*, 79.

Most Sikhs, however, accept that he died in 1708 and was the last of ten authoritative gurus, passing his authority on to the completed Sikh bible, the Guru Granth Sahib.

Sikhs experienced a brief period of autonomy under the powerful leader Maharaja Ranjit Singh. The maharaja had come into possession of the famous Koh-i-Noor diamond before it later became part of the British crown jewels. Ranjit Singh was able to carve out an autonomous territory for the Sikhs that lasted until ten years after his death. He supported the preservation of the holy Sikh bible, which he installed in his palace.[35] After Ranjit Singh died, his empire would be taken apart by the British and the jewel claimed for the crown. The words of the gurus remained alone as a Sikh possession.

Sikh Doctrine

Sikhs are monotheists. They believe in a creator God who is primary and fundamental to the universe. The idea of Ek Onkar conveys the idea of God's oneness and unity, that one must keep in mind the name of God constantly—a notion called Nam Simaran. Sikhs must adhere to the appreciation of God and not let their own pride or self-centeredness get in the way; that pride is called *haumai*. The high monotheism of Sikhism is much like that of Islam, but Sikhs accept that the soul continues its voyage in reincarnation (called *awagaun*) until it overcomes its personal obstacles and achieves unity with God. Some of those obstacles include the five evils of anger, lust, greed, ego (or pride), and attachment.[36] While Hindus have called escape from reincarnation *moksha*, and Jains have called it *kevala*, the Sikhs have used the term *mukti*. When a Sikh attains the realm of truth (*sach khand*), one is able to attain the liberation from reincarnation called *mukti*. There have been many names for God in the Sikh religion. One that conveys well God's highness and eternity is Akal Purakh, the "Timeless Being" or the "One beyond Time."[37] The Sikh Mul Mantar affirms this high God, and the Japji prayer of the Sikhs reminds them of God's ever-pervasive reality.

The essential ethics of Sikhism, or of any religion, may be found in the behaviors they reject. "Countless fools, blinded by ignorance, countless thieves and

35. Singh, *Guru Granth Sahib*, 222–29.
36. Singh, 137.
37. Singh, 6.

embezzlers, countless impose their will by force. Countless cut-throats and ruthless killers. Countless sinners who keep on sinning. Countless liars, wandering on their lies. Countless wretches, eating filth as their ration. Countless slanderers, carrying the weight of their stupid mistakes on their heads."[38] In these few lines, we find injunctions against many of the major things that world religions proscribe: theft, use of force, murder, slander, and lying among them. A Gurkish, or Sikh who is loyal to the words breathed through the guru, would not do any of these things, for committing these sins means one has turned away from God.[39] Hard work, honest living, abstention from intoxicants, and good ethics are vital Sikh values.

Heeding the words of the gurus (the Gurbani) is a way of trying to ensure the correct moral practice. Guru Amar Das wrote, "Blessed is he who gives ear to the Guru, heeding his message of Truth. Only by grace can we come to the Lord, a mystery others ignore. Deprived of God's name we must wander astray; only the Name brings us joy."[40] Meditating on God's name and God's words contained in the Sikh scriptures is paramount.

Most monotheistic religions must confront the idea of predestination. Religions that affirm one high God that knows all often also conclude that God ordains all events and that everything unfolds according to God's plan. For the Sikhs this notion of predestiny is called *hukam*. Muslims have also considered predestiny, and the Protestant John Calvin was famous for his doctrine that there is an elect group who are predestined for salvation but may not know it. If God knows all, God must also know the destiny of our soul. As Guru Gobind Singh once wrote, "All this he knows and all that lies within, reading the deepest secrets of every human heart."[41]

Sikhs have rejected the caste system as forcefully as Buddhists have rejected it. Since the time of the first guru to the last, caste plays no role in the status of an individual. The fifth guru, Arjan, wrote, "What makes you a Brahmin, and I merely a Sudra? If blood runs in my veins does milk flow in yours?"[42] There is not a formal priesthood in Sikhism, but the *gurdwaras*, or "temples," are often under the power of certain families or groups, and control over them has been a source of some

38. Beth Wright and Christopher Partridge, *A Study Companion to World Religions*, 2nd ed. (Minneapolis: Fortress, 2013), 191.
39. McLeod, *Textual Sources*, 76.
40. McLeod, 48.
41. McLeod, 56.
42. Singh, *Sikhs*, 36.

conflict and controversy.[43] Sikhs believe in supporting their religion, that a tenth of one's disposable income should go to the support of the faith.

Every day Sikhs pray and meditate on the name of God, an act called Nam Simaran. A traditional Sikh prayer called the Japji affirms one high, creator God, and it opens, "There is one supreme being, the eternal reality, the creator, without fear and devoid of enmity, immortal, never incarnated, self-existent, known by grace through the true Guru."[44] Sikhs recite the prayer every day.

Since the days of the first Khalsa, the first ritual initiation of five intercaste Sikhs by the guru Gobind Singh, Sikh men will take the name of Singh, meaning "lion," and Sikh women will take the name of Kaur, meaning "princess." Sikhs are not supposed to gamble, drink liquor, or take intoxicants, nor are Sikh men supposed to shave their hair, as a sign of devotion to God. This ritual contrasts sharply with Jain monks, who remove or pluck their hair out, and Buddhist monks, who shave their heads.

Sikhs have repudiated Hindu idols but in other respects have appropriated elements of Hinduism. One Sikh excerpt reads, "The Guru's words is the mystic sound, the voice of the scriptures immanent in all. Shiva, Vishnu, Brahma and Parvati, all are but manifestations of the one divine Guru."[45] Another asserts that Sufis have also been seeking the same wisdom: "Listening to the Word, one comprehends the wisdom of Sufi masters. Listening to the Word, the blind find their eyes opened."[46]

Guru Arjan made clear the Sikhs' relationship to Hinduism and Islam:

> I do not keep the Hindu fasts or [the Muslim fasts during] the month of Ramadan. I serve him, and him alone, who is my ultimate refuge. I believe in one lord, who is also Allah. I have broken off with the Hindu and the Turk. I do not go to Hajj or worship at Hindu pilgrimage places. I serve only him and no other. I offer neither Hindu worship (*puja*) nor Muslim prayers (*namaz*). Holding the only formless one in my heart, I worship him there. We are neither Hindu nor Muslim. My body and soul belong to the one

43. Grewal, *Sikhs of the Punjab*, 159.
44. Singh, *Guru Granth Sahib*, 91.
45. McLeod, *Textual Sources*, 87.
46. McLeod, 88.

> who is called Allah and Ram. Kabir has uttered the truth; meeting with Guru and pir I have met the lord.[47]

In the span of just five centuries, Sikhism has established itself as a significant world religion. It has done so walking a fine line between two major world religions. Having a lineage of gurus, a sacred text, temples, and accompanying rituals, it has come to stay in the religious landscape of India and the world.

Mainstream Sikhs support the idea that there were ten gurus, from Nanak to Gobind Singh, that they received the divine words and expressed it in their bible, the Guru Granth Sahib (or Adi Granth). Sikhs affirm one creator God whose name and importance must be remembered. They accept not only the *Guru Granth* as their text but also the *Guru Panth*, or the community of Sikhs created by the initial Khalsa by Gobind Singh. Known as the twin doctrines (of the text *Granth* and community *Panth*), many Sikhs feel bound by them.[48]

There have been divisions, offshoots, and controversies in Sikhism. The Nirankaris and Namdharis have emerged, among others, as sects within Sikhism. The Nirankaris wanted to preserve the integrity of the Sikh community and guard against practices that seemed more oriented toward Hinduism. Founded by Baba Dayal, the Nirankaris have continued a leadership of gurus but still recognize the authority of the original ten. The Namdharis have a different view: that the lines of gurus did not really end with the original ten. Thinking that Guru Gobind Singh did not die in 1708 but went into brief seclusion and continued to live until 1812 (which would have made him 137 years old), they believe he passed his authority to an eleventh guru, Balak Singh of Hazro. For Namdharis the line of gurus didn't end and continues until this day.[49] The ascetic order of the Udasis (also known as the Mahants) has already been mentioned, and yet other perspectives on Sikhism exist. Pashaura Singh once counted seven significant schools of Sikhism.[50]

In response to pressures on their community, Sikhs have desired to restore and preserve the integrity of the community. The Singh Sabha and Akali Dal were organizations and movements that emerged in this way. It can be argued that Sikhs

47. Singh, *Guru Granth Sahib*, 174.
48. McLeod, *Textual Sources*, chap. 1.
49. McLeod, 122–27.
50. Singh, *Guru Granth Sahib*, chap. 8.

did not fare very well at the moment of partition, when India and Pakistan were sundered in two. Their homeland of the Punjab was also divided, they received no sanctuary state of their own, and this added political pressure to the religious incentives that already existed to preserve themselves.

Sikhism and the Politics of Partition

At the time of India's partition, the Sikh city Amritsar fell on the Indian side of the border. No Sikh state was created, but the desire to possess a land of their own appealed to many Sikhs. V. S. Bhatti introduced the idea of a sanctuary state called Khalistan (land of the pure) as early as the 1940s.[51] Sikhs were a much smaller community than either Hindus or Muslims, and no state called Khalistan was ever created. When partition happened and communal rioting ensued, many Sikhs died in the violent aftermath. The romantic, historically inspired movie *Partition* offers one perspective on that tragedy.

The idea for an independent state for the Sikhs did not die during the partition, however. It was kept alive and succinctly expressed decades later in the Anandpur Resolution of 1973, which claimed that at partition, Sikhs had been bullied into joining the union of India. The Sikh organization called the Akali Dal was instrumental in passing this resolution, and it caught the imagination of many who longed for independence. It became the foundation of the Khalistan movement to realize an autonomous region for the Sikhs.[52]

Those who supported the Anandpur Resolution and a separate state called Khalistan were from a variety of backgrounds, intending to support the Sikh community. They argued that if Muslims had been allowed a sanctuary to safeguard themselves against a Hindu majority, Sikhs should be allowed a similar opportunity in Khalistan. From the Sikh point of view, it seems fair and logical, but what may seem fair or logical is not inevitably what becomes a reality in politics. Radicals make political waves, and conservative leaders try to respond; disagreement and conflict are basic to politics.

Jarnail Singh Bhindranwale was a militant who supported the idea of a *dharamyudh*, or "holy war," in support of creating a Sikh state of Khalistan. Bhindranwale

51. Grewal, *Sikhs of the Punjab*, 172.
52. Grewal, 212.

had been a suspect in violent murders, and in the summer of 1984, he and a few thousand other armed militants lodged themselves within the holy precincts of Amritsar, ready for a fight. Their violent threat put the Punjab region on edge and Indian politicians on sharp notice; a crisis would ensue.

The idea of an independent Khalistan, though perhaps a good one, might be difficult to implement in that region. Even if it were not done with the threat of force, as Bhindranwale used, it would require carving out a territory on the boundary of two nuclear-armed states, India and Pakistan, who have fought wars over that border. Getting a mutual concession of both states to a third party, the Sikhs, on this explosive boundary is a process that is fraught with great difficulties from the outset.

The prime minister of India at the time, Indira Gandhi, was facing a difficult policy choice of how to engage Bhindranwale and his militants. She chose to use force, and on June 4, 1984, launched "Operation Bluestar," in which the Indian military overwhelmed and killed Bhindranwale and his militia. There were seven hundred soldiers killed and five thousand other casualties, and several sacred Sikh sites were damaged, the Akal Takht in particular. The operation did put an end to the immediate crisis. India offered to repair the damage done to the sacred precincts. Many Sikhs were outraged.[53]

Two of Indira Gandhi's personal bodyguards, Beant and Satwant Singh, were Sikhs. Indira Gandhi expressed complete confidence in them, affirming that "India is secular."[54] Sadly, this confidence was misplaced, and on October 31, 1984, her protectors became assassins, gunning down the beloved prime minister. One assassin was killed, and the other was captured and would later be executed. Rioting ensued, and thousands of Sikhs were killed in vengeance for the murder of Indira Gandhi. It left a bitter memory between Sikhs and Hindus and was truly tragic. Given this, it is remarkable that since the assassination, a Sikh prime minister, Manmohan Singh, has served in that political office as a Congress Party leader from 2004 to 2014. That the member of a religious minority, which had been embroiled in the assassination of a beloved prime minister, could also fulfill that office is also

53. Grewal, chap. 10.
54. Ramachandra Guha, *India after Gandhi: The History of the World's Largest Democracy* (New York: Harper Perennial, 2007), 565.

a promising sign that the forces of political forgiveness and reconciliation are still alive in Indian politics.

What Fits?

The Sikhs believe in Nam Simaran, the constant memory of God's exalted reality. To forget God, to neglect God's wishes, is to fall away from *sach khand*, which is God's realm of truth. If these basic ideas were to be translated into other religions, a Jew, a Christian, or a Muslim would probably agree with them. Either God or Allah should be respected and neither forgotten nor neglected. The ideal of exalting one God is an element of Sikhism that is reflected by other faiths as well.

Yet here is where the rigors of logic apply with some difficulty. Someone who is not a Sikh must ask, Is *their* scripture correct? Is it general devotion to a deity that matters or proper dedication to the one true expression of divine truth? One could affirm and champion one's own view of God, whatever it may be (Christian, Muslim, Jewish, atheist, or another), but does one negate and demean the culture and view of the other? What price do we pay for certainty? Especially when the world is so full of competing views and asserted facts, a humble spirit and mind back away from absolute claims in order to avoid demeaning or negating the authenticity, *the humanity*, and the potential benefit of another person's religion. Such a spirit does not overrate its own wisdom. Such a mind is able to see oneself in the customs, traditions, and beliefs of others and conclude that greater community and greater peace is possible. Universalism, in whatever faith it is held, chooses the love and unity of humankind over the affirmation of an infallible, isolated perspective. It is willing to sacrifice a strident certainty for the hope of a more encompassing truth.

No perspective is perfect, and having many different, competing ones out there may instruct us further on how to assemble the puzzle of life. Universalism, while it may seem good to some, to others might undermine that complete faithfulness, the Nam Simaran, which Sikhism maintains as central. When a Muslim is kneeling, submitting to God in prayer, does he doubt Allah? Does he think of Buddhism? Certainly no more than a Buddhist thinks of the Kaaba or Allah when meditating. When a Jew is touching the mezuzah on the door, does he think of Sikhism? Universalism, a view of what is binding and true in *all religions and perspectives*, requires thinking "outside the box" and in a manner that must be admitted to risk undermining the felt authenticity of religion itself. Simply put, seeking what is common to all religions may cause some doubt about what is ultimate and true in each particular religion. Doubt, or the capacity to doubt, might lead to a broader perspective of truth, but it might also lead to being consumed by many endless doubts. This perhaps is where Nam Simaran and the teaching that "there is neither Hindu nor Muslim" might help us. Perhaps, with hope, we are all indeed the children of the God we address by different names. With the confidence that God calls to us all in separate ways, we can join hands together.

What Doesn't Fit?

We must see by now how the abstract principles of a given faith might be compatible, in loose form, with those of another religion but specific rituals and beliefs are not. These unique particulars give religions a great deal of their force but may also render them incompatible with each other. Sikhs believe in both reincarnation and God. Buddhists agree with the former but disagree about the latter. Christians, Jews, and Muslims agree about there being a God but not about reincarnation, nor about many of the particulars of the Sikh faith. The *langar*, or "community meal," of Sikhs is a wonderful idea, but could it substitute for the communion of Christianity or the Passover of Jews? Certainly not for either Christian or Jew.

Sikhism has challenged the ideas of God becoming incarnate. The incarnation of Vishnu as Krishna and Rama would seem to be in question. What, however, about the Christian belief of God incarnate in Jesus? Here Muslims or Jews might go along with the Sikh view, but a Christian would probably dissent. Universalist Sikhs see God or the sacred in all religions. The Sikh Baba Virsa Singh was once quoted,

> From childhood, I kept questioning God, "In order to love Jesus, must one become a Christian, or just love?" He told me "It is not necessary to become a Christian. It is necessary to love him." I asked "To believe in Moses, does one have to observe any special discipline or just love?" The divine command came "Only love." I asked "Does one have to become a Muslim in order to please Muhammad or only love?" He said "One must love." "To believe in Buddha, must one become a monk or a Buddhist?" He replied "No. To believe in Buddha is to love." God said "I created human beings.

> Afterward, human beings created sectarian religions. But I created only human beings, not religions."[55]

The assertion of our common humanity bonded by our capacity to love is welcoming, and I have always loved this quotation for this reason. Hopefully, we are all children of God bound and saved by things as simple as love. There is also a too-pliant flexibility in this quote, however, a tendency to sweep important and conflicting facts and details under the rug. When religions directly assert conflicting ideas, their legitimacy can seem challenged. But might God have spoken to different cultures in languages and ideas amendable to their needs? Does that difference benefit and challenge our own understanding? The striking differences in religion force us to rethink the puzzle of life, hopefully in ways that make us better. The picture puzzle of religion will never be finished or fully clear, but it may be sufficiently clear enough to affirm our common bonds and humanity.

55. Fisher, *Living Religions*, 426.

11 East Asian Religions

Summary of East Asian Religions

Far more religions have existed than can be treated comprehensively in one textbook. If one tried, the result would be large and unwieldy. And yet, I must say something of the religions of East Asia: Confucianism, Daoism, and Shinto. Some scholars see Confucianism not as a religion but instead as a philosophy of life. I tend to agree. Confucius introduced no new religion, no new deity or metaphysic. Daoism is more mystical and abstract. Both of these emerge in ancient China and find homes elsewhere in Asia, becoming popular and enduring teachings. Shinto emerged in Japan. We will look at each in turn and then ask at the end what they might agree upon and what might keep them apart.

Confucianism

Is Confucianism really a religion? In Chinese tradition, *chia* is the name for a school of philosophical thinking, while *chiao* indicates a religious teaching.[1] Whether Confucianism is, properly speaking, a philosophy (*chia*) or a fuller religious teaching (*chiao*), Confucianism makes use of religious ideas that preceded it. Confucius did not reject religion, but neither did he intend to create a new one. He organized Chinese ways of thinking into a system of social and moral thought that he believed would preserve and protect civilization. Although not so successful in his own lifetime, Confucius's thought became so important to Chinese civilization afterward that it can be revered like a religion, whether it properly can be called one or not.

Confucius lived from 551 to 479 BCE. He was known as "Master Kung" or "Kung Fu Tzu." As a young man, Confucius loved learning and worked at various jobs. He wanted nothing more than to be a political court advisor, where his thought could really matter. He worked as a keeper of granaries for a while and even secured a

1. Partridge and Dowley, *Introduction to World Religions*, 395–96.

government post to the local lord of the State of Lu in east central China. There he briefly put his political ideas into practice, but rivals were able to distract the lord of the State of Lu with dancing girls and worldly delights, things trivial and unimportant to Confucius. A political lord or master should be an exemplar of morality, the classic "Confucian gentleman," who would not have idle time to waste. Confucius and his master did not see eye to eye, and Confucius resigned from the only political job he ever had.[2]

He tried for many years to find employment elsewhere and to get his ideas recognized. While he did not find success in politics, he became recognized as a teacher. His students found his thought compelling, and through their dedication and devotion, organized parts of his writings, the *Analects of Confucius*.[3] When Confucius died, his thought had not yet entered into the mainstream of Chinese civilization, but that would soon change.

In Confucius's day, the Zhou (Chou) dynasty was beginning to fall apart. Fighting and political chaos threatened the foundations of the Zhou civilization. Feudal landlords were battling each other in a ruthless game of ambition and power seeking. This time would come to be known as the period of Warring States, when the power of the Chinese Zhou dynasty finally collapsed and the short-lived Qin dynasty replaced it. Around the time of the Qin dynasty, construction began on the Great Wall of China. The wall exemplifies the feeling of danger and insecurity that pervaded the times. Walls are normally built only in response to a grave need. The danger of invasion and the feeling of political insecurity were real.

The Great Wall of China is a remarkable achievement, but it is still a wall. Left unprotected, walls are conquered by ladders. Soldiers need to police the walls and watch out for invaders. Those soldiers need training and discipline. They must have weapons and know how to use them. More than brick and mortar, sword and shield were needed to keep China intact and safe. Confucius understood this. Moral discipline, hard work, honor, and commitment are required of soldiers, masons, generals, farmers. All of Chinese civilization needed to work together to stay strong. Confucius believed his thought was the invisible moral brick and mortar of human minds that could bind a sagging order together.

2. Jennifer Oldstone-Moore, *Confucianism* (New York: Oxford University Press, 2002), 14.
3. Ames and Rosemont, *Analects of Confucius*, 7–8.

Filial piety, the Confucian hierarchy known as *xiao*, is an integral part of this order and social harmony. There are five basic relationships in the hierarchy that, if practiced dutifully and with respect and honor, were supposed to unite society:

1. *Family*: kindness of father for loyalty of son
2. *Siblings*: grace of older brother for respect of younger
3. *Gender*: right conduct of husband for obedience of wife
4. *Social*: humanity of older friend for deference from younger
5. *Political*: benevolence of ruler for loyalty of subjects

In a nutshell, "The ruler must rule, the minister minister, the father father, and the son son."[4] Every minster, father, and son had to fulfill his role with moral integrity. What this meant is that while deference was owed to an authority, usually to elders, males, and heads of family or state, this deference was not completely unqualified. Benevolent reciprocal treatment, the silver rule of "do not impose on others what you yourself do not want," was required.[5] This reciprocity was called *shu*. According to Confucian rules of etiquette, proper behavior means respecting the humanity in all peers above and below you and trying to provide what society expects of you to the best of your ability. The appreciation of the humanity of the other, an idea called *jen* (also written *ren*), is a part of this. If deference was expected, so was proper moral behavior.

Famously, Confucius also said that "the excellence of the exemplary person is the wind, while that of the petty person is the grass. As the wind blows, the grass is sure to bend."[6] It is important to understand, however, that the exemplary person was the leader trying to be a true Confucian gentleman, a *junzi*. This is a person who understands and respects humanity (*jen*). That person cannot command any respect if this is not truly understood or if proper action is not taken. The wind that blows is the earned respect of a leader acting properly or rightfully. That wind will not blow, and the grass (meaning the people serving the leader) will not bend if action is arbitrary, authoritarian, or immoral. Only when the humanity of the other is understood and respected and the *shu*, or the silver rule, obeyed

4. Ames and Rosemont, 156.
5. Ames and Rosemont, 189.
6. Ames and Rosemont, 158.

will the social and moral winds blow and the deference of the people naturally bend to their leadership.

When the Zhou dynasty finally collapsed, a brutal and short-lived Qin dynasty replaced it. Confucian texts were ordered to be destroyed; Confucian scholars were in grave peril. Had not the brutality of the Qin undermined its own authority, Confucianism might have been exterminated, but this is exactly what Confucius had predicted. A brutal, authoritarian leader will not command the hearts and loyalty of men or women. The Qin dynasty lasted only from 221 to 206 BCE.

Mencius (372–289 BCE) was known as the second Confucian sage. He had the same prediction as Confucius: "When one by force subdues men, they do not submit to him in heart. They submit because their strength is not adequate to resist. When one subdues men by virtue, in their hearts' core they are pleased and sincerely submit."[7] Mencius believed that human nature was essentially good: "Human nature is good just as water seeks low ground. There is no man who is not good; there is no water that does not flow downwards."[8] He thought there was an essential moral energy, or qi, that the human heart could direct. Confucian discipline was the channel to guide this spiritual qi. Unleash the waters of human benevolence in a trained and disciplined way and social life would be improved.

The third Confucian scholar, Hsun Tzu (Xunzi), lived around 300 to 230 BCE. He believed that Confucian discipline was needed, but for reasons different from those of Mencius. Hsun Tzu had a pessimistic view of human nature. He wrote, "Human nature is evil; any good in humans is acquired by conscious exertion. Now the nature of man is such that he is born with a love of profit. Following the nature will cause its aggressiveness and greedy tendencies to grow and courtesy and deference to disappear."[9] Moral character had to be acquired by consistent study and practice. If left without the dam of Confucian ethical discipline, the selfish and untamed waters of human nature would be destructive, in Hsun Tzu's view.

After surviving the Qin dynasty, Confucian teachings were revived during the Han dynasty (202 BCE–220 CE). Master Kung Fu Tzu would not know that his teachings would become so widely acclaimed, but they did. From 1313 to 1905 CE, Confucianism was part of the required civil service exams in China that were

7. Wright and Partridge, *Study Companion*, 99.
8. James Fieser and John Powers, *Scriptures of the East* (New York: McGraw Hill, 2004), 164.
9. Fieser and Powers, 165.

necessary for getting a government post.[10] For centuries before that, it had also been practiced and embraced. A man who in his own fleeting life span was largely spurned later flourished in China!

As with many religious traditions, competing schools of thinking exist in Confucianism. Mo-tzu (470–391 BCE) founded a school of thinking known as Mohism. While he endorsed Tien Ming, or the idea of the "Mandate of Heaven" that was needed for imperial rule, Mo-tzu did not approve of the Confucian hierarchy. His belief was more egalitarian. He was concerned with war and peace. Mo-tzu was likely a craftsman who was also part of an order of professional soldiers. His belief was the opposite of Einstein's famous maxim that "you cannot simultaneously prepare for and prevent war." Mo-tzu argued that by being most prepared to fight, you would be able to deter aggression. Mo-tzu did not believe you *should* fight. You should have arms but be reticent to use them. War was neither desirable nor good. The Chinese Dao De Jing states this mindset most beautifully: "Weapons are the tools of violence; all decent men detest them. Weapons are the tools of fear; a decent man will avoid them except in the direst necessity and, if compelled, will use them with the utmost restraint."[11] These are not the words of Mo-tzu, but they echo his attitude toward the just use of force: careful, measured acceptance.

Han Fei Zi (280–233 BCE) was another rival thinker in a school named *legalism*. The name seems odd, for it espoused the harsh application of legal force as a way to ensure absolute obedience. Treachery and deceit were the constant concern. As Han Fei Zi once expressed, "Prepare as you may against those who hate you, calamity will come to you from those you love."[12] Yet the harsh pessimism and the brutality that the Qin dynasty espoused led to a counterrebellion and the demise of the Qin. When the Han dynasty replaced it, it sought the Tien Ming, or the "Mandate of Heaven," and so chose the more moderate Confucian doctrine that the Qin had forcibly set aside.

Confucianism accepted that religious ideas and practices were conducive to a good and orderly state. Confucianism is a hierarchical system dependent on a responsible and benevolent chain of authority, and what could be a higher authority

10. Diané Collinson, Kathryn Plant, and Robert Wilkinson, *Fifty Eastern Thinkers* (New York: Routledge, 2000), 217.
11. Lao Tzu, *Tao Te Ching*, trans. Stephen Mitchell (New York: Harper Perennial, 2006), 31.
12. Collinson, Plant, and Wilkinson, *Fifty Eastern Thinkers*, 255.

than God? There have been many deities and views of the divine in Chinese history, and as more a philosophy than a religion, Confucianism deferred to these traditional beliefs, embracing them as part of a heavenly sanctioned order. If the authorities ceased to reflect the humanity and benevolence expected of them, they might lose their respect (*te*) or the authoritative command and sway that they held over the people.

Daoism

China has its fair share of deities. Nu Wa was the goddess figure who is said to have first molded human beings of earth. Taiyi was the name of the high God at one time, and the Yellow Emperor was a grand figure, one of five great emperors, and said to have existed thousands of years ago. Legend says he played a founding role in Chinese civilization. At the end of his great reign, he ascended into the heavens on the back of a dragon and became divinized.[13] But the central idea of the Dao is very different from these other notions of the gods. Daoism does not personify the God, does not give it a human face. Instead of God, Daoism speaks abstractly about a great impersonal force that directs the cosmos and is the center of all.

Personification and anthropomorphizing are all common traits of religion. On the one hand, it may seem absurd to personify God, to say God is an old guy with a beard sitting on a throne. That delimits the divine to its conventional and worldly aspects. Humans tend to personify God so we can relate to God. Our image of the divine is not the ultimate—it is the penultimate, as Joseph Campbell would say; it is the nearest and next best thing we can imagine.[14] Hans Küng once observed that "the term 'person' also is merely a cipher for God"—that is, a stand-in for what we cannot fully know.[15] The God of our imagination may not actually be God in full view but a reflection of the part revealed to us so that we can understand. One cannot converse with or relate to a brick wall, but one can relate to and converse with a person.

Daoism, however, has avoided all of this. God is not the center; the Dao (also written Tao) is the center of all things:

13. Julia Ching, *Chinese Religions* (New York: Orbis Books, 2005), 23–25.
14. Joseph Campbell, *The Hero with a Thousand Faces* (Novato, CA: New World Library, 2008), 222.
15. Jammer, *Einstein and Religion*, 113.

Man follows the earth.
Earth follows the universe,
The universe follows the Tao,
The Tao follows only itself.[16]

This cosmic center cannot be fully understood. The Dao De Jing explains this at the very beginning of its text: "That Tao that can be told is not the eternal Tao. The name that can be named is not the eternal Name. The unnamable is eternally real. Naming is the origin of all particular things."[17] Whatever image we have of the Dao, it is not the Dao as it is in its perfection and totality.

Daoism asserts that this pervasive cosmic force has both yin and yang aspects, which are opposite and complementary. Neither is stronger or better than the other, and both are absolutely essential to life. The yin aspect of the Dao is associated with things dark, receptive, cool, and female. The yang aspect of the Dao is bright, assertive, hot, and male. Yin and yang, dark and bright, cool and hot, these are the opposites of the known universe. They are dualities by which we come to know and appreciate things through their distinctness from each other. One might imagine that good and evil could be part of this duality, but neither good nor evil can be assigned to yin or yang. The Dao suggests a sacred and natural world that exists beyond these human distinctions.

Who created Daoism? What is its origin? Some have ascribed its founding to Lao Tzu. We do not have much concrete information on Lao Tzu, who may have been a Chinese scholar or archivist sometime between the third and sixth centuries BCE. There is even a tale of Confucius and Lao Tzu meeting and swapping wisdom, but it would be difficult to substantiate this story with other sources. Lao Tzu is said to be the traditional author of the Dao De Jing (Tao Te Ching), which translates to "The Way and Its Power." Before he went into retirement, legend says, a border guard asked him for his wisdom, and he left behind the short but memorable Dao De Jing. For Daoists like Lao Tzu, understanding the sacred Dao was like trying to discern the immense powers behind the universe that direct all things, man, the natural world, the earth, even the cosmos. The Dao De Jing reads, "There was something formless and perfect before the universe was born. It is serene. Empty. Solitary.

16. Tzu, *Tao Te Ching*, chap. 25.
17. Tzu, chap. 1.

Unchanging. Infinite. Eternally present. It is the mother of the universe. For lack of a better name, I call it the Tao."[18] When we personalize the sacred, we give it a face and call it a god or goddess. Daoism does the opposite, assuming the highest power is beyond our conception. Names given to it are just conventional labels.

While some have argued that Lao Tzu is the founder of Daoism, I have come to understand the matter differently. Lao Tzu is an important contributor to the Daoist tradition but not its founder. Daoism comprises a collection of teachings and sayings from Chinese culture, and the Dao De Jing should be seen as a confluence into which many streams flow but not as the initial or only source of the river.

Water is an important concept in Daoism. It describes the power and flux of the Dao. The Dao De Jing tells us, "Nothing in the world is softer and weaker than water but nothing is superior in overcoming the hard and strong; weakness overcomes strength and softness overcomes hardness. Everyone knows this, and no one practices it."[19] Rock is a traditionally yang-like or hard substance, yet running water erodes it and washes it away over the course of time. Wind too is a force very yin-like but has great powers of erosion and also of destruction with tornadoes and hurricanes. What is yin-like can become yang-like, and the two interpenetrate and are not fully distinct from each other. There is a mysterious and deep connection, a mutual interdependence and flow of energy, influence, and power.

Knowing this great cosmic flow, understanding the interpenetration and the interdependence of both yin and yang, is essential to the idea of *wu wei*, which has been variously translated as "actionless action, or non-action," "pure effectiveness," "uncontrived action," or even "non-intervention."[20] Of these the terms, the ones that best fit my understanding of *wu wei* are "pure effectiveness" and "uncontrived action." The Daoist master who has studied and fully appreciated the Dao will not seek to manipulate it but advantageously receive it. This means getting the most done without overexertion because one has fully understood a phenomenon in all its aspects and knows best how to "go with the flow." One cannot control the currents of the ocean or the winds of the seas, but if one is an experienced sailor and navigator, one can plot a course to best use them to one's advantage to sail from

18. Tzu, chap. 25.
19. Fieser and Powers, *Scriptures of the East*, 186.
20. First definition from Fisher, *Living Religions*, 183; second from Tzu, *Tao Te Ching*, vii–x; third from Partridge and Dowley, *Introduction to World Religions*, 270; and fourth from Collinson, Plant, and Wilkinson, *Fifty Eastern Thinkers*, 243.

one point to another. The expert sailor gets the most accomplished while doing the least, while the novice gets frustrated, upset, and stuck in the windless doldrums.

The Dao is said to have a tangible energy that interpenetrates life. This energy is called qi, or "chi" in the Chinese conception. Mencius believed that this qi, or chi, had a formative aspect around the human heart and that the benevolent person could direct its energies for good. Hence Confucianism and Daoism do not remain wholly independent. Confucianism was more morally and socially oriented, while Daoism was more mystical and cosmic. Indeed, one did not have to be either a Confucianist or a Daoist; one could be both in Chinese culture. Qi, or chi, was responsive to wisdom benevolently directed.

The flow of qi, or chi, has been explored in countless different ways in Chinese culture. In the study of acupuncture, energy fields inherent to the human body are tapped into and subtly manipulated for better health. Tai chi chuan is a fluid Chinese exercise that is said to bring about better health and vigor. This energy is not limited to the human body but said to exist in the earth itself, in the flow of energy through rocks, through streams, and even in buildings and living spaces. This last aspect has been known as feng shui, an ancient art thought to bring greater harmony to the energy of our living space and the world around us. More than just ergonomics or the convenience, feng shui adherents maintain that this energy makes tangible and real differences in our lives.

There was also a field of Daoism that explored the possibility of longer life, even immortality. The pursuit of elixirs to prolong life or cheat death was widely practiced in China. One legend records how Master Wei Po Yang may have unexpectedly found it, but if he did, the recipe is lost to history.[21] The intriguing figure of Chuang Tzu (369–286 BCE) may have also been interested in the mystical and supernatural powers that the study of the Dao was reported to offer. The opposite of Confucius in many regards, Chuang Tzu spurned the post of a political advisor and craved nothing more than his own solitude and the power of connection with the Dao.[22]

The Dao is popularly reflected in the *Star Wars* movies. George Lucas's concept of the Force reflects the all-pervasive idea of qi, or chi. His Jedi, like the Daoist master, cannot manipulate the Force but must accept it and let it flow through them. They get the most done when they receive the force peacefully, although the

21. Ching, *Chinese Religions*, 107.
22. Collinson, Plant, and Wilkinson, *Fifty Eastern Thinkers*, 249–50.

practitioners of the dark side mistakenly try to manipulate it. The idea of the Force is not identical to that of Daoism, because the light and dark aspects of yang and yin in the Dao are not as adversarial and antagonistic as the Force in *Star Wars*. In Daoism there seems to be an idea of an ultimate force or energy that transcends (but includes perhaps in some way) our conventional ideas of good and evil. There is no face of this great force, or Dao. It is timeless, eternal, but real.

Shinto

Shinto is one of many religious influences in Japan. Buddhism has also played a major role, but only Shinto is indigenous. Shinto is a faith rooted in nature. It is a pantheistic faith that embraces the spirit of wilderness. Shrines and sacred places are located throughout Japan, nestled in places believed to have a strong connection to native spirits called *kami* and to the landscape itself. Mount Fuji, the famous volcano of Japan, is also imbued with the sacred spirits of the kami. The central point in Shinto is to maintain a harmonious relationship with the naturally occurring spirits, an auspicious and good relationship that is called *kannagara*. So long as this positive state of kannagara is maintained, it bodes well for the Shinto believer, but if there is any corruption, evil, or disharmony that disrupts that state, one can fall into a state of impurity called *tsumi*. The negative and dangerous spirit called *oni*, or *obake*, may plague the self.

To restore purity and the state of kannagara, one has a number of options: donning a white robe, or kimono, bathing in a rapidly flowing waterfall while chanting and clapping one's hands are said to dispel negative energy. Positive energy, or *ki*, rains down over the shoulders, washing away the negative tsumi.[23] This ritual of waterfall immersion is called the *misogi* and is a popular Shinto practice. During a business opening or wedding ceremony, a Shinto priest may perform a blessing with a ritual wooden rod called *oharai*. Mobile Shinto shrines may be paraded around an area to dispel negative spirits. This rite is called the *mikoshi*. Whether by ritual waterfall, the *misogi*; the blessing of a Shinto priest with a rod, the *oharai*; or the mobile Shinto shrine called the *mikoshi*, the point is to restore and maintain that positive energy and the auspicious relationship with the spirits, or kannagara.[24]

23. Thomas P. Kasulis, *Shinto: The Way Home* (Honolulu: University of Hawaii Press, 2004), 50–52.
24. C. Scott Littleton, *Shinto* (New York: Oxford University Press, 2002), 23–27.

The name of the religion, *Shinto*, refers to the "way of the kami," seeking always a good relationship with the spirits.[25]

There are many sacred areas in Japan where the presence of the kami is thought to be especially strong. Like a sanctuary in nature, they are often demarcated by *torii*, or Shinto red gates, to show the presence of the sacred refuge. The *torii* are entered and a ritual ablution is often performed before a meditative experience of orientation. Interrupting the routines of ordinary life to connect with a greater force or meaning about us is a common aspect of most religions. Whether it is a break for prayer or meditation, there is a need to get oriented. To "tie us back" to the sacred world around us. This is also true of the Shinto sanctuaries demarcated by the *torii*.

Shinto is not a heavily moralistic religion, though the Japanese do have a rich sense of morality. Buddhism and Confucianism have also been an influence and have contributed to the cultural ethos of the people. There is in Shinto a link between the sacred past and the Japanese emperor: Amaterasu was believed to have a divine connection to Japan's imperial ancestry.

Amaterasu is the goddess of sun, although she is not the first kami, or "divine spirit," of the Japanese pantheon. Long before Amaterasu, the first creator God or spirit was called (at least by one name) Amenominakanushi. Amenominakanushi created the cosmos, the world, and two of the most important and earliest Shinto spirits, Izanagi and Izanami. Izanagi was male and Izanami was female, and in their union, they gave birth to many of the divine kami of the Shinto pantheon. They also took a jeweled spear and, standing atop a rainbow bridge, stirred the ancient waters of earth until out of the bubbles and froth the islands of Japan were formed. They were cocreators of the Japanese nation and culture.[26]

A tragedy befell Izanagi and Izanami. During the birth of fire deity Kagutsuchi, Izanami caught fire and died, going to the realm of *yomi*, a place of filth and decay. Stricken with grief, Izanagi determined to go into the afterworld to rescue his beloved Izanami, but when he arrived, she did not recognize him and assaulted him. Besmeared by the corruption of death but surviving the assault, Izanagi fled in failure and purified himself by bathing. The ritual of bathing is important for Shinto, as it is for many other religions. In the act of purifying himself, Izanagi

25. Hori Ichiro et al., eds., *Japanese Religion: A Survey by the Agency for Cultural Affairs* (New York: Kodansha, 1972), 13.
26. Littleton, *Shinto*, 23–24.

miraculously gave birth to three deities. The goddess of sun Amaterasu sprang from his left eye. The moon god Tsukiyomi emerged from his right eye, and the temperamental storm god Susanoo leaped from his nose. It is one of the most unusual narratives, but stories of gods and goddesses asexually conceived and born are not rare in religion.

Bereaved for his lost wife, Izanagi retired from the heavens and offered the place of the exalted queen of the kami to his daughter Amaterasu. As the sun goddess, she became the most important of the Japanese kami, with a divine connection to them and to the emperor. Not satisfied with this arrangement, however, and upset with his lot as the god of storms, her brother Susanoo stormed into the heavens and demanded that Amaterasu share rulership with him, just as their parents Izanagi and Izanami had once done. Defiling her heavens, and even killing some of her servants, his boorish behavior was an insult, and Amaterasu fled to a cave to escape Susanoo's temper tantrum. Of course, as the goddess of sun, this means that the world was then submerged into eclipse, and her servant kami had to coax her back out with a mirror and a sacred rope called a *shimenawa*. Successful in doing so, the earth then returned to sunlight.

The hapless Susanoo was fined a thousand tables of food for his shameful behavior, and he embarked on a heroic quest to redeem himself. Encountering a man and woman who were about to lose their last daughter as a tribute to an eight-tailed and eight-headed dragon, they agreed that if Susanoo rescued their daughter from being consumed by the dragon, she would be betrothed to Susanoo. Accepting the deal, Susanoo cleverly got the dragon drunk on rice wine, enabling Susanoo to take advantage. Slaying the dragon, he recovered the sacred sword Kusanagi from its entrails and won the hand of the daughter in marriage.[27]

The *Kojiki* and the *Nihon Shoki* are two of the oldest texts in Japan, which speak about the exploits of the kami of the Japanese pantheon. Both date from the eighth century CE and appear to be commissioned not only to tell of the heroic exploits of these Shinto deities but also to bolster their connection to the imperial throne. Emperor Tenmu is said to have supported them, and Empress Genmei continued that support. After elaborating on the age of the gods, the texts tell the story of

27. Robert Borgen and Marian Ury, "Readable Japanese Mythology: Selections from Nihon Shoki and Kojiki," *Journal of the Association of Teachers of Japanese* 24, no. 1 (April 1990): 61–97. See also Fieser and Powers, *Scriptures of the East*, 209–14.

humanity, including the story of Emperor Jimmu in the sixth through seventh centuries BCE. In this mythology, Japan is known as a Shinkoku, a divine nation that is exalted and special.[28]

Religious texts and traditions present us with a sacred view of the world about us. They present a reason and a purpose to our being here. The essence of religious myths gives human beings a meaningful place and standing in the world about us, a metaphysical and moral map of our lives. We know where we are, why we are here, and where we are going. There is of course a fundamental tension here with modern science. Science has discovered many wonders in our bodies and our universe but not a definite reason for our being here. The method and goals of science and religion are not identical. Science looks for objective facts and verifiable theories. Religion looks for meaning and morality. There is an important, sometimes complementary, sometimes oppositional, role between the two.

In the Shinto tradition, we also see variation. The Shinto scholar Motoori Norinaga (1730–1801) viewed the afterworld of *yomi* as a bad place, much like the grim place that Izanami died and went to. The Shinto scholar Hirata Atsutane (1776–1843), however, had a much different perception, seeing this world as a testing ground for the afterlife, with a heaven awaiting us if we passed the test. Atsutane had studied Norinaga's thought, but he had also been exposed to the work of Christian missionaries and been influenced by their views. He believed in heaven (*ten*), earth (*tsuchi*), and afterlife (*yomi*); should we pass the test of earth, a fine paradise of heaven awaits.[29] This hope and expectation are, as we have seen, not uncommon.

What Fits?

The hope of a life to come is a major aspect that many world religions share. If it is not an afterlife, it is a release from reincarnation and the earthly travails that accompany it. Asian religions like Shinto and Buddhism have expressed elements of this hope. The desire to have a continuance of life—an ongoing connection with loved ones gone—seems, to me, a healthy and functional feature of the human

28. John S. Brownlee, *Political Thought in Japanese Historical Writing* (Waterloo: Wilfrid Laurier University Press, 1991), 15–19.
29. Richard Devine, "Hirata Atsutane and Christian Sources," *Monumenta Nipponica* 36, no. 1 (Spring 1981): 37–54.

mind. We do not need to argue it is only for those who fear death, for everyone fears death just as much as they want to cling to life. If some have seen religion as a crutch for the fearful who wish to escape death, one might also turn the same criticism against the morbidity of a pessimism that dismisses the afterlife without firm proof. Hope is a resource, a gift to be prized just as much as critical reason is a tool needed to keep it from going astray.

Rudolf Otto (1869–1937) once wrote that "if one subjects everything to reason our religion will lose its mystery and its supernatural character. If one offends the principles of reason our religion will be absurd and ridiculous. . . . There are two equally dangerous extremes, to shut reason out and to let nothing else in."[30] This is a simple but striking point. If one seriously considers the cosmos, there is a lot we have explained but much more we have not. Our world is still imbued with a deep mystery, though oftentimes our conventional lives, our daily habits and routines, cause us to ignore that mystery. Religion embraces that mystery and helps us anchor ourselves meaningfully in a world that is not yet fully intelligible.

East Asian religions try to juggle the mysterious parts of our world with the rational parts. Daoism has a deep sense of the mystery and rhythm in the cosmos. We see that order, that rhythmic harmony, in nature and can feel its tranquility resonating inside us. If Daoism supplies the mystery of the transcendent, then Confucianism provides a rational philosophy for the social order. East Asian religions and philosophies have found a balance between what is mysterious and opaque and what is rational and known. Any time religion fails to keep the balance between the mysterious and the rational, it may be in need of revision or replacement; it may have become either too fantastic or too quotidian. The religions that have survived are probably those that have kept that balance and remained compelling to their adherents.

What Doesn't Fit?

Cultures are connected to religion. There are very few Muslims in Japan. Asking the average Japanese person to show reverence to the Kaaba is not going to click with them. I can imagine an Arabic businessman visiting Japan yearning for the

30. Rudolf Otto, *The Idea of the Holy*, trans. John W. Harvey (New York: Oxford University Press, 1971), xviii–xix.

home of Mecca and the familiar precincts of the Kaaba or a direction (mihrab) to pray to and face Mecca. I could also imagine a Japanese businessman in Saudi Arabia wishing for a Shinto shrine to pay homage to, the sight of Mount Fuji or a red gate. Sacred space is prescribed by religion, and the sacred space of *the other culture* is often proscribed, alienating and forbidden. All religions have this sense of rootedness and connectedness, and while it gives us meaning, it can also set us apart. That is part of the paradox of religion, of what fits and what does not fit. Religions connect us to nations, cultures, and traditions that are a part of humanity and give us rules of conduct that instruct us toward benevolence. At the same time, this cultural and religious rootedness may make us feel estranged and alienated when far from our sacred turf. We all have a few pieces of the puzzle of life that we consider sacred to us, and we hold these dear. We cannot always figure out the pieces of the puzzles that others bring to bear, but I think it commendable, even necessary, to try.

Conclusion

Universalism and the Religious Puzzle

Summary of Universalism

Think of a puzzle finished around the edges but incomplete in the middle. At the edges, the puzzle appears complete. Imagine those parts as the various world religions we know of today. From its own viewpoint, each religion offers a total explanation of life. What happens, however, when you zoom out and the picture of the puzzle becomes larger? Soon you see differing traditions, differing ideas, and no complete picture about the puzzle of life you are building. There are gaps of understanding. What is the common image? Puzzle pieces, ideas from different religions, may fit together in some places but not in all. There are bridges, parts where pieces may connect to each other, but they are incomplete.

You are left with a problem. You may not wish to insist your picture of the world is total. To make one's own religion absolute crowds out the other religions that also claim to possess a legitimate view of the whole. To throw all the other pieces of the puzzle off the map, to say that they do not belong, to fill the whole of life with just your puzzle pieces may seem rude, even irrational. Yet this is the problem that religions face today. One can affirm one's own tradition and deny all others. Alternatively, one can accept the other traditions as legitimate. But this latter choice only leads to more complicated questions. How do these traditions historically relate? How can we *affirm* their history meaningfully, morally, so that they offer a common religious picture of a greater world we live in?

Universalists are people who pursue this more complicated alternative. They view all religions as legitimate but as parts of a larger picture puzzle that is unsolved. No one needs to be ashamed of or deny their tradition. On the contrary, a Universalist view has to begin building the puzzle from *somewhere*, so you have to begin in one place, affirming yourself and your tradition. What is difficult is to establish a vision of the whole of humanity's religious histories. What do they add up to and mean together? Is there actually one meaningful puzzle to build? We might be able to use religions like a compass for an overarching principle of good conduct, which provides a spiritual map to orient and direct our lives. The compass may be imperfect, and the map may be incomplete. Like a puzzle still under construction, we are still trying to build our way to understand each other as one people, one world, and one civilization united by an idea, religious or otherwise, that blesses us all to the exclusion of none. That project is Universalism. To conclude this book, we will look at one vision of Universalism as expressed in the life and teachings of Mohandas Gandhi.

Gandhi's Universalism

When Louis Fischer saw a picture of Jesus on the wall of Gandhi's ashram, he asked if Gandhi was a Christian. Gandhi responded, "I am a Christian, and a Hindu, a Moslem, and a Jew."[1] He meant that he affirmed all religions as equals. He was of course foremost a Hindu, but he believed that many religions responded to a "felt want" or basic spiritual need in humankind.[2] He read the Bhagavad Gita, the Qur'an, and the Bible at his prayer meetings. He attracted advocates of all faiths.[3] In a pluralist world, what could be more appealing? He told us that wherever we come from, our faith may be good.

Gandhi's ideas ring true. But there have been problems with making Universalism work as a religious view. Parts of the puzzle are still incomplete. His universal view is on the safest ground when standing for the simplest principles of morality. When trying to account for a more full-blooded model of religious thinking, however, it encounters difficulties. Simply put, religions do not all affirm the same thing, but they do affirm a few common basic ideas.

The strength of a universal view based on Gandhi's idea is threefold: (1) it affirms the equality of religions and their believers, (2) it says truth transcends all religions but is also vitally captured by many of them, and (3) it imagines God as a caring parent, giving a genuine message to all the world's peoples.

1. Louis Fischer, ed., *The Life of Mahatma Gandhi* (New York: Collier Books, 1962), 335.
2. Gandhi, *Selected Works*, 6:270.
3. Fischer, *Life of Mahatma Gandhi*, 450.

Most people know Gandhi as the great advocate of nonviolence. They may have forgotten his Universalism, that all religions are equal, providing a basic moral map and spiritual compass that can guide us through life. The compass needle of any given religion may not point to the exact same magnetic moral north, but with the correction of a compassionate and reasonable mind, they point the way. We might, in a world full of different religions, converge on one place, like pathways up the same mountain.

We have found some good moral ideas to suggest the direction of that spiritual compass. Religions can firm a few basic moral values, as stated in the introduction:

1. Follow the Golden Rule—do unto others as you would have them do unto you, or love your neighbor as yourselves.
2. Accept God or a Sacred Purpose in your life.
3. Do not lie.
4. Do not kill, or more specifically, murder.
5. Do not commit adultery, or "unchaste acts."
6. Do not steal.
7. Do not be possessive of or greedy about material things.
8. Respect one's elders, or authorities.

These are important directions; this list does not pretend to be final. They will not include everything that all religions regard to be essential. This must be accepted, and like a real compass, they will point not to the exact same "moral magnetic north" for all peoples but hopefully near enough to it. Corrections need to be made based on reason.

I must stress here that not everyone needs to accept a Universal framework; I have tried to show there are distinct advantages and disadvantages to it, as there are to any viewpoint: traditional, atheist, agnostic, scientific, or others. Recall in our trilemma of belief, no choice may come easily. If there is something you have learned here, I hope it is the need to take all viewpoints seriously. I offer my view to show how I try to make sense of an urgent and complex problem in religion and hope it fosters growth in your own viewpoint, wherever it may take you. Indeed, if God did make us with such striking similarities as well as differences, it seems that Sacred or godly purpose was to make us think and puzzle.

Gandhi condemned religious intolerance, believing that "the growing spirit of toleration towards all religions is a happy augury of the future."[4] Yet we have seen terrible religious rivalries persist. He would have grieved deeply to see the events of 9/11 and the grinding acrimony oftentimes felt between members of differing religions. In his own India, the rise of a Hindutva (nationalist pro-Hindu) mindset has challenged his principles.[5] His idea of Universalism, of the comparative equality of world religions, has been tested deeply since his death. He believed in a happy augury in the future, but that future does not seem to have arrived. Can we still get there?

Concerning the three strengths of a universal view, the first is that it asserts the equality of religions and therefore the equality of persons believing in them. It can unify and push back against hatred and alienation. His belief in nonviolence, or ahimsa, was deeply linked to his views of human equality. The closing words of his autobiography expressed that belief: "My uniform experience has convinced me that there is no other God than Truth. And if every page of these chapters does not proclaim to the reader that the only means for the realization of Truth is Ahimsa, I shall deem all my labor in writing these pages to have been in vain."[6] Gandhi's nonviolence was deeply rooted in and inseparable from his religious ideas.

The second appealing aspect of Gandhi's Universalism is its assertion that truth transcends religions but is also in part captured by them. He believed in a view beyond any one single religion. Neither the Hindus nor the Muslims nor the Christians had a monopoly on truth. All religions had an essential sliver of this truth; enough of a sliver to make them comparably equal and invaluable. Yet even on the surface, one can tell religions do not say the same thing, nor are they exactly pointed in the same direction. Just to take Hinduism, Christianity, and Islam, one can see they have different scriptures, varying ethical emphases and ideas, and distinct notions about God. Somehow he saw past these differences and simply affirmed that no religion was true to the exclusion of others. He explained, "I came to the conclusion long ago, after prayerful search and study . . . that all religions were true, and also that all had some error in them, and whilst I hold my own, I should hold others as dear as Hinduism. . . . So we can only pray, if we are Hindus, that

4. Gandhi, *Selected Works*, 6:272.
5. Guha, *India after Gandhi*, 576–633.
6. Gandhi, *Gandhi, an Autobiography*, 503–4.

not a Christian should become a Hindu, . . . but our inmost prayer should be that a Hindu should be a better Hindu, a Muslim a better Muslim, and a Christian a better Christian. . . . I broaden my Hinduism by loving other religions as my own."[7]

Gandhi rejected the need of conversion, writing, "I disbelieve in the conversion of one person by another. My effort should never be to undermine another's faith but to make him a better follower of his own faith. This implies the belief in the truth of all religions and respect for them."[8] This was his view, yet he learned some of this from his Jain friends. Before leaving for England to study law, he swore an oath to a Jain monk not to touch wine, women, or meat.[9] He had a sustained correspondence with a Jain friend, Raychandbhai, that was influential.[10] One can see in his thought the Jain idea of *anekantavada*, which affirms that there may be many legitimate viewpoints. Buddhism also influenced him. The famous Buddhist parable of the blind men and elephant appealed to him. In this parable, each blind man clings to a different part of the elephant, giving a partial understanding of what the elephant is but none the complete picture.[11] Since no one man can understand all in this parable, so no religion also has a monopoly on truth. Gandhi elaborated, "It has been my experience that I am always true from my point of view and am often wrong from the point of view of my honest critics. I know that we are both right from our respective points of view. . . . The seven blind men who gave seven different descriptions of the elephant were all right from their respective points of view, and wrong from the point of view of one another, and right and wrong from the point of view of the man who knew the elephant. I very much like this doctrine of the manyness of reality."[12]

This is a vast departure from the perspective of religion as a revealed and permanent truth. Other believers might reach for their Tanakh, their Bible, or their Qur'an, and by citing it, they claim also to relay an eternal and undeniable truth. As moved as Gandhi was by the Bhagavad Gita, he did not make absolute claims for it. He admired the Gita, stating, "The book (the Gita) struck me as one of priceless worth. The impression has ever since been growing on me with the result that I

7. Fischer, *Essential Gandhi*, 212.
8. Fischer, 212.
9. Gandhi, *Gandhi, an Autobiography*, 39.
10. Dundas, *Jains*, 263.
11. Bodhi, *In the Buddha's Words*, 183–90.
12. Long, *Jainism*, 165.

regard it today as the book *par excellence* for the knowledge of Truth."[13] For him, many religions had sufficient truth in them, their errors could be corrected, and none needed to capture it all. He rejected untouchability, though practiced by many Hindus, because of its moral failings. Scriptures could point to a truth but did not necessarily capture it entirely or flawlessly. He wrote, "Scriptures cannot transcend Reason and Truth. They are intended to purify Reason and illuminate Truth. . . . It is the spirit that giveth the light."[14] No one scripture, even the Gita or the Vedas, might capture it all. He further wrote, "I do not believe in the exclusive divinity of the Vedas. I believe in the Bible [and the] Koran to be as much divinely inspired as the Veda."[15]

Gandhi's belief that no one religion captures truth fully but that religions are pathways up a common mountain is eye-opening for some and repugnant nonsense to others. Scriptures and religions may themselves provide the principle for correcting their errors so that a wiser, more compassionate understanding can emerge. Yet how many are willing to share in this claim? Many believers would balk at the idea of their religion having errors in need of correction. They do not wish to be told that they are "in the dark" with an incomplete view like the blind men and the elephant. Gandhi's appreciation of religion was universal, broad minded, his only dogma being a passionate desire to find an overarching truth that connected humankind at various levels. I do not maintain it is a perfect view, nor for everyone. Simply put, the image of the puzzle being built is not perceived to be the same by all people, nor the ideas of how to make it.

The third element of Gandhi's Universalism is his compassionate model of God as parent. This God cares equally for all people of earth and so he provides to each of them a sacred wisdom tradition. Why should this God give all wisdom to just one group of earth's peoples? Why not share this wisdom with the whole world? To champion just one religion might seem a form of spiritual nationalism, an arbitrary favoritism God should not allow. Assuming we are all children of God, why not believe we all received a compatible sacred message? Gandhi's Universalism embraces all because all are God's children. All have received a form of vital

13. Gandhi, *Gandhi, an Autobiography*, 67.
14. Fischer, *Essential Gandhi*, 135.
15. Fischer, 213 (brackets in the original).

spiritual truth. They have seen it differently, been moved in different ways, and this difference accounts for their variety.

Yet affirming this idea comes with some assumptions and problems. For example, it might cut away the idea that Jews are the chosen people of God; that Muhammad was the last and final prophet, whose Qur'an gave a final and correct form of God's message; or that Christians alone are saved through faith in Jesus Christ. As rational and compelling it may be to think that all religions have a share in truth, that none has a monopoly on truth, there are still pervasive elements of many religions that affirm otherwise: that truth is locked up in one tradition, or one indispensable faith. Possibly, some faith or faiths have all the correct puzzle pieces. And is there really a God or parental spirit governing this universe? We cannot be sure, just as we cannot be sure if a given traditionalist isn't right in affirming one view.

Some thought Gandhi went too far, including one Hindu man who became his assassin. On January 30, 1948, before one of his prayer meetings, Nathuram Vinayak Godse assassinated Gandhi. Godse had a militant view opposed to Gandhi and an entirely different reading of the Bhagavad Gita. Godse did not see the Gita as an allegorical battlefield, a spiritual struggle between good and evil, as Gandhi saw it.[16] Godse did not agree that its ultimate value was nonviolence. He saw the Gita as a real battlefield and believed that Gandhi had to be a casualty on it. For Godse, Hinduism gave him a license to kill Gandhi.[17]

A religious view that is benevolent, that includes and transcends in its thinking, can be rationally compelling. How could it fail? And yet before his assassination, Gandhi felt a deep failure. He had not been able to teach his beloved India nonviolence *and* tolerance. The bold dreams he had of living to the ripe age of 120 had begun to fade. He had become estranged from his eldest son, Harilal, and his most trenchant rival, Muhammad Ali Jinnah. In fact, if there was just one, *and only one*, person whom Gandhi arguably had to convince of his message, it would have been Jinnah. As the leader of the Muslim League, Jinnah had become an ardent proponent of the division or partition of India, an idea that Gandhi could not bear: "My life's work seems to be over. I hope God will spare me further humiliation. . . . I shall perhaps not be alive to witness it, but should the evil I apprehend overtake

16. Mohandas K. Gandhi, *The Bhagavad Gita according to Gandhi*, ed. and trans. John Strohmeir (Berkeley: Berkeley Hills Books, 2000), 27.
17. Yogesh Chadha, *Gandhi: A Life* (New York: John Wiley & Sons, 1997), chap. 48.

India and her independence be imperiled, let posterity know what agony this old soul went through thinking of it. Let it not be said that Gandhi was a party to India's vivisection."[18] The violence that consumed India at the brink of its partition was not just a failure of nonviolence; Gandhi felt it was his failure to teach India that Hindus and Muslims were one. He had not, in his mind, been able to convince enough Hindus and Muslims that there was no essential division between them, that they could be brothers.

Gandhi had a Muslim friend named Abdul Ghaffar Khan. Khan, the "Frontier Gandhi" of the Pashtuns, affirmed the spirit of the Islamic notion of Ahl-Kitab, or "People of the Book" (or those who received a genuine religious message), in a widely encompassing way. Khan, like Gandhi, had read comparatively in religion and argued for a more Universalist reading of it: "But I kept on reading the Gita, which I read thrice. I think at the back of our quarrels is the failure to recognize that all faiths contain enough inspiration for their adherents. The Holy Koran says that God sends messengers and warners for all nations and all peoples, and they are their respective prophets. All of them are *Ahle Kitab*, men of the Book, and the Hindus are no less *Ahle Kitab* than Jews and Christians."[19]

When one person objected that this was not the traditional Muslim view, Abdul Ghaffar Khan replied,

> I know. But they fail to see that the Hindus and their books are not mentioned in the Holy Koran because the list there is not exhaustive but merely illustrative. The Holy Koran simply lays down the principles, namely, that those who have inspired books, come within the category of *Ahle Kitab*, and I am absolutely certain that the meaning of the texts includes all people who have inspired books to govern their faith and conduct. And I would go even further and would say that the fundamental principles of all religions are the same though details differ, because each faith takes the color and flavor of the soil from which it springs.[20]

18. Chadha, 433.
19. Tendulkar, *Abdul Ghaffar Khan*, 173.
20. Tendulkar, *Abdul Ghaffar Khan*, 173.

For Khan, it was natural to assume religions would vary but also foolish to believe they did not each have sufficient principles for moral guidance. For example, most religions contain some form of the Golden Rule: do unto others as you would have them do unto you. Confucius saw it as a silver rule: do not do unto others what you do not wish them to do to you.[21] Rabbi Hillel the Elder is also said to have described the core of Judaism in the same way.[22] Jesus reported it in the gospels: "Love your enemies, do good to those who hate you. . . . If anyone strikes you on the cheek, offer the other also."[23] Jesus said the double love command was the core of religion: to love God and one's neighbor as oneself.[24] Muhammad said, "None of you is a believer so long as he does not wish for his brother what he wishes for himself."[25] The Qur'an also reiterates a form of the Judeo-Christian ethic of loving one's own kind and doing good deeds.[26] Gandhi learned this lesson from the Bhagavad Gita 2:55–57: "They live in wisdom who see themselves in all and all in them, who have renounced every selfish desire and sense craving tormenting the heart."[27] The Buddha said, "As a mother cares for her son, her only son, all her days, so towards all things living a man's mind should be all-embracing, friendliness for the whole world."[28]

Here we have a principle—or principles—that can be used to point the moral compass of religions toward a magnetic north. In many other respects, however, the map of the world they also affirm will still have obstacles and disagreements. Did God become incarnate just once, as Christians maintain; nine times with the different avatars of Vishnu; or not at all, as Islam insists? Or is it silly to even think of a God at all, as Buddhism asserts? Some religions have ideas of a soul and afterlife, others of reincarnation, while Buddhism challenges the notion of the permanent soul or self. The obstacles to a common sense of religious belonging are many, but there are also a few powerful uniting directions.

Making sense of the sacred then is finding a moral and spiritual map and compass, a way of coming to terms with the world that will sustain you and guide you

21. Ames and Rosemont, *Analects of Confucius*, 153.
22. Wylen, *Settings of Silver*, 201–2.
23. Luke 6:27–29.
24. Matt 22:37–40.
25. Küng, *Islam: Past, Present and Future*, 657.
26. Dawood, *Koran*, v. 42:23, or p. 341.
27. Easwaran, *Bhagavad Gita*, 95–96.
28. de Bary, *Buddhist Tradition*, 38.

in times of need. No person or religion may do this perfectly by themselves, for all good accomplishments require hard work. Religion is no exception. The more you try to understand it and foster the better morals of religion, the more it may give back to you in time of need. And times of need are abundant in our lives. Religions *do not* agree on everything, but they *can* agree on some things. This is a reason both for hope and for caution, to proceed with careful optimism toward a better future.

Martin Luther King Jr. was deeply inspired by Gandhi and wrote, "I believe this man, more than anybody else in the modern world, caught the spirit of Jesus Christ and lived it more completely in his life. His name was Gandhi, Mohandas K. Gandhi."[29] King accepted the nonviolence and Universalism of Gandhi. King stated about the world's religions, "Religion at its best has always sought to promote peace and good will among men. This is true of all the great religions of the world. In their ethical systems, we find the love ethic standing at the center. This is true of Judaism, this is true of Christianity, this is true of Islam, of Hinduism and Buddhism, and if we go right through all the great religions of the world we find this central message of love and this idea of the need for peace, the need for understanding and the need for good will among men."[30] A universal view of religion, I think, is sober minded and realistic. It does not presume that one's own background or viewpoint is best. It tries to work toward a healthy integration of one's view with those of other traditions and perspectives. This is not easy. This is, in fact, very hard because the image of life's ultimate meaning (the puzzle that we are all at work building every day) is *not* very clear. We must be patient. We must be realistic.

Moral realism is something I very much appreciate. Reinhold Niebuhr defined Christian realism as "the disposition to take all factors in a social and political situation, which offer resistance to established norms, into account, particularly the factors of self-interest and power."[31] Good morals are not always easily realized. The sin entrenched in our hearts and political institutions resists their fruition. Societies do not often allow what is right. Long before Niebuhr, the ex-slave Frederick Douglass understood that struggles for justice were long and hard. He wrote, "The struggle may be a more moral one; or it may be a physical one; or it

29. King, *Radical King*, 24.
30. King, 97.
31. Reinhold Niebuhr, *Christian Realism and Political Problems* (New York: Charles Scribner's Sons, 1953), 119.

may be both moral and physical; but it must be a struggle. Power concedes nothing without a demand. It never did, and it never will."[32] Niebuhr elaborated on this struggle: "Man's capacity for justice makes democracy possible; but man's inclination to injustice makes democracy necessary."[33]

Niebuhr's realism is much better known in terms of the Serenity Prayer: "God, give me grace to accept with serenity the things that cannot be changed, courage to change the things which should be changed, and the wisdom to distinguish the one from the other."[34] For Niebuhr and many Christians, as well as persons of other faiths, religion means trying to adhere to good morality, even when the world around does not seem to support it. This requires great inner strength and courage. I don't think that *only* religious persons have this strength and courage, but religion certainly can help. Gandhi, King, and Niebuhr all observed that secular people and atheists can often share more benevolence and justice than the so-called faithful.

A Universalist religious view, I believe, will become an increasingly *realistic* view. In a globalized world, it is increasingly difficult to map out everything according to one reference point to the exclusion of all else. Phones and satellites, TVs, and internet technologies have brought down long-standing barriers, but cultural walls of misunderstanding persist. A Universalist tries to think outside of the box, to build puzzles of meaning where others were perhaps afraid to build them. Being a Universalist does not require you to abandon your point of view, only to root it in a larger world context. Being a Universalist and a realist at the same time means you must know that belief does not determine our reality. I can believe that I am Olaf, the world's only living, walking, and talking snowman who can stride the sands of Saudi Arabia without melting, but that cannot make it so. Beliefs do not determine our *actual* reality; they determine a mental one. Beliefs are established by interpretation and create only a mental reality in which we live and in which we are trying to make sense of the world.

The puzzle of life's full picture is incomplete and does not make full sense. There may be a future vision that can put them together but none that is fully resolute with one picture and one interlocking fit. The puzzle of life in its center remains

32. Frederick Douglass, *Frederick Douglass on Slavery and the Civil War—selections from His Writings*, ed. and with an introduction by Philip S. Foner (Mineola, NY: Dover, 2003), 42.
33. Reinhold Niebuhr, *The Essential Reinhold Niebuhr: Selected Essays and Addresses*, ed. Robert McAfee Brown (New Haven, CT: Yale University Press, 1986), xii.
34. Niebuhr, xxiv.

a mystery, incomplete, something to be pondered. Puzzlement, though, is not always a negative thing. It is also a call for more understanding. That is OK. For to love one's neighbor, to do good to one's neighbor, you have to also *understand* your neighbor. Bereft of a comprehension of who you really are, I cannot understand you and cannot love and appreciate you as much as I should. And understanding is not an easy thing. It is just as difficult as love.

We can believe in our texts and traditions, but this does not establish a reality for them. They are true, not true, or partly true. I hope, however, that it is not so much the text that matters as your devotion to truth and the purity of your heart and mind. Whether there is a God or judgment or reincarnation, I sincerely believe that it is the purity of one's heart and the dedication to love and truth that will matter most. If there is no God or judgment or reincarnation, then purity, truth, and love in our hearts may be all that matter.

Bibliography

al-Bukhari, Muhammad. *The Hadith*. Self-published, Amazon Digital Services, 2015. Kindle.

Al-Djazairi, S. E. *The First Caliphs*. N.p.: MSBN Books, 2016. Kindle.

Ames, Roger T., and Henry Rosemont, trans. *The Analects of Confucius—a Philosophical Translation*. New York: Ballantine Books, 1999.

Armstrong, Karen. *Buddha*. New York: Penguin, 2004.

——. *A History of God*. New York: Alfred A. Knopf, 1993.

——. *Muhammad: A Biography of the Prophet*. New York: HarperSanFrancisco, 1993.

Aslan, Reza. *Not God but God: The Origins, Evolution and Future of Islam*. New York: Random House, 2006.

Avedon, John F. *In Exile from the Land of Snows*. New York: Harper Perennial, 1997.

Bainton, Roland H. *Here I Stand: A Life of Martin Luther*. New York: Meridian, 1995.

Bell, Rob. *Love Wins: A Book about Heaven, Hell and the Fate of Every Person Who Ever Lived*. New York: HarperOne, 2005.

Bengtsson, Jesper. *Aung San Suu Kyi: A Biography*. Washington, DC: Potomac Books, 2012.

Bhutto, Benazir. *Reconciliation: Islam, Democracy and the West*. New York: HarperCollins, 2008.

Bodhi, Bhikku. *In the Buddha's Words: An Anthology of the Pali Canon*. Boston: Wisdom, 2005.

Borgen, Robert, and Marian Ury. "Readable Japanese Mythology: Selections from Nihon Shoki and Kojiki." *Journal of the Association of Teachers of Japanese* 24, no. 1 (April 1990): 61–97.

Boyce, Mary. *Zoroastrians: Their Religious Beliefs and Practices*. New York: Prentice Hall, 2001.

Brownlee, John S. *Political Thought in Japanese Historical Writing*. Waterloo: Wilfrid Laurier University Press, 1991.

Buck, William. *Mahabharata*. Berkeley: University of California Press, 1981.

Campbell, Joseph. *The Hero with a Thousand Faces*. Novato, CA: New World Library, 2008.

Carpenter, Humphrey. *J. R. R. Tolkien: A Biography*. New York: Houghton Mifflin, 2000.

Cerrina, Jean Akhtar. *Islam's Peaceful Warrior: Abdul Ghaffar Khan*. Bloomington, IN: Xlibris Corporation, 2003.

Chadha, Yogesh. *Gandhi: A Life*. New York: John Wiley & Sons, 1997.

Chadwick, Robert. *First Civilizations: Ancient Mesopotamia and Ancient Egypt*. Oakville, CT: Equinox, 2005.

Chimnoy, Sri. *Commentaries on the Vedas, the Upanishads, and the Bhagavad Gita*. New York: Aum, 1996.

Ching, Julia. *Chinese Religions*. New York: Orbis Books, 2005.

Clothey, Fred. *Religion in India: A Historical Introduction*. New York: Routledge, 2006.

Collet, Sophia Dobson. *The Life and Letters of Rammohun Roy*. Edited by Dilip Kumar Biswas and Prabhat Chandra Ganguli. Calcutta: Brahmo Mission, 1962.

Collinson, Diané, Kathryn Plant, and Robert Wilkinson. *Fifty Eastern Thinkers*. New York: Routledge, 2000.

Cywiak, Samuel, and Jeff Swesky. *Flight from Fear: A Rabbi's Holocaust Survival Story*. Palm Coast, FL: Independent, 2010.

Dalai Lama. *Freedom in Exile: The Autobiography of the Dalai Lama*. New York: HarperOne, 1991.

Darwin, Charles. *The Autobiography of Charles Darwin*. Edited by Nora Barlow. New York: W. W. Norton, 1958.

——. *From So Simple a Beginning*. Edited by E. O. Wilson. New York: W. W. Norton, 2006.

Dawood, N. J., trans. *The Koran*. New York: Penguin, 2003.

de Bary, Theodore. *The Buddhist Tradition in India, China, and Japan*. New York: Random House, 1972.

Devine, Richard. "Hirata Atsutane and Christian Sources." *Monumenta Nipponica* 36, no. 1 (Spring 1981): 37–54.

Dillenberger, John. *Martin Luther: Selections from His Writings*. New York: Random House, 1962.

Doniger, Wendy, and Brian K. Smith. *The Laws of Manu*. New York: Penguin Classics, 1991.

Doniger O'Flaherty, Wendy. *The Rig Veda*. New York: Penguin, 1981.

Douglass, Frederick. *Frederick Douglass on Slavery and the Civil War—selections from His Writings*. Edited by and with an introduction by Philip S. Foner. Mineola, NY: Dover, 2003.

Dundas, Paul. *The Jains*. 2nd ed. New York: Routledge, 2002.

Easwaran, Eknath, trans. *The Bhagavad Gita*. Berkeley, CA: Nilgiri Press, 2007.

——. *A Man to Match His Mountains: Badshah Khan, Non-violent Soldier of Islam*. Berkeley, CA: Nilgiri Press, 1984.

Eaton, Richard Maxwell. *Rise of Islam and the Bengal Frontier, 1204–1760*. Berkeley: University of California Press, 1993.

Eck, Diana L. *Darsan: Seeing the Divine Image of India*. 3rd ed. New York: Columbia University Press, 1998.

Eshleman, Andrew. *Readings in Philosophy and Religion: East Meets West*. Malden, MA: Blackwell, 2008.

Esposito, John. *Unholy War: Terror in the Name of Islam*. New York: Oxford University Press, 2002.

Esposito, John, and Dalia Mogahed. *Who Speaks for Islam? What a Billion Muslims Really Think*. New York: Gallup, 2007.

Fieser, James, and John Powers. *Scriptures of the East*. New York: McGraw Hill, 2004.

Finocchiaro, Maurice E. *The Essential Galileo*. Cambridge, MA: Hackett, 2008.

Fischer, Louis, ed. *The Essential Gandhi: An Anthology of His Life, Works, and Ideas*. New York: Vintage Books, 1983.

——. *The Life of Mahatma Gandhi*. New York: Collier Books, 1962.

Fisher, Mary Pat. *Living Religions*. 7th ed. Upper Saddle River, NJ: Prentice Hall, 2008.

Freud, Sigmund. *Civilization and Its Discontents*. Translated by James Strachey. New York: W. W. Norton, 2010.

Friedman, Richard Elliot. *Who Wrote the Bible?* New York: HarperSanFrancisco, 1997.

Gandhi, Mohandas K. *Gandhi, an Autobiography: The Story of My Experiments with Truth*. Translated by Mahadev Desai from Gujarati. Boston: Beacon, 1993.

——. *Satyagraha in South Africa*. Translated by Valji Govindji Desai from Gujarati. 6th ed. Ahmedabad, India: Navajivan, 2001.

——. *The Selected Works of Mahatma Gandhi*. Vol. 6. Edited by Shriman Narayan. Ahmedabad, India: Navajivan, 1968.

Grewal, J. S. *The Sikhs of the Punjab*. New York: Cambridge University Press, 1998.

Guha, Ramachandra. *India after Gandhi: The History of the World's Largest Democracy*. New York: Harper Perennial, 2007.

Hammurabi. *Hammurabi: The Oldest Code of Laws in the World*. Transcribed by David Pierce. Translated by C. H. W. Johns. Edinburgh: T&T Clark, 1903.

Hanh, Thich Nhat. *The Art of Living*. New York: HarperOne, 2017.

——. *At Home in the World: Stories and Essential Teachings from a Monk's Life*. Berkeley: Parallax, 2016.

——. *The Heart of the Buddha's Teaching*. New York: Broadway Books, 1998.

——. *Living Buddha, Living Christ*. New York: Riverhead Books, 1995.

——. *Peace Is Every Step*. New York: Bantam Books, 1991.

Hobbes, Thomas. *Leviathan*. Edited by C. B. MacPherson. New York: Penguin, 1985.

Holmes, David L. *The Faiths of the Founding Fathers*. New York: Oxford University Press, 2006.

Hume, David. *Dialogues concerning Natural Religion*. Edited by Martin Bell. New York: Penguin, 1990.

Huxley, Thomas Henry. *Agnosticism and Christianity—and Other Essays*. New York: Prometheus Books, 1992.

Huyler, Stephen P. *Meeting God: Elements of Hindu Devotion*. New Haven, CT: Yale University Press, 1999.

Ichiro, Hori, Ikado Fujido, Wakomoto Tsuneya, and Yanagawa Keiichi, eds. *Japanese Religion: A Survey by the Agency for Cultural Affairs*. New York: Kodansha, 1972.

James, William. *The Will to Believe and Human Morality*. New York: Dover, 1956.

Jammer, Max. *Einstein and Religion: Physics and Theology*. Princeton, NJ: Princeton University Press, 1999.

Jefferson, Thomas. *The Jefferson Bible: The Life and Morals of Jesus of Nazareth*. Radford, VA: Wilder, 2007.

Kant, Immanuel. *Grounding for the Metaphysics of Morals*. Translated by James W. Harrington. 3rd ed. Cambridge, MA: Hackett, 1993.

Kasulis, Thomas P. *Shinto: The Way Home*. Honolulu: University of Hawaii Press, 2004.

Khan, Yasmin. *The Great Partition: The Making of India and Pakistan*. New Haven, CT: Yale University Press, 2007.

King, Martin Luther, Jr. *Martin Luther King Companion*. Selected by Coretta Scott King. New York: St. Martin's, 1993.

——. *The Radical King*. Edited by Cornel West. Boston: Beacon, 2020.

——. *A Testament of Hope: The Essential Writings and Speeches of Martin Luther King, Jr.* Edited by James M. Washington. New York: HarperCollins, 1986.

Kinsley, David. *Hindu Goddesses: Visions of the Divine Feminine in the Hindu Religious Tradition*. Los Angeles: University of California Press, 1988.

Küng, Hans. A *Global Ethic: The Declaration of the Parliament of World Religions*. New York: Continuum, 1995.

——. *Islam: Past, Present and Future*. Translated by John Bowden. Oxford: Oneworld, 2007.

Kyi, Aung San Suu. *Freedom from Fear—and Other Writings*. New York: Penguin, 2010.

Leakey, Richard. *The Origin of Humankind*. New York: Basic Books, 1994.

Lewis, Bernard. *The Crisis of Islam: Holy War and Unholy Terror*. New York: Modern Library, 2003.

Littleton, C. Scott. *Shinto*. New York: Oxford University Press, 2002.

Long, Jeffrey. *Jainism: An Introduction*. New York: I. B. Tauris, 2009.

Mango, Andrew. *Ataturk: The Biography of the Founder of Modern Turkey*. New York: Overlook, 2002.

Mann, Gurinder Singh. *Sikhism*. Upper Saddle River, NJ: Prentice Hall, 2004.

Marx, Karl, and Friedrich Engels. *On Religion*. New York: Dover, 2008.

McLeod, W. H. *Textual Sources for the Study of Sikhism*. Chicago: University of Chicago Press, 1999.

Meeks, Wayne A., ed. *The HarperCollins Study Bible*. New York: HarperCollins, 1993.

Muesse, Mark. *The Hindu Traditions*. Minneapolis: Fortress, 2011.

Narayan, R. K. *The Ramayana—a Shortened Modern Prose Version of the Indian Epic*. New York: Penguin, 2006.

Niebuhr, Reinhold. *The Children of Light and Darkness*. New York: Charles Scribner's Sons, 1944.

——. *Christian Realism and Political Problems*. New York: Charles Scribner's Sons, 1953.

——. *The Essential Reinhold Niebuhr: Selected Essays and Addresses*. Edited by Robert McAfee Brown. New Haven, CT: Yale University Press, 1986.

——. *Man's Nature and His Communities*. New York: Charles Scribner's Sons, 1965.

——. *Moral Man and Immoral Society*. Louisville, KY: Westminster John Knox, 2001.

Nigosian, Solomon Alexander. *The Zoroastrian Faith: Tradition and Modern Research*. Montreal: McGill Queen's Press, 1993.

Oldstone-Moore, Jennifer. *Confucianism*. New York: Oxford University Press, 2002.

Otto, Rudolf. *The Idea of the Holy*. Translated by John W. Harvey. New York: Oxford University Press, 1971.

Paine, Thomas. *The Age of Reason*. Sioux Falls, SD: NuVision, 2007.

Parikh, Vastupal. *Jainism and the New Spirituality*. Toronto: Peace, 2002.

Partridge, Christopher, and Tim Dowley. *Introduction to World Religions*. 2nd ed. Minneapolis: Fortress, 2013.

Phipps, William. *Darwin's Religious Odyssey*. Harrisburg, PA: Trinity, 2002.

Plato. *The Last Days of Socrates*. Edited by Christopher Rowe. New York: Penguin, 2010.

——. *The Republic*. Translated by Raymond Larson. Arlington Heights, IL: Harlan Davidson, 1979.

Prabhavananda, Swami, and Frederick Manchester. *The Upanishads: Breath of the Eternal–the Principal Texts Selected and Translated from the Original Sanskrit*. New York: Mentor Classic, 1957.

Prebish, Charles S., and Damien Keown. *Introducing Buddhism*. 2nd ed. New York: Routledge, 2010.

Robertson, Bruce Carlisle. *Raja Rammohun Ray: The Father of Modern India*. Oxford: Oxford University Press, 1995.

Rodrigues, Hillary P. *Introducing Hinduism*. New York: Routledge, 2006.

Rogerson, Barnaby. *The Heirs of Muhammad*. New York: Overlook, 2006.

——. *The Prophet Muhammad: A Biography*. Mahwah, NJ: HiddenSpring, 2003.

Roy, Rammohun. *The English Works*. New York: AMS, 1978.

Russell, Bertrand. *Why I Am Not a Christian: And Other Essays on Religion and Related Subjects*. Compiled by Paul Edwards. New York: Simon & Schuster, 1957.

Singh, Patwant. *The Sikhs*. New York: Doubleday, 1999.

Spink, Kathryn. *Mother Teresa: A Complete Authorized Biography*. New York: HarperCollins, 1998.

Stern, Jessica, and J. M. Bergère. *Isis: The State of Terror*. New York: Ecco, 2015.

Stetson, Eric. *Christian Universalism: God's Good News for All People*. N.p.: Sparkling Bay Books, 2008.

Tendulkar, D. G. *Abdul Ghaffar Khan*. Bombay: Popular Prakash, 1967.

Thakur, Minni. *Raja Rammohun Roy: His Social, Political and Economic Ideas*. New Delhi: Deep & Deep, 1987.

Trautmann, Thomas. *India: Brief History of a Civilization*. New York: Oxford University Press, 2016.

Tzu, Lao. *Tao Te Ching*. Translated by Stephen Mitchell. New York: Harper Perennial, 2006.

Ware, Kalisstos. *The Orthodox Way*. Crestwood, NY: St. Vladimir's Seminary Press, 1979.

Wiesel, Elie. *Night*. With a new translation by Marion Wiesel. New York: Hill & Wang, 2006.

Wilcox, Clyde, and Carin Robinson. *Onward Christian Soldiers: The Religious Right in American Politics*. Boulder, CO: Westview, 2011.

Wintle, Justin. *Perfect Hostage: A Life of Aung San Suu Kyi, Burma's Prisoner of Conscience*. New York: Skyhorse, 2007.

Wolpert, Stanley. *A New History of India*. 7th ed. New York: Oxford University Press, 2004.

Wright, Beth. *A Study Companion to World Religions*. Edited by Christopher Partridge. 2nd ed. Minneapolis: Fortress, 2013.

Wylen, Stephen. *Settings of Silver: An Introduction to Judaism*. New York: Paulist, 2000.

Yusuf Ali, Abdullah, trans. *The Qur'an: A Guide and Mercy*. 26th ed. New York: Tahrike Tarsile Qur'an, 2010.

Zoroaster. *Hymns of Zoroaster, the Gathas*. Edited by M. L. West. New York: I. B. Tauris, 2010.

Index